1994

THE PHILIPPINES IN CRISIS

THE PHILIPPINES IN CRISIS

DEVELOPMENT AND SECURITY
IN THE AQUINO ERA
1986-92

W. Scott Thompson, D. Phil.

St. Martin's Press
New York

First published in the United States of America in 1992

Printed in the United States of America

ISBN 0-312-05593-5

Library of Congress Cataloging-in-Publication Data

Thompson, W. Scott (Willard Scott), 1942-
      The Philippines in crisis / W. Scott Thompson.
        p. cm.
      Includes index.
      ISBN 0-312-05593-5
      1. Philippines—Politics and government—1986- 2.
Philippines—Economic policy. 3. Philippines—Economic
conditions—1986- 4. Philippines—National security.   I.
Title.
DS685.614.T47   1992
959.904'7—dc20   91-40742
                                     CIP

Table of Contents

to
Heidi Thompson,
Richard Lewis, Jr., and Alain Rouvez
for happy spirits and noble friendship in complicated times

Prologue

In the late 1980s and early 1990s, while Washington contemplated the "end of history" as liberal democracy became the goal of many of its longtime adversaries, a sideshow went on in Southeast Asia, part of that "vast bulk of the Third World . . . very much mired in history," destined to be "a terrain of conflict for many years to come," as Frank Fukuyama put it.[1] But that third world was a substantial majority of the world's people, and there were few places in it where "history" was being more actively fought out than in the Philippines.

The question of the relevance of democracy to developing countries is hardly new. Two decades ago I undertook a comparative study of the Philippines and Thailand. My analytical purpose was to see how internal political arrangements related to success in foreign policy. At the time, the Philippines was a rambunctious democracy, Thailand a tired autocracy. Looking through the prisms of development and security, as in this volume, I found that democracy had served the Philippines, if only because in its bargaining with the United States—over issues where Washington was *demandeur*—more claimants had to be paid off. Fewer people have to be satisfied in a dictatorship.

On the other hand, I observed that, in all,

from an internal perspective, Thailand appeared to have done rather better, emerging at the end of this period as she did with a new elected government....One was bound to have misgivings examining what was happening to the Philippines, no matter how impressive economic progress was thought to be....The imposition of martial law, the imprisonment of some of her most distinguished citizenry, the silencing of the press, the ever-increasing enrichment of the president and his family, all cast a heavy pall over the archipelago.[2]

Much is lost in political analysis from not facing where one went wrong. The pride involved prevents one from seeing where premises, scholarship, or reasoning were at fault, so one learns from one's mistakes only how to make new ones. Suffice it that I nonetheless concluded that, at least with respect to foreign policy and relations with the United States, the Philippines had done better than Thailand, as of the mid-1970s.

Moreover, the implication of Filipino foreign policy success and the seemingly dire prospects for Thailand as the Indochinese wars continued to rage in the region led me to leave the reader with the clear impression that the Philippines would also end up the better off of the two in the long run.

By the end of the 1980s, a decade and a half after the Vietnam war's end, Thailand was the newest "NIC," or newly industrializing country; in contrast, the Philippines was poorer than before with no prospect of joining that list at any time before the end of the century, even in the best of circumstances. The easy explanation for my incorrect prophecy is that, first, no one could have foreseen the rapacity of the Marcos family and the speed with which its intelligent leader would dissipate the opportunity that he so clearly foresaw (and, for the first few years, undertook) to modernize and galvanize his country; nor the speed with which his countrymen would accommodate him.

And, second, few foresaw the skill with which Thailand could convert its opportunity at the end of the region's main war to make itself a haven of stability and growth. The explanations explain nothing. Why was Marcos so able to corrupt his country's institutions—and why was Thailand so adaptive in moving ahead? The latter question must wait for another volume, but the former one, while not the subject of this book, during a sabbatic leave granted by Tufts University's Fletcher School of Law and Diplomacy, is implicit in the question we ask of the Aquino era—namely, why did the republic revert so readily to its old mold?

Every developing society has two basic challenges: finding and distributing resources for the country's development, and maintaining order. The challenge to the Philippines to satisfy these twin needs was formidable in the period of this study, which focuses on the nexus of these two concerns, in an environment characterized by a commitment to democracy. As it turned out (and all too often so turns out), the first challenge was at least in appearance easier than the second, with the result that I give much more attention herein to the questions of order (namely ending the insurgency and putting down coups) than to resources (namely getting foreign aid and using it wisely).

So that is what the book is about; what it is not about is a comprehensive history or analysis of the Aquino era as a whole. True, most of the key themes of that period are viewed herein, but readers must await other studies for a full view of this turbulent time. I have, for example, not once mentioned the formidable problems of Mindanao, in particular the Muslim rebellion there, for which numerous solutions were proposed and tried. Mindanao, however, no matter how bloody a conflict, was a marginal one for the republic as a whole; it did not threaten the central control that an old elite had therein, whereas the New People's Army did—toward the end of this period, the Young Officer's Union did also.

In 1989 the Carnegie Endowment for International Peace, the Asia Foundation, and the Philippine-American Foundation (the Manila-based administrator of Fulbright grants) provided me with research support and awarded me grants to carry out the research reported in this book. I would like to thank Dr. Thomas Hughes, president of the first, for his scholarly enthusiasm over many years, and Dr. Alan Choate, of the second, for his encouragement and thoughtfulness amid whatever difficulties I found myself. Dr. Juan Francisco, the executive director of the third, was always incredibly helpful, as were Alex Collata and Luzviminda Cabrera. Manuel Perito, Jr., in Manila, and Enrique Ortiz, John Luddy and Vesco Koutzev in America were ideal research assistants, a term that well describes Mary Pyche and Kris Ratnavale, my always cheerful secretarial assistants at Fletcher and Carnegie respectively. Tony Abaya, Nicholas Alonso, Ken Baranda, Alman Battiao, Ben Benitez, Ambassador Peter Koch, Ambassador Alejandro and Cherito Melchor, Michael Houlihan, General Fidel V. Ramos, Pepito Reyes, Josie and Ernesto Rufino, Teresita and Francis Sionil-Jose, and Angelita and Meliton Salazar, in Manila, are all thanked for their encouragement and help. James Clad's manuscript comments were invaluable. The Institute for Philippine Culture is thanked for its generosity in allowing me to cite its annual surveys of Filipino attitudes. As one gets older, one may ask better questions—but research abroad becomes more difficult: not necessarily because of a decline in agility or willingness, but because of the increasing difficulty of breaking away from entanglements at home. In the United States, my beloved colleague and mentor, the late Robert L. West, Alain Rouvez, Nicholas Edwin Scott Thompson, and Paul Rakowski are thanked for coping with these during my absence as well as with assisting my project in a variety of substantive ways.

Editors and their staffs are seldom as encouraging as Simon Winder and his, particularly Laura Heymann, who brought this long project to a swift conclusion and helped create order out of chaos.

It seems pious and pretentious to add that the mistakes, obviously, are mine alone. Having been so wrong before (I hope heuristically), in the present instance I hasten to add it humbly.

W. Scott Thompson
Fletcher School of Law and Diplomacy

NOTES

1. Kenneth Jensen, ed., *A Look at "The End of History"* (Washington, D.C.: United States Institute of Peace, 1990), p. 21.
2. W. Scott Thompson, *Unequal Partners: Philippine and Thai Relations with the United States, 1965-75* (Lexington, MA: Lexington Books, 1975), p. 161.

1

Introduction: Three Ways Out

It was a revolt within the Armed Forces of the Philippines (AFP), made successful by President Marcos's own cousin General Fidel V. Ramos, that occasioned the 1986 "People Power" revolution, exemplary even in a period when many other peoples were throwing off the yoke of tyranny. But the four American helicopters that descended on Malacañang Palace at nine in the evening of 25 February 1986 symbolized the American role in the crisis; they were so much larger than what the Philippine Armed Forces could muster. They took Ferdinand Edralin and Imelda Romualdez Marcos, their family, and their close friend (and most prominent of the business cronies) Eduardo "Danding" Cojuangco from the palace to Clark Air Force Base, hence to an ignominious American exile. There was no way out, other than this, from the great crisis of 1986, itself the product of Marcos's own engineering. The old Philippine republic was overthrown.[1]

The new one was already born: several miles from the palace the courageous widow in yellow had already taken the presidential oath of office amid tumultuous celebration at the stunning, indeed historical, victory that People Power had wrought. Its popular name, "EDSA," for "Epifanio de los Santos" after the vast intersection where the victory took place, was indicative of its miraculous nature. It would have seemed ungallant at the time to note that the new president had chosen to take the oath at the posh Club Filipinas, in one of the city's richest enclaves, among the cheering upper middle and upper class supporters who brought her to power; but in time that fact became salient.

For a year and a half President Corazon Cojuangco Aquino—she is Danding Cojuangco's first cousin—had a tabula rasa on which to start the work of rebuilding democracy. Merely by ending the unvirtuous economic structures of "crony capitalism" that Marcos had created to enrich his friends and by capitalizing on the prosperity of the Asian region, she brought rapid growth to the Philippines for three years and opened the doors to stability, itself so critical a prerequisite of democracy-building. But reform, also an essential element for the rebuilding of democracy, was slower and the benefits accrued even more unequally than is usually the case. One result was an attempted coup d'état a year and a half after the EDSA revolution. It brought to a pause the feeble attempts at reform that her government had initiated and substituted a concentration of effort to appease the military.

The next two years after the 1987 coup attempt were marked by a gradual, and then rapid, deterioration of the polity's health, with the late 1989 coup attempt—the seventh since Aquino took office—ending a second phase of this long-term crisis, one dominated by the AFP, whose demands and problems were then much larger. But then, the appetite comes with the eating, it is said.

Only in the third phase of crisis were the issues indeed truly joined: it was then clear that one set of the competing elites was attempting to restore what we can loosely call the Marcos infrastructure, that factions within the military were disinclined to trust democratic institutions, and that the nascent political structures created in the first phase were too weak to compete with these other forces. It was the determination of the most decorated Philippine soldier, General Fidel V. Ramos, that his country not become a "banana republic," riddled by military coups.[2] The economic forces at work tended to reinforce his own efforts to prevent such an occurrence, but at the time of writing it was not clear that those two sets of forces were strong enough to prevent the destruction of the polity—or its steady deterioration into precisely what General Ramos so dreaded, a banana republic.

Thus this book conveniently divides into three phases, with the claims of democracy, security, and development differing in each.

This book is also about three players who dominated the republic in the Aquino era, but dominated it *ad seriatim*. Corazon Cojuangco Aquino reigned throughout the three periods of this book, but only barely ruled in one of them—the first. It is through her that we examine the attempts to reinstitutionalize democracy in the Philippines, while development plans were reinvigorated.

The second period saw the emergence of General Ramos, also known as "Eddie" in a country of first names, from the shadows in which his powerful cousin Ferdinand Marcos and *his* cousin General Fabian Ver had kept him, as he perfected his strategy for defeating the Communist revolution in the countryside that threatened the republic's survival. This is a period of security concerns, in which the seemingly more threatening dangers, especially that of the Maoist New People's Army, were reduced almost to manageable proportions.

The last period, however, was dominated at times in numerous substantive ways and certainly symbolically, though never in formal position, by Aquino's extraordinary cousin, Eduardo "Danding" Cojuangco, whose descent from the skies on the eve of the 1989 coup set the pace for the politics of the third period. His political program, which followed the strategy he had followed throughout his life, was to increase growth rapidly in the Philippines through shrewdly chosen investments. The period ended with the presidential election of 1992, in which he was a prime contender.

Corazon Aquino

To have underestimated Ninoy Aquino's widow was a mistake many regretted. Anyone knowledgeable of Philippine social structure would know the role of the woman was always significant. And if Cory Aquino stayed in the background as a wife and was overshadowed in the public eye by her always effervescent and usually overwhelming husband, it had to be remembered that she was a Cojuangco, a member of the richest landowning family of the republic. She had substantial interests to look out for and defend.[3]

"Only the uninformed and naive would consider [her] politically innocent, for . . . in her is a confluence of the political gifts and propensities of both sides of her family. Politics is in her blood," Isabelo Crisostomo writes in a biography.[4]

The awe in which she was held abroad, and the expectations seen for her rule in her first years of power, are well expressed by David Steinberg, a longtime student of Philippine history:

> During the long years in which her husband was incarcerated and she lived a private terror, she grew in stature and wisdom. Corazon Maria Aquino exhibits a quality of Grace that confounds both her allies and her foes alike. This transcendental dimension stems from a deep piety, suffusing all of her political actions. The historical trajectory has been altered and she has the potential of

breaking her nation free from a destiny that offered little hope for the masses and made the likelihood of social revolution [sic] very high.[5]

Yet it was equally a mistake to assume that Cory Aquino had acquired powers and skills of statecraft by miracle. She was no mere housewife, but she was perforce also learning politics on the job. If she felt at ease with heads of state, it was as aristocrat and Ninoy's widow; mastering Filipino politics was something else. She was tough enough to resist all those—such as her vice president—who assumed that once installed, she would be content with ceremony; once installed, however, she was not tough enough to lay out and demand any basic reforms beyond ridding the country of the immediate heritage of the Marcos entourage, for which her motivation was manifestly obvious. Or was she on a cleft stick—wanting to rid the country of Marcos's vestiges but unwilling to give up the privileges of class that might be entailed for her family and herself?

What she symbolized was powerful enough to gain history's largest honorarium, as Senator Robert Dole quipped after she had addressed the American Congress and netted an additional $100 million for her country. It was powerful enough also to keep herself, family, and friends in office for a good six years. But what it turned out she had in common with Marcos is that, presented a once-in-a-generation opportunity to institute basic reform, she, like Marcos with Martial Law, threw away the chance. And, perhaps on a smaller scale, she seems, like Marcos, to have permitted those around her, including her own family (or especially her own family), to obtain the material profit of governance.[6]

Thus it was frequently asked, when the tone and burden of her administration veered from reform in the first year to—once a congress had been elected—conservative politics as usual as in the pre-Marcos era: Was she pushed that way by the military, by the Americans, by business interests? Or was that her natural resting place, where she would have ended up in any case? The answer is both, but the second question is the more salient one. There was absolutely nothing in her intellectual or social preparation indicating the slightest interest in serious social reform. Thus when David Steinberg in his congressional testimony spoke of "the extraordinary quality of her own person not only to celebrate the triumph of good over evil that she spearheaded, but also to underscore my conviction that social justice can start to happen, that the Communists can be defeated,"[7] he was simply illustrating the American weakness for—to quote Dr. Johnson—the triumph of hope over experience, as so many did of these events.

She was not interested in the intricacies or substance of reform, which she well showed by putting land reform off for over two years after coming to office, by which time it was probably too little and too late. "[W]hen EDSA catapulted her to the presidency," Teodoro Benigno, once her press secretary, said, "she had all the power to effect the reforms that were then probably necessary and even imperative, including land reform. When she had the maximum power, she had the minimum knowledge of the presidency."[8]

She also lacked the conventional language of political and economic reform (though of course she could use it in prepared speeches around the country).[9] She was not part of the international culture of economic developers—roving World Bank or International Monetary Fund (IMF) officials, for example—and land reform was an especially distant (and threatening) concept. Unfortunately, it was difficult for her to learn these languages on the job. "She is more of a talker than a listener,"[10] an American who dealt with her frequently commented. And since she believed, in a quite literal sense, that she had God on her side, such language was never considered salient.

It is important to note that her husband had a fair amount of opportunism about him; he could deal between left and right to his own advantage (for example, keeping the old Huks and New People's Army [NPA] at bay with personal deals in his own province, sometimes, indeed, on the grounds of his wife's great hacienda, while maintaining close friendships with numerous conservative Americans). As president he would have been simply more competent than most Filipino leaders, and probably less corrupt, if only for lack of need, given Cory's wealth—and principle.

Corazon Aquino was something else. Her family was serious. Her father was a Chinese banker and one of the richest men of the Philippines, owner of a six-thousand-hectare hacienda in central Tarlac, where she grew up. Her maternal grandfather was a famous senator, two uncles were congressmen. Small wonder that she found nothing unusual—or exceptional—about having, as president, a brother, brother-in-law, cousin, and uncle in Congress. And it was a close-knit family. Even as president, Corazon Aquino attended the weekly family breakfasts presided over by Don Pedro Cojuangco, her older brother. It was classicly Chinese.

The ties with the United States were also serious; early in the postwar era her family started a newspaper that " 'dedicated itself to the promotion of Filipino-American understanding,' "[11] according to one study. She spent her last three years of high school and then college in America—at a sister school of her Manila Catholic school, a convent school in New York, and then the little-known College of Mount St. Vincent, also in New York.

While in America, those who knew her found her a deeply principled woman devoted to her family—defined in Philippine extended terms—and to her God. Her religion was serious. In school, her "strong faith became evident early when she joined the Sodality of Mount Sinai Vincent, a club for especially religious students, to study Roman Catholic liturgy," according to her biographer.[12] Many disbelieved the sincerity with which she applied prayer to statecraft and found incredible the notion that she truly believed that prayer alone, unaccompanied by galvanizing leadership, was sufficient to deal with the republic's ills. But it was true, and it is true that she so believed, and assumed that unanswered prayers were divine tests. As statecraft faltered, prayer groups at Malacañang Palace took on new life.

Beyond prayer was her sense of what her most perceptive observer, Teodoro Benigno, called "the seasons" of which she was a creature. "She moves in terms of seasons. She thinks that things will come to pass. She feels that time has a way of resolving problems, of healing wounds, of pacifying passions."[13]

In the Philippines we have seen all too clearly how rapidly power corrupts. Power used to achieve needed social goals ennobles. Aquino's major defect was in her inability to *use* power, to harness it, corruptly or nobly. She had no instinct for the jugular, no sense of how to place "her" people in key positions throughout the government in order to achieve her program, as Margaret Thatcher did by moving Nicholas Ridley and others around various ministerial posts, *pour encourager les autres*. Power, Bertrand Russell reminds us, means "I talk you listen." Aquino knew she had a right to be listened to, but she never had a talking agenda beyond getting rid of the Marcos legacy, and that she overdid to an extent that almost destroyed her other agendas. Her only effective network was that provided by her avaricious younger brother, who tightly controlled patronage, and whose corruption was widely believed to have attained Marcos-like levels by the end.

Indeed her problem was in what she thought she had a right to, her sense of entitlement. It may seem to beg a question to say that her upbringing, her "breeding" as she would call it, made a sense of class entitlement inevitable; how then do we explain the earthy feel for the jugular displayed by her equally well-born and wealthy cousin Danding Cojuangco, whom we discuss below? For that matter, her husband, though far less wealthy, arguably descended from an equally luminous family, and no one ever accused him of reticence in the use of power.

The distinction, quite apart from genetics, is in the enormous gap in the style of upbringing of boys and girls among the *Ilustrados*. The "macho" values permeating all other classes in the Philippines drove culture among wealthy boys as well (as Benigno writes, "Ninoy was essentially the quint-essential macho."),[14] but the girls were reared to be ladies. Though they might well play a role in running family finances or businesses beyond what was normal in the past generation in equivalent American households, they were not involved in the rough-and-tumble of Filipino politics; Imelda Marcos was the first woman politician in the Philippines to wield a political knife—and her motivation, as a child of a dispossessed branch of a rich family, was only too well known.[15]

Corazon Aquino's personal strength and courage were never in question. But she had no political instincts worthy of her heritage, and so the government that was administered under her name lasted for six years with only such direction as was imposed from without.

Her class status—referred to precisely as such by Professor Felipe Miranda—did bring with it "the idea that the people around her whom she knows personally could be trusted to help her since after all, she particularly would mean well in a democratic sense."[16] In fact, as we see below, many of them were hardly deserving of such trust.

There was also the question of her husband's heritage. Teodoro Benigno seems once again to have found its essence—in Corazon Aquino's "reacting against the personality of Ninoy."

> Having been married to a very gifted, talented politician, who was an element of nature and who, as a matter of fact, dominated everything he set his mind to, including of course, Cory Aquino, or most especially, Cory Aquino [coming to office] was a very traumatic experience for her.

The effect, he said, was for her to surround herself not with the competent politicians of the sort Ninoy attracted, but rather with people who were "like shadows going in and out of the office," with whom she was comfortable, and through whom she emerged from "the cocoon of Ninoy.... These people inside have the 'good news syndrome.' "[17] Her cabinet could not call her directly, it was noted; Marcos's could.

One thing that gave her strength and helped her survive was her own stubbornness. At a press conference, asked whether she might "cave in" to Congress on a particular issue, she replied, "I never caved in when Ninoy was in prison for seven years. I never caved in either when we were living in the United States. There were never any deals or any compromises, and I know what my duties are. I will do exactly what I believe is right and I will pursue this plan of action."[18]

General Fidel V. Ramos

Fidel Ramos was born in 1928 to Narciso Ramos, a worldly—and kindly—diplomat who ultimately became foreign secretary, and to a sister of Ferdinand Marcos's mother. He graduated from West Point in 1950 and also gained a degree in civil engineering from the University of Illinois. He did service in Korea as a reconnaissance platoon leader and later was operations officer with the first "Philcag"—Philippine Civic Action Group—in Vietnam. No one in or out of the armed forces doubted the brilliance of his future, either by his own competence or his inheritance. His classmates knew he was marked; one noted that he was the first in their class to have his own car, which in the early 1950s meant real wealth when young captains made token salaries. Though his family was not rich, it was more than comfortable.

He was not one to take a stand, for most of his life, which in part explains his willingness to go along with martial law, when he might well have taken a long sabbatical leave at the least. But he had never done so, and only in his sixth decade, when he had a great opportunity to make a difference, did he seize it.[19]

It can also be said that Ramos was always a seemingly unassertive person whose comparative advantage was staff organization. But whereas Filipinos are thought to be great planners though bad executors, Ramos carried out his plans, he made things happen. It was on this that his reputation grew.

He played a key role in martial law as commander of the Philippine Constabulary, the national police, and his visage in that period reflected ambivalence about its achievements.[20] He was proud that law and order had been restored, that almost a half-million guns had been collected; he was not eager for the return of the old politics—but was ashamed to have been a part of a collective that tortured and bullied.

"People's Power" of 1986 permitted his atonement, as he, along with Minister of National Defense Juan-Ponce Enrile, played the critical role in mustering the gun barrels to get his cousin out of power and out of the country. From then on he became the country's first democrat. He put down seven rebellions; in the most important one he could have himself taken supreme power. He defeated the coup attempts not by ordering his opponents down; it is unlikely that would have worked in any circumstances given the divisions of the country. Rather it was, as on one occasion, by circulating all night from camp to camp, from group to group, using the powers of reason and good sense. Only when the rebels started firing did he order that the guns be manned. He was not the "macho" strong man the Philippine polity was reaching out for at the end of the period of this book[21]—and he may have let his personal behavior be guided by his need to conform to that national need. Still, as his country's most decorated soldier, he more than adequately symbolized the order the polity wished to see in high office. He was running for the presidency and was determined to achieve it constitutionally.

In his frequent trips around his country, usually sitting on the edge of an open helicopter looking out over the archipelago, he displayed both humility and courage. His instructions to bases where he was to visit always included strict orders that there be no fuss, no colors, that he would eat "with the men" in the mess, and that security be kept to an absolute minimum—to the extent, in NPA-infested territory, that his traveling companions were positively terrified for his (not to mention their own) survival. He showed compassion for the poor, an open heart for NPA guerrilla returnees from the hills ("it's their country too," he told a group of European human rights activists), and an absolute determination that his country shape up in democratic ranks. He could not be poor, but his life style seemed to suggest, on the whole, that he had been far less corrupt than opportunity had otherwise allowed.[22]

Ramos thought a great deal about his country's problems, and in his speeches during his stint as Secretary of National Defense (SND) he showed a profundity that few public officials in any country ever manifest. In late 1988 he said that "Our history as a people has been one of failure to reach a stable basis for national consensus, of opportunities to put the nation on course missed or misused." He went on to speak of the ruling elite ("which has too much and a majority that has too little"): "And this fundamental imbalance has caused our society to be in constant danger of being violently overthrown and fed the discontent of the masses even as we struggle for nationhood."[23]

Before the return and ascendance of Danding Cojuangco, Ramos had an almost straight shot at the palace. His standing in the polls put him far ahead of the competition. For during 1988 and 1989 Ramos all but mastered the insurgency that had plagued the republic for two decades. Although successes have many fathers—and there are many claimants for the success in reducing the Communist Party of the Philippines/New People's Army to manageable proportions in these years—there can be little doubt that the strongest claim to paternity goes to Ramos, who formulated the strategy and had the tenacity to stick with it until results started coming in.

Ironically, it was the factionalism in his own organization, the Armed Forces of the Philippines, with the coups that resulted, which in the end probably weakened his standing in the presidential sweepstakes. It was one thing for him to look loyal—and to look good—putting down coups. But after the nearly successful coup attempt (hereafter the Great Coup) of 1989, what stood out was an army on which the government could not rely to keep itself in power, whether or not Ramos remained loyal.

His only way out of the dilemma, many concluded, was to perform an "inside," or so-called constitutional, coup, in which, presumably, Mrs. Aquino remained in Malacañang Palace, with all executive power going to him and his associates.[24] It was a prospect that he found uncongenial in the extreme, though by 1991, as the country's political and economic situation deteriorated, many thought that he could no longer resist the pressures to undertake precisely such action.

Eduardo (Danding) Cojuangco

Even before his return in late 1989 Danding Cojuangco was talked of, in knowledgeable circles, as the strongest possible presidential candidate. A former governor of Tarlac, his power in Marcos's court was legendary, though in 1990 he was trying to create an image separate from Marcos. One columnist called him "the lean and hungry Cassius who would whisper into the emperor's ears, and the emperor would brighten and nod, clap his hands and summon his courtiers," and recounted the story according to which Danding slapped the face of the First Lady's powerful brother in the presence of President Marcos,[25] presumably for *lèse-majesté*.

Though he was "crony #1" of Marcos, he was a crony with a difference. Everything he had ever touched turned to gold; his enterprises throughout the archipelago thrived and his employees celebrated him. On his return he had a network even with four years of rust that outshone everyone else's. Danding's fortune was largely in the Philippines; he believed in his country.[26] Born to great wealth, he multiplied it by orders of magnitude and was always thought to relish the position of power behind the throne. But on his return it became clear that to recoup the properties the Aquino government had sequestered he would have to sit on the throne. Within six months of his return the 1992 presidential election, still two years away, seemed a forgone conclusion, if the same trends prevailed—and if indeed the election were held.[27]

As he retrieved his sequestered properties, including his voting rights in the giant San Miguel Corporation, he revealed the extent of his network and fortune. Wherever he went around the archipelago, great crowds followed— whether because he was "Mr. Basketball" in a country where that is the most popular diversion, or because he gave off the scent of victory. In the last part of this period, whatever the outcome was to be at the presidential polls, he gave the appearance of having cousin Cory's government on the run.

These three people, so close in age and upbringing, symbolized the spectrum of the Filipino elite. There was a woman who as psychological symbol of the Virgin Mary could cleanse her country of the sins of a ruthless dictatorship that had been visited upon it; a modest soldier, atoning for his past, and thus symbolizing the role of so many in the republic; and a tough and sometimes ruthless politician, who seemed to be telling the nation to end its self-mortification and get on with development. And if Danding were not to succeed, the country might choose from between the Cojuangco extremes—extremes including those represented by the two cousins. But it was on this spectrum that Filipinos and Filipinas were likely to find themselves.

NOTES

1. There is a substantial literature on the events leading up to and including the Epifanio de los Santos (EDSA) coup. See in particular Raymond Bonner, *Waltzing with a Dictator* (New York: Vintage Books, 1988), and for a local military perspective, see Col. Hector M. Terrazona, *After Edsa*, Vol. I (Manila: Hector M. Terrazona, 1989).

2. Interview, General Fidel V. Ramos, October, 1989.

3. President Aquino listed her assets at less than twenty million pesos in 1989, or less than a million dollars. It was a standard joke among Filipinos that politicians understated their assets by at least an order of magnitude; then the problem was that requirements of publication had to be consistent with what had been declared to the Bureau of Internal Revenue. It little mattered how personally rich she was; her family was rich on an international scale, and became vastly richer as a result of her presidency. It was unlikely that she would fail to benefit materially to any extent she wished upon leaving Malacañang Palace. It was commonly understood in the meantime that her immediate family was benefitting from her office on a large scale, and attention was periodically focused in the press on her sons-in-law in particular.

4. Isabelo T. Crisostomo, *Cory: Profile of a Presidency* (Quezon City, Manila: J. Kriz Publishing Enterprises, 1986), p. 14.

5. Committee on Foreign Affairs, US House of Representatives, Hearings and Markup before the Subcommittee on Asian and Pacific Affairs (February 25, March 3, 4, 5, 11, 12, 17, 18, 1987), p. 585. Hereafter, "Hearings and Markup."

6. Increasingly, toward the end of this period, knowledgeable Filipinos talked of the "certainty" that Mrs. Aquino too had benefitted materially—and directly. Nor would all agree that the scale was any different from the Marcos period, especially when they figured in the potential profits from the base lands to be captured through presidential favor from the U.S.-Philippines Bases agreement. That remained to be seen. But in all fairness, it must be added that it took years for direct evidence of Marcos corruption to emerge, so the question of how Aquino era corruption and that of the Marcos period stacked up also remained to be seen—though it seemed highly unlikely that even presidential brother Peping Cojuangco could have amassed the scale of wealth the Marcoses did. In any event, the Aquino clan had many fewer years.

7. "Hearings and Markup," p. 585.

8. "The Presidency," *Solidarity* Seminar Series on Public Issues, No. 20, *Solidarity* 125 (January-March 1990), p. 147. Hereafter "The Presidency."

9. For example, her May Day speech in 1986, pledging an "economic revolution that will lift us from poverty, underdevelopment, and economic injus-

tice." Cited in Lucy Komisar, *Corazon Aquino: The Story of a Revolution* (New York: George Braziller, 1988), p. 178.

10. Though Mrs. Aquino in some respects was conscious of being a listener. During the chaotic month of November 1986, when Defense Minister Enrile attempted a coup and was sacked, she said in a speech that it had been said that "Marcos was the first male chauvinist to underestimate me. He was not the last to pay for that mistake. . . . One distinct quality I have observed in the men who would discount my abilities, diminish my role, or who cannot bring themselves to imagine that I shall rule this country . . . is their ability to outtalk me at every opportunity. . . . [But] I would like to think that I have managed to have the last word." *Ibid.*, p. 243.

11. Jose Syjuco, quoted in Rosalinda Piñeda-Ofreneo, *The Manipulated Press: A History of Philippine Journalism since 1945* (Manila: 1984), p. 71, cited in "The Philippine Press System, 1811-1989," by Doreen G. Fernandez, *Philippine Studies* 37 (1989).

12. Crisostomo, *Cory: Profile of a Presidency*, p. 36.

13. "The Presidency," p. 147.

14. *Ibid.*, p. 174.

15. See for example the irreverent and often highly informed *Imelda and the Clans, A Story of the Philippines*, "by her dissident niece" Betriz Romualdez Francia (Manila: Solar Publishing Co., 1988).

16. "The Presidency," p. 150.

17. *Ibid.* It was widely assumed that the (at least unconscious) reason President Aquino kept Ninoy's friends at arm's length was her own discomfort with her knowledge that they had gone around with her husband in his not infrequent "womanizing" on the town.

18. Interview by Amando Doronila and Paulyn Sicam, 3 July, in *Manila Chronicle* (8 July 1990), in Foreign Broadcast Information Service-East Asia-90-134 (12 July 1990), hereafter FBIS-EAS.

19. Stories in the Philippines that I could not confirm state that Ramos at some point early in his career made a serious mistake, which his subsequent life was an attempt to compensate for. Varying stories were told, no proof was ever found. The point is that people believe it of him.

20. Based on interviews with the author, 1979-89.

21. It was common knowledge that Ramos, despite his exemplary public behavior throughout his adult life to his wife, the registrar of the International School, had a mistress who often reportedly traveled with him, which was widely thought to help his image where it was deficient. One columnist brought it almost into the open, in asking why Cardinal Sin was endorsing Executive Secretary Orbos for the presidency, instead of his EDSA comrade—"and it seems religion has nothing to do with it" (Ramos being a Protestant). "Will the honorable Cabinet member . . . stick to his guns and insist that there is absolutely no, repeat no, basis to the unfair charges alluding to his personal life? Or will he divest himself, once again in a timely fashion, of certain encumbrances that may compromise his bid for the

highest public office in the land?" "Eddie's Empowerment," Armando Malay, Jr., *Newsday* (2 April 1991).

22. Published assets mean little in the Philippines; Ramos listed the value of his house in the extremely exclusive "village" of Ayala Alabang as around $100,000, which from its outward appearance was surely an order of magnitude less than its replacement cost. However, even as Secretary of National Defense he traveled in small cars with minimal or no security.

23. "Nation Building and National Security," Speech of Sec. Fidel V. Ramos, 81st Foundation of the Philippine Columbian Association (11 December 1988).

24. See infra, p. 288. Also see FBIS-EAS-90-174, "Listen to Ilagan, Quezon City Eagle Broadcasting Radio in Tagalog (4 September 1990): "It appeared that when rumors of a coup d'etat were flowing in the country—it was said that Secretary Ramos would be involved in a constitutional coup."

25. Teodoro Benigno, "Mr. Crony Tiptoes into Town," *Philippine Star*, 29 November 1989.

26. See for example "Danding speaks out!" undated, published by "Friends of Danding," in which he emphasizes his development hopes for the Philippines.

27. See Peter Waldman, "Closest Marcos Crony Is Favorite to Succeed Aquino in the Philippines," *Wall Street Journal* (2 April 1990), p. A1. See also John McBeth, "Tough Nut to Crack, Cojuangco Provides Serious Challenge to Aquino," *Far Eastern Economic Review* (8 February 1990), pp. 8-9.

2

Democracy and Development

In the wave of third world democracy-building during the 1980s, the restoration of democratic hopes in the Philippines stands out, thanks to the depravity of the old order and the clarity of the democratic hopes of the new middle and upper-middle-class elite that brought Corazon Aquino to power.

Political Structure

But what of the "democracy" that was restored? One problem in examining Philippine democracy is the illusion, which many of its western students maintain, of the apparent similarity of institutions in that country and in the West, particularly in the United States, which provided the explicit model. A presidency, a Senate, and a House of Representatives hid two more pervasive underpinnings of Filipino politics. One is the Malay basis of the society, a consensus culture that only *appeared* to be making its political bargains through the superficial institutions of popular power in Manila. It is in some ways more instructive to compare Filipino culture with its sister Malay-based state Malaysia, of which several authorities argue that "the strong curbs placed on political conflict and dissent may be seen as reflective of Malay cultural values, which appreciate strong authority and fear conflict and dissention."[1]

The other is the Spanish heritage; representatives of the King of Castile held the islands as personal property, as King Leopold had held the Congo. It was to be exploited—and it was. The tradition flourished for four hundred years. Notions of individual rights did not develop, not even in the revolution against the Spaniards that a nascently imperialistic America so shrewdly exploited. But a form of personalism ironically did develop, in considerable contrast to Malaysia (but not in contrast to equally-Malay Indonesia), as an outgrowth of the mixed ethnic heritage of the ruling elite and the fact that social status among the ruling *mestizos* arose almost purely from, in David Steinberg's words, "wealth and consumption,"[2] as opposed to descendence from a precolonial elite.

To appreciate the pattern maintenance that Aquino conservatism represents, as we will argue, it is useful to note what Frank Golay, the authority on Philippine political economy in the first republic, had to say over two decades ago.

> A distinguishing characteristic of the Philippine political system . . . is its monolithic conservatism. This is explained in part by the failure of the "new men" who precipitated the Philippine revolution in the waning years of the 19th century and were superseded by members of the cacique elite imbued with Hispanic-clerical and class loyalties and with political power rooted in the semifeudal organization of Philippine rural society. The land-based oligarchy steadily tightened its grip on the independence movement and used the increasing self-government granted by the Americans to perfect a political system designed to perpetuate its political dominance. The power of this oligarchy has remained firmly rooted in dispersed satrapies based on ethnic and regional loyalties.[3]

Nothing much changed in the ensuing two decades. We might say that the struggle for political order and thence democracy is that of finding a balance between the tendency of the state to become all-powerful or totalitarian, on the one hand, or "subsystem dominant," where the claims of the state on behalf of the majority are subordinated to the interests of a class, on the other. This latter position has almost always been the case of the Philippines in the twentieth century. As Professor Tony Smith has written, the "autonomy of the state from social forces was not attained" under the Americans, and instead "sixty families" ruled, circulating through the medium of elections and never allowing an effective state to rise.[4] True, Marcos had a chance, and indeed to some extent used it, to restructure the state after he proclaimed martial law and greatly cut the power of the landowning oligarchy. But his achievement of personal power largely overshadowed the increased efficiency of the state, and in the end there were few positive accomplishments left from the early days of martial law. As we will see, the oligarchs were swift to put the old system back in place after they had got rid of Marcos. The system returned to what Paul Hutchcroft refers to as "patrimonial plunder," to describe the system before *and* after Marcos.[5]

The system was not a construct of western social scientists; Filipinos talked openly (and talked incessantly) as to how their values inhibited efficiency or reform. In a memorandum on human rights—and their consistent enforcement—to the AFP's chief of staff, Secretary of National Defense Ramos, for example, noted that "We are all aware of how the Filipino cultural trait of 'pakikisama',[6] worthy as it may be, often frustrates our efforts at enforcing discipline and upholding justice for all." Arguing for "transparency"—the latest American borrowing—he ruled that officers would be held accountable for *not* upholding their duty to report violations, that is, in contradistinction to their cultural inclinations.[7]

Similarly, in a budget justification, General Mariano Adelem accounted for the fatness of the officer corps by noting the "defect" in the promotional system, "given the culture of Filipinos"—those bypassed for promotion couldn't be kicked out; it just was not possible.[8]

In direct contrast is the patience and perseverance of the Filipino, which helps to explain why there is so much tolerance of so much that is wrong.

In the period of this study the republic was beset by repeated and grave challenges, some of them natural disasters, most of them man-made, but the public attitude was generally one of patience. Senate President Jovito Salonga said that after the December 1989 coup, "you had the drought, then the earthquake, then the brownouts, the rains and the typhoons and the floods and of course the energy crisis, the confrontation in the Middle East and the great probability of an increase . . . in the price of oil and basic commodities. So in a way [Cory's problems are too serious]. . . . We will have more difficult times. But I think the Filipino will smile, survive and overcome."[9] The following table is revealing.

In the first question, in which figures are percentages of total responses, we find "God" dominating, as it would in a very Catholic country; it is hard to imagine a Filipino *not* so responding. But in the second, which notes the frequency among the first three items mentioned, we get a more revealing indication of values than the rote response of the first; God and personal perseverance are tied at the top; government, fate, and family are roughly equal, in the fourth decile.

The Philippines is an attentive polity and political culture; the degree of political awareness in the country, despite its geographic nature, is remark-

ATENEO PUBLIC OPINION SURVEY[10]

Questionnaire Item	Survey area		Socioeconomic Class		
	RP	Metro Manila	ABC	D	E
• *Factor which the respondent considers as most important for his/her own and his/her family's progress—First rank*					
God	57	65	64	56	55
Personal perseverance	37	30	33	37	40
Government	2	2	1	2	2
Fate/Luck	2	1	1	3	1
Family/Relatives	2	2	1	2	2
Non-relatives one knows	0.2	0	0	—	0
• *Factors which the respondent considers as important for his/her own and his/her family's progress—Frequency of mention among first three ranked items*					
God	94	93	94	93	94
Personal perseverance	94	96	94	93	94
Government	39	44	45	39	35
Fate/Luck	32	19	23	30	40
Family/Relatives	34	36	33	36	31
Non-relatives one knows	5	9	5	6	4
• *Most important thing the respondent considers he/she should do for his/her own progress—First rank*					
Pray	45	51	40	47	44
Good work	39	28	38	39	40
Study	10	16	15	9	9
Maintain good relations	4	3	5	4	6
Lodge petitions with the government	1	1	1	1	1
Nothing, just wait to be lucky	1	—	—	—	1
• *Things which the respondent considers he/she should do for his/her own progress—Frequency of mention among first three ranked items*					
Pray	83	81	78	83	85
Good work	95	96	96	94	94
Study	41	58	50	40	38
Maintain good relations	67	57	64	70	66
Lodge petitions with the government	7	4	7	7	7
Nothing, just wait to be lucky	4	1	3	3	6
Boot-licking	1	1	0	1	1

able. Almost all the voting public can identify the country's main players. Extraordinarily, in socioeconomic class E—the bottom third—two thirds of the Ateneo respondents knew of Foreign Secretary Manglapus, and the percentage continued to grow with time; in the 1990 survey it was up almost to three fourths. Four fifths in 1989 had heard of General Ramos, and that number went up slightly as well; the not very visible Education Secretary, Lourdes Quisumbing, was recognized by well over half the respondents. In the ABC group combined, all those figures were in the ninth decile.[11]

Yet whither the commitment to democracy, for all that sophistication? As we will see, the armed forces were riven by factions ready to seize power at any convenient opportunity; a fifth of the nation's barangays (villages) were Communist-influenced or held (perhaps at the point of a gun, though one suspects that NPA justice, and redistribution of local wealth, were equally salient); surveys showed that, especially among the D and E groups, the commitment to democracy was contingent on results that were hardly in evidence during the Aquino era; several of the strongest candidates for the 1992 presidential election, if such an election was held, were authoritarians who, while no doubt keeping the forms of democracy, seemed highly

	ATENEO PUBLIC OPINION SURVEY[12]				
	Survey area		Socioeconomic Class		
Questionnaire Item	**RP**	**Metro Manila**	**ABC**	**D**	**E**
• *Possibility of the Filipino people completely losing faith in peaceful means of promoting democracy*					
February 1988					
Possible	50	58	55	49	50
Undecided	21	19	21	22	19
Not possible	23	21	22	23	23
March 1990					
Possible	40	49	41	43	35
Undecided	23	12	21	26	21
Not possible	30	37	34	26	34
• *Possibility of the Filipino people choosing a military government over a civilian government*					
March 1990					
Possible	31	33	28	32	30
Undecided	21	9	20	25	16
Not possible	42	57	47	37	46

unlikely to maintain its spirit. In short, the prospects for democracy in the Philippines were modest at best. When soldiers struck in the Great Coup, there was no "People Power" to hold them back, but there were cheers, of a modest sort, for the rebels.

Democracy, we would argue, is less a set of rules about the division of power and manner of elections than a habit of working together, sharing power, in a spirit of tolerance. Tolerance is not how one describes the Filipino polity. Yet consider the results of the Ateneo survey in 1990.

Across the board, all classes showed more faith in democracy in 1990 *after* the Great Coup than before, and despite all other evidence that the polity was not working. It is hard to interpret this other than by our newly identified characteristic of perseverance in the Filipino psyche, which we saw in the preceding table.

A critical defect in the country's polity is in the relationship of power and money, which are related in every society. But to a degree not found elsewhere, politics in the Philippines is seen as the start of the road to success and fortune—unlike, for example, the United States where it tends to be the end of the road. General Ramos made the point very well when he noted:

> We are talking about a society that emerged from colonial rule with an economic and political elite whose privileges were rooted in the patronage it acquired from the country's colonizers. The point is significant because it is the basis of the belief, still prevalent to this day, that political influence is the indispensable root of material benefit.[13]

Formal political structures created in the Aquino era reflected all the other uncertainties in the polity. It is understandable that the constitution-drafters of 1986-87 wished to ensure that everything a piece of paper could do to prevent another Marcos from coming to power would be done. The central arm of his dictatorship was martial law; though he suspended it in 1982, he had already created—using its umbrella—sufficient power to keep the results of martial law in place. Small wonder, then, that Section 18 of the new constitution required the president, in the event of rebellion, to submit to the Congress a report on any proclamation of martial law (and/or revocation of habeas corpus) within forty-eight hours; and gave Congress, "by a vote of at least a majority of all its Members in regular or special session," the authority to revoke the proclamation. As Teodoro Benigno put it, the constitution was "almost without teeth," framed with "an ogre in mind . . . a political monster of such hideous proportions that they had to box [the president] in with a lot of constitutional constraints."[14]

National Character

The defects in the bargaining structure of the Philippine polity is understandably related to national character. There is no absence of guilt assessment. Senator Leticia Shahani, herself one of the most distinguished Filipinas of her generation, gave a "privilege" speech in the Senate just after the 1987 coup attempt, on the "weakness of the Filipino character." "Ours is a sick nation, gravely afflicted with the interlocking diseases of poverty, passivity, graft and corruption, exploitative patronage, factionalism, political instability, love for intrigue, lack of discipline, lack of patriotism and the desire for instant self-gratification."[15] In calling for the creation of a commission of inquiry into these alleged defects and their remedies, she worried about the self-destructive urge among Filipinos that she feared was generalized into a "policide" culture—meaning the murder of the state, or "sui-policide."[16]

In some ways, however, her very speech illustrated part of the problem. The defects she mentioned were hardly novel; what a commission would do besides further publicize them was also not clear—as indeed one of her colleagues, Senator Vicente Paterno, noted. If, he argued, "we continue . . . to flagellate ourselves and look only at our weaknesses, who else is going to praise the Filipino in this world . . . ?"[17] he asked. Trollope had the Duke of Omnium say it no better.

There is another trait worth noting in the same article. Filipinos talk themselves down. Mr. "Teddyboy" Locsin, a Filipino *Ilustrado*, sometime Aquino speechwriter and supporter of the new order, once accused his country of "congenital cowardice" as one of its strongest characteristics, on the basis of its reluctance to protest martial law,[18] though in fact until the early 1980s there remained much support for Marcos, thanks to the lower classes' desire for order.

Filipinos also talk too much, it is said, and the talk is often unrelated to reality; *The Economist* had a sidebar saying "Filipinos talk too much for their own good." "The problem is that the torrent of words (memorably described by one foreign diplomat as 'fluency without meaning') can obscure the need for action."[19]

Most observers have noted the defective sense of nationalism in the Philippines, defective only manifestly in its difference from other third world patterns. One journalist wrote that "we remain strangers to public demonstrations of love of country, of patriotic zeal and fervor. Many Filipinos feel self-conscious about singing the national anthem, about reciting the pledge of allegiance. . . . Perhaps, this is because we are still groping with our sense of nationhood."[20] In fact such "public demonstrations" had become extremely frequent—at Rotary meetings, official gatherings of almost any sort, and the start of school, Filipinos demonstrated their nascent nationhood. It was their doubt about it that was unusual.

The central structure of Filipino culture is *utang na loob*—or the structure of reciprocity that pervades daily existence. In all cultures there is the reality of reciprocity; there is usually the myth, and occasionally the reality, of ideals. In the Philippines *utang* is right on the table, there need be no excuse or "beating around the bush" because *utang* is a central and explicit societal value. It is important for us here because it helps to explain why the new republic could not shake off the patterns of the old republic.

Another implication of *utang* is the aversion on the part of the old political culture to issues and causes, nowhere better illustrated than in an editorial on "ingratitude"—the animadversion for *utang*—by Teddyboy Locsin. The article was in celebration of the journal's hero, Ninoy Aquino.

> *Utang na Loob* is the foundation of civilized society.
>
> It is the mark of a real man. This is known from Sicily to Sorsogon, from Canada to Cagayan. If you cannot be grateful, get out of politics, get out of our lives. The only ones who denounce *utang na loob* are fickle women, and the cause oriented [sic] who are sissies, anyway. The most disgusting animal on earth is the ungrateful.[21]

True, loyalty is a vital ingredient in any functioning governmental system.[22] Successful governments are driven, however, by ideals and ideas, just as President Aquino's was in its first year. The quotation makes clear why such an uproar ensued when, a generation earlier, an American ambassador called the Philippines "ungrateful."

Filipinos have never had a strategic sense as a nation; in some way because they never had to, as wards of a superpower. But it is difficult to have a discussion in Manila on national goals; life is pleasant, enjoyable, even amid strife and hardship. An example is the demographic explosion. With one of the highest growth rates in the world, the population was doubling approximately every twenty-seven years. At the current growth rate of 2.8 percent, the population would reach 150 million in thirty years. The issue is not whether there is or is not land on which another 50 or 100 million Filipinos could live, it is whether there are the services, the infrastructure, the schools, not to mention the resources for purchasing essentials, locally and from abroad.

Yet this subject is a difficult one to discuss in the Philippines, because of the very strong position the church takes. It is hard to get Filipinos to focus on the components of national strategy, to see the consequences of no improvement, for example on this issue. At a conference of the Solidarity Seminar on Public Issues, made up of senior professionals, one person insisted that there was no relation between growth rate and economic development. "It's not a necessary causal relationship," it "depends on what you do with your people." But *there* was the problem; more people has historically meant more pressure on resources in the archipelago.[23]

Operationally, the Marcos population program died in 1986—and was not replaced with anything until 1988, when Congress enacted legislation that declared birth control to be the nation's second-highest priority, behind only the insurgency. In fact nothing happened; it was even alleged that Popcom, the Population commission, funded "pro-life" interest groups.[24] John Blackton, a senior U.S. Agency for International Development (AID) official in Manila, in a paper on counterinsurgency, wrote that "the willingness of the Philippines to tackle this problem can be just as vital (in the long run) as the defeat of the insurgent movement."

> That the Aquino government appears unwilling or unable seriously to address the population problem is disturbing. It would be futile to succeed in defeating the insurgency, especially by military means alone during the guerilla phase, if the end result is a country which is not politically and economically viable, and which might therefore fall to the communists at some time in the future, perhaps without a shot being fired.[25]

"New" versus "Old" Politics

Between 1986 and 1990 the Philippines was attempting to salvage what of the past was not destroyed in a twenty-year autocracy and to fuse it onto new structures. But the clutter of the past made this difficult. Those attempting to introduce new political ideas (or ideas new to the Philippines) of equality and populism were outmanned—and outgunned—by old elites that knew what to do to recapture power and how to use it for their own wealth and aggrandizement.

In fact there should be little surprise in this. It was the professional middle and upper classes that constituted "People Power," and if some of these envisaged real economic reform—by way of redistribution—they were sufficiently entangled with those who wanted no economic reform as to get nowhere. Learned scholars generated "yellow books" envisaging historic economic change. The reality was that in the first year the government all but dealt in a vacuum. For one thing, there was no money; an American embassy official recalled how they had jiggled the books of their own project plans to get a few hundred million dollars of real money into the Filipino vault. The military was always restive and demanding more power, until Minister of National Defence Enrile finally overplayed his hand by involving himself in a coup.

But most important, all initiative was in Corazon Aquino's hands. Why did anyone delude himself into believing she had any interest in economic reform—because she had "cause" radicals at her side? Those—most conspicuously her executive secretary, Joker Arroyo—had their own hobby horses (in Joker's case, bringing errant officers to trial). What is the reason to believe Corazon Cojuangco Aquino would seize the estates of her own people, in a country where one's own people, one's extended family, is the highest social obligation? What is the reason to believe that Aquino had any desire to reduce her own standard of living and that of her family, below the extraordinary level of luxury that she had enjoyed her entire life (except in Boston).[26] Where is the evidence that she was a Roosevelt, either Roosevelt, as "traitor" to her class?

What happened is that the international community (including no small number in the Philippines itself) was so fixated on Marcos and his evils that it was assumed, without evidence, that the dragon slayer, the widow in yellow, would right all the other wrongs in the archipelago. Everyone was in something of a trance. Aquino never had any intention of real socioeconomic reform; at least there is no evidence beyond the boilerplate rhetoric of reform in her first years. It was late 1989 before she even began talking of help to the poor, which is a very different thing from restructuring society for their benefit.

The cause alliance that had brought her to power was called the "rainbow coalition" after the EDSA revolt. The monumental Davide Commission report, which reported on the great 1989 attempted coup, noted its problem:

> From this diverse array of forces was drawn the political leadership for the post-Marcos government, led by President Aquino. [It] was studded with prominent erstwhile Marcos cabinet members and politicians, side by side with veteran political leaders who fought Marcos and the "best and the brightest" non-political types. Their main challenge was to revive democracy and restore basic freedoms. . . . They assumed that the factors that bound them together in the so-called "rainbow coalition" were sufficiently strong to overcome deep-seated disagreements on social reform and economic policy. Unfortunately, much more is required of political leaders.

The report then reviews the governing elites of neighboring countries and finds, correctly, a coherence wholly lacking at home. "Elites in these countries think as one in moving their countries ahead. The ruling elite has a clear consensus indicative of a disciplined process of decision-making."[27]

While the conventional view is that Aquino moved to the right after the August 1987 coup attempt—when she caved in to numerous military demands, including the sacking of Joker Arroyo—her moves to the right actually came much earlier. Thus the traumatic month of November 1986, dominated by coup moves and for most of it a standoff between her circles and Enrile's, was a series of negotiations with Enrile as to how many concessions she should make even then to the right. Most critical was her firing of labor secretary Augusto "Bobbit" Sanchez, who was considered too pro-labor. James Clad, the respected reporter of the *Far Eastern Economic Review* then in Manila, doubted the wisdom of the move. "He carried progressive credentials that would allow him to make the KMU [the radical union Kilusang Mayo Uno (May 1)] bite their tongue and accept strike settlements. . . . He had given a progressive tone to the government. Now [with the appointment of corporate lawyer Franklin Drilon] it was contracting into a technocratic center of business people with strong U.S. links."[28]

In fairness to Mrs. Aquino it must be pointed out that from the moment of her inauguration, power was divided in the republic. It was not just that Juan-Ponce Enrile thought himself more entitled to the presidency than Aquino, by virtue of his moves as defense minister in ousting Marcos. It was that he was a power to himself, as were his senior lieutenants, particularly Gregorio "Gringo" Honasan, of whom so much more was to be heard in subsequent years. It was common to wonder why Aquino did not fire Enrile, when he was openly provoking her with public attacks on a daily basis in the fall of 1986, as his subalterns allegedly planted bombs around Metro Manila to frighten the populace. But her reported response had reality in it: "What if I fire him and he doesn't want to vacate his office? Who's going to enforce it?"[29] Small wonder, then, when the president dares not fire her own minister, that this coup was not even officially investigated, although General Ramos ordered an inquiry at the armed forces level; no charges were ever filed against the known plotters. The Davide Commission, which in the process of exhaustively investigating the 1989 coup attempt reviewed all past ones, quoted a source as saying

that Ramos's moves [in 1986] had always been conciliatory, not wanting to deepen the cleavages existing within the AFP. He said if the "iron fist" has been used, the military leadership was not sure about the sentiments and reactions of

149,412

the troops in the field. For his part, Ramos maintained that as [Chief of Staff] there was not much he could do inasmuch as the plotters were mostly under the jurisdiction of [Enrile's Ministry of National Defense] and answerable to someone else.

Two months later came another coup attempt. General Ramos had to spend five hours at night with Gringo Honasan and, reportedly, a hundred Reform the Armed Forces Movement (RAM) officers, all senior alumni of the 1986 People Power coup. They were demanding leniency for loyalists and an airing of their grievances on radio and television. It is hard to square the notion of governmental authority with a situation in which a colonel who has already helped stage one coup is still in command of troops and in a position to spend a night negotiating with the armed forces chief of staff.

The result is what Father Bernas, the distinguished constitutional lawyer and sometime pastor to the presidency, termed a "Nation in Crisis." It was his data even that provided the analytical context for the term—a Ford Foundation-funded annual "public opinion survey" that plumbed the depths of societal evolution (and on which we have already drawn, as the "Ateneo" surveys). A glimpse of what was happening in the latter phase of this study is grasped by a single entry. The survey popularized the breakdown of Filipino groups into A through E socioeconomic classes, as we have seen. In August 1988, after a year of rapid economic growth, about half of the population as a whole saw its "present quality of life compared to six months ago" as the same, but for every two who saw it as better, three saw it as worse; a year later, over three times as many saw it as worse, so rapidly were conditions deteriorating. In the E category of least advantaged, the ratio had gone from roughly two to one to *five* to one. And whereas in 1988 all groups expected their quality of life to improve in the coming six months, in August 1989 the population as a whole divided more pessimistically, with the E category seeing it as worse within six months by over two to one. When the cashiered colonel "Gringo" Honasan said, in an interview on the eve of the 1989 coup attempt, that a coup was a function of a "clear signal" of the masses to its military, he was not speaking hypothetically. Democracy was to be in a state of siege, at the very least.

NOTES

1. Larry Diamond, "Introduction: Persistence, Erosion, Breakdown, and Renewal," in Larry Diamond, Juan J. Linz, and Seymour Martin Lipset, *Democracy in Developing Countries, Vol. 3, Asia* (Boulder, CO: Lynne Rienner Publishers, 1989), p. 16.
2. Cited in Karl Jackson, "The Philippines: The Search for a Suitable Democratic Solution, 1946-1986," in *Ibid.*, p. 235.
3. Frank Golay, "Some Costs of Philippine Politics," *Asia* 23 (Autumn 1971).
4. Tony Smith, "America and Democracy in the Philippines," manuscript, p. 32.
5. Paul Hutchcroft, "Oligarchs and Cronies in the Philippine State: The Politics of Patrimonial Plunder," *World Politics* 43 (April 1991), pg. 414-450.
6. Defined as the maintenance of good relations, to the exclusion of other considerations, being good-hearted to one's friends, and thus eliciting similar treatment.
7. Memorandum, SND, Camp Aguinaldo, to Chief of Staff, AFP (1 December 1989).
8. Joint Committee, National Defense and Finance, Senate (27 June 1988).
9. Interview by Rey Arquiza with Senate President, *The Manila Chronicle* (9 September 1990), Foreign Broadcast Information Service-East Asia-90-176, (Sept. 1990), p. 49. Hereafter FBIS-EAS.
10. Ateneo de Manila University, *Public Opinion Survey*, August 1989 (Quezon City: Ateneo de Manila University, 1989), Table 15, pp. 51-52. Hereafter, Ateneo Survey. Roughly, A class is the rich elite, B and C are the middle classes, D is the lower-middle class, and E is the proletariat.
11. *Ibid.*, Table 5.
12. Ateneo Survey (1990), Table 19, p. 61.
13. Speech of Secretary Fidel V. Ramos, 81st Foundation Day of the Philippine Columbian Association (11 December 1988).
14. Teodoro Benigno, "Here's the Score: How Does the Republic Cope," *Philippine Star* (26 February 1990).
15. Senate Hearings, Vol. 1, No. 37 (17 September 1987), p. 958.
16. *Ibid.*, p. 960. Shahani had distinguished herself in Philippine diplomacy and international organizational work prior to entering politics. As General Ramos's sister she had additional authority.
17. *Ibid.*, p. 966.
18. "Surely ... a people who will kneel in Ilocano [Marcos] ordure for 11 years and stir only to scoop it up and inhale it, cannot qualify as a nation of congenital heroes," he replied to his critics a week later. "On Cowardice," *Philippine Free Press* (16 September 1989), p. 17.
19. "Survey, The Philippines," *The Economist* (7 May 1988), p. 15.

20. Melinda Quintos de Jesus, "Human Factor: EDSA Passions," *Philippine Star* (27 February 1990).

21. Theodoro L. Locsin, Jr., "On Ingratitude," *Philippine Free Press* (9 September 1989), p. 11.

22. Paul Nitze, the American strategist, made the revealing comment—for a nonideological person who, like Filipinos, had traversed both sides of the spectrum in his long career—that "loyalty is the only thing that counts in government."

23. Solidarity Seminar Series on Public Issues, no. 21, "Population Growth and National Development," *Solidarity* 126 (April-June 1990): 106. This speaker was not identified, because he/she, along with five others, did not agree with the conclusions.

24. Frank Jiang, "Pasturing a Fecund Flock," *Far Eastern Economic Review* (11 October 1990), p. 62.

25. John Stuart Blackton, "Counterinsurgency: Winning Within the Rule of Law," USAID (Manila: June 1989). Provided to the author by the Philippine Government.

26. Where Ninoy and Cory had a ten-room brick comfortable but not ostentatious house, without uniformed staff; in 1991 dollars the house would be worth approximately $750,000. Mrs. Aquino worked endlessly in those years around the house, entertaining Ninoy's friends and coping with children and family. It was also her happiest period, she told her neighbor, this author.

27. Davide Commission, *Republic of the Philippines*, "The Final Report of the Fact-Finding Commission" (pursuant to R.A. No. 6832) (Manila: October 1990), p. 100. Hereafter, "Davide."

28. Cited as interview with Clad, in Lucy Komisar, *Corazon Aquino: The Story of a Revolution* (New York: George Braziller, 1988), p. 241, and interview by author with Clad, Washington, D.C., 1989.

29. Komisar, op. cit., p. 230.

30. Davide, op cit., p. 183.

31. Ateneo Survey, p. 17.

32. Michael Dueñas "Another Coup?," *Philippines Free Press* (1 December 1989), p. 2.

3

Prospero and Caliban: Decolonization and the United States

The study of state behavior usually, and in the case of third world states almost always, includes the study of the attempts of polities to align their internal possibilities to the realities of the international environment. To examine where a state is moving, on a spectrum of behavior from "extreme maladaptation" (South Vietnam, which went out of existence), to "ideal adaptation" (Japan, moving from defeated power to economic superpower), requires an inspection of the state's internal behavior and its drive mechanisms and then an examination of the foreign policy possibilities. This requires an understanding of the historical, geographic, and economic realities in which the state finds and defines itself. For the Philippines, these realities to an extraordinary extent involve relations with the United States.

This study is of the Philippines; it makes no attempt to update, and is different from, the numerous studies of Philippine-American relations,[1] especially those that attempt comprehensiveness. Nevertheless, it is difficult to contemplate the study of either Philippine domestic or foreign policy without so much examination of the connection with the United States as to make this almost a distinction without a difference.

The role of the United States in the Philippines is on all levels exceptional—economic, military, social, and, perhaps most important, psychological. To find a parallel, where the echoes and reverberations are as pronounced from the larger to the smaller nation as in this dyad, takes one perhaps to France with Senegal or the Ivory Coast; but those African states' reinforcements and links in Francophone (and even Anglophone) Africa are more salient than those of the Philippines in Southeast Asia. There is in fact no parallel—there is no dyad that was as strong, in the Aquino era. As a result, the United States appears to be a major actor in this book.

The degree of psychological dependence in the archipelago on the United States, the source of the occasional intensity of the rebellion against the former colonial power, is well shown by a formerly oft-cited quote from the independence day address—then celebrated on the fourth of July, no less—of the Philippine republic's first president, Manual Roxas. "Our safest course, and I believe it true for the rest of the world as well, is in the glistening wake of America whose sure advance with mighty prow breaks for smaller craft the waves of fear."[2]

Apart from the obvious, the quote reveals a less frequently remembered fact that distinguishes the Philippines from the rest of the colonial world. Other nations attaining their independence at World War II's end—like those a generation later—got it from declining powers, scuttling empire because they had lost the will to hold it and lost the means to subsidize it, once "native" demands increased. The Philippines got its independence from a traditionally "anticolonial" power (ambiguous though that term is for the United States) that was very much on the rise. Whereas the gap in power would decline between (for example) India and Britain (as, later, between Algeria and France), it would increase between Manila and Washington. The Philippines, ruled by the colonizer's own ruling class, had been special in an America that had few world responsibilities. With its new self-imposed responsibilities, and those conjoined through alliances around the globe, the United States could think less and less often of the country where its elite had governed.[3]

Filipinos did not cease to think of America and Americans. As we see throughout the book, Americans played critical roles at every level of Philippine society and of its polity. And in the Aquino government's moment of extreme weakness, near the end of the period we are studying, with the Great Coup of 1989, Washington had to intervene with its Air Force to save the regime, flying stunning flights over Manila with its most competent aircraft. A perceptive observer wrote in the attempted coup's aftermath that, as a result, "the Philippine power structure has been stripped naked for all to see." And the preeminent observation was that "the predominant political power in the Philippines is the United States of America."[4] It was not a position to be envied.

For the growth in dependence on the United States that the U.S. Air Forces's "persuasion flights" occasioned had an obvious and powerful down side, the predictable equal and opposite reaction to such enormous dependence. Luis Beltran, a perceptive and outspoken journalist, argued in early 1990 that "most Filipinos have begun to feel that they are no longer masters of their own destinies."

> You get that feeling when people discuss what will happen in the 1992 presidential elections and someone invariably asks: "But who will be the American candidate?" Or if someone brings up the matter of the US bases and other people abruptly cut him off by saying: "The Americans will leave when they want to. It's no longer for us to decide."[5]

As Conrado Estrella, governor of the Philippine Constitution Associations, put it, "Some things cannot be done because the Americans would not be pleased."[6]

The obsession with the Americans is also illustrated, in its most demeaning aspect, by Emil Jurado's prediction that "the RAMboys won't mount a kudeta [coup d'état] these days since the American media are now preoccupied with the Mandela release in South Africa and the reunification of . . . Germany."[7]

At all points it should be remembered that the public discussion of the relationship with the United States, even at its most heated, always also bore the imprint of those seeing the benevolent side of the American presence. Nestor Mata, a venerable columnist who alone had survived the plane crash in which President Magsaysay was killed,[8] reminded his readers, at the time of the 1990 Cheney flap—when Mrs. Aquino refused to receive the American defense secretary—that it was "not the Americans, after all, who allowed graft to flourish inside [Aquino's] government, who turned their heads when presidential appointees, relatives, and friends were accused of the same charges once levelled against those in the past regime. . . . Nor was it the Americans who picked the . . . incompetents, the inefficient, the dolts [for her cabinet]."[9]

The fact that there was an insurgency in the hills with anti-Americanism as part of its logo, and that it had become de rigueur to attack the bases, did not mean the dependency syndrome had come to an end; in some ways they were both illustrations of its continuation. What the United States continued to hold was an authority position. Periodically Washington has had to be called in to solve underlying problems that the republic could not solve for itself. Ambassador Alejandro Melchor made a list going back to the Stonehill case in 1965, which an aide of Robert Kennedy settled from Hong Kong, up to the extraction of President Marcos in American helicopters: "If there was one person Marcos took seriously, it was Reagan; once he got the word [during the EDSA revolution] from the White House, then he was willing to leave," said the man who knew Marcos's mind the best—and who was in the White House situation room advising the US administration on how to cope with the evolving situation in Marcos's last few days.[10]

For the United States was not just—like all other colonial powers in reference to ex-colonies—richer, more sophisticated, better governed. It was the world center in so many ways. And by the time Manila had heard that the American advantage had begun to dim, as Soviet power grew in the late 1970s and early 1980s, given understandable lags in Filipino perception,[11] something better came along—crisis in the Communist bloc. America was back to the fore. So the authority relationship never really dimmed; this was the agonizing fact for radicals who wanted the island republic to stand on its own.

Why did the United States still seem to have an extraordinary hold on the Philippine mind, almost a century after the conquest? "Because you spoiled us," his Eminence Cardinal Sin put it—this from the second most powerful and assuredly the most astute political figure in the Philippines. "The proof is from the war. We all—except the Laurels and a few others—went up to the hills and never saw the Japanese during the war. We waited for the Americans, and when they came [through the Visayan Islands, where the cardinal grew up] we celebrated, running ahead of the soldiers asking for chocolates." The cardinal then added, looking down at his feet, "And then they forgot about us."[12]

There was the other side, the sense of ingratitude, the highest form of Filipino cultural sanction. War pensions, reparations, whatever: America did not do enough in the perception even of those most supportive of the relationship.

Yet the ultimate balance sheet was always positive to all but a fringe, at least within the elite. The cardinal could very bluntly remind us of President Quezon's oft-quoted statement that he would rather the Philippines be governed like hell by Filipinos than celestially by Americans: "and look what we have," his Eminence noted, "Hell." Had the Americans stayed, he went on, there would not have been the corruption, the filth, the trash;[13] this from arguably the most politically powerful prelate in any country since the sixteenth century.[14]

Most of the governing elite in Manila have had formative experiences in the United States. The Marcoses, however much Madame courted European dukes and duchesses, knew where real power for their country lay. She cultivated it in unusual ways, sometimes in remarkable fashion.[15] The president had the good intention of establishing—and made a down payment on—a chair, in his name, at Tufts University's Fletcher School of Law and Diplomacy.[16] The president's cousin, General Fidel V. Ramos, who was to unseat him, was a graduate of West Point, and the extraordinarily capable executive secretary (at the start of martial law), Alejandro Melchor, graduated from the U.S. Naval Academy two years later.

The new republic after 1986, though talking of diversifying its international connections, looked no less to America—where a flattering reception gave Corazon Aquino not only a one hundred million dollar addition to the Philippine aid bill, as we have seen, but such a frenzy of adulation, receptions, and hype that even the most reluctant of protégées would have been put back on track.

Aquino, preeminently, had spent considerable time in America coping with her husband's large needs and learning the republic's dynamics. They spent their exile—and last days together—in Boston. The United States was always seen as the only place from which a campaign against Marcos was pertinent, yet the irony of that fact was generally lost on the élite in exile: the pertinence was derived from American salience to *Marcos*, yet the élite in exile remained comfortable in America—both psychologically and materially.[17]

America was seen as both good and evil, but assuredly as the only place to go.[18] As Cardinal Sin noted in response to the interviewer's reference to Foreign Secretary Raul Manglapus's position toward the U.S. bases: "A ha! But where did he spend his exile? He went to the United States. A ha! Now he denounces the United States because for a short time he is a big man!"[19] And it might be added, it was an *American* hitman whom Manglapus added to his payroll, allegedly to murder Colonel "Gringo" Honasan and his fellow army rebels who threatened the regime's survival. Of course, Manglapus denied the 1991 charges—but they had the ring of truth. Otherwise, why had he received him in his home, as he admitted doing? Surely not just to "discuss 'events'," as he claimed. The issue, of course, was whether the Aquino administration was morally superior to that of Marcos's.[20]

But America was other things too. Senator Ernesto Maceda held the Wendy's and 7-Eleven franchises for the Philippines. In what led to a major political crisis not long before the 1989 coup attempt, Congressman Nicanor de Guzman got 314 guns in Los Angeles—or at least shipped them from there—with the almost certain assistance of the president's brother, Jose Cojuangco, Jr. Green cards, status, prebends, legitimacy—America offered a mixed bag. And if *Ilustrado* families always distributed largess among all presidential campaigns to ensure that family interests would be cared for in the next administration, they did so nationally: someone of their number usually lived stateside.

Washington, of course, used the credits it accumulated. It was widely thought that the most salient American card was the green one—liberally distributed to politicians to keep them in line, or in *utang*. *Two-thirds* of Aquino's cabinet owned them—but as we see, even green cards could not keep the Philippine Senate in line on the issue of the bases.

The American hand remained important in other ways that even transcended the historic connection. It was Japan that held the significant monies for large-scale international bailouts—but Japan was not, in the late 1980s, yet ready to take the front seat—and the Philippines was even more unwilling to let it—in a rescue mission. The people running the country—in their late fifties, early sixties—had childhood, indeed adolescent, memories of the vicious wartime occupation. Memories were still fresh in the late 1980s, and the Japanese knew it.

So it was the United States that had to orchestrate the external salvation of the country. And it was, of course, Americans—two congressmen (Stephen Solarz and Jack Kemp) along with two senators (Richard Lugar and Alan Cranston) who proposed the "mini-Marshall" plan, from which so many blessings (and problems) flowed, about which we hear in the next chapter.

It is worth noting the role of the embassy itself in the period of this study. American ambassadors have at times been considered (and have been) veritable proconsuls, and often as the second most powerful personage in the republic;[21] a strong diplomat like Henry Byroade, who stood at Ferdinand Marcos's side as he contemplated martial law, is the classic model.[22]

Washington was fortunate at the time of the 1986 revolution to have Steven Bosworth as ambassador. Bosworth was a former career officer who was recalled to duty, on his own terms. He was not looking to a post beyond Manila and was able from the start to call the shots as he saw them; he needed the Marcos family for nothing. His influence on official Washington during the events of late 1985 and early 1986 was immense. Likewise, during Aquino's first year, he was able to play a stabilizing role.

In 1987, however, Washington sent Nicholas Platt, who had a more conventional profile as a successful foreign service officer, with visions beyond Manila in his future. He arrived inauspiciously at the time of the August coup attempt. Thereafter, he simply rolled with events in the republic, and the embassy was again and again caught off guard. He treasured and valued his access to Malacañang Palace, but was not known in reform circles. The embassy position on the bases was to maintain the status quo, well beyond the point at which such was practicable in Filipino politics, indeed even in American politics. As for the Great Coup of December 1989, the embassy privately gave assurances in November that all was well, even on the eve of the coup, and no sooner was the dust dry on those events but the ambassador was putting a gloss on depressing postcoup developments. Small wonder that the U.S. embassy provided no ballast, good or bad, to Aquino's government in the last two phases of this study.

Development Diplomacy: The Philippine Side

Development and security are national affairs in a highly intrinsic sense; they are all about keeping the nation a nation—or making it one, especially in the developing world. Yet their attainment is foreign policy-intensive. Third world states need external assistance for both development and security. Ministries of foreign affairs have as their theoretical purpose the preservation and regulation of boundaries between the home state and foreign powers, and in practice are there to help get aid for development and security.

In the Philippine case the national mission was complicated by the absence of any precolonial—or postcolonial, for that matter—diplomatic tradition. Throughout Asia and Africa, Britain and France had, in varying degrees, prepared their wards for independence by training the brightest and best of their civil servants for foreign service, often in their own ministries. In a few of these states the struggle for independence had sharpened the sense of necessity of good representation abroad. In the Philippines the American governors made no such efforts; the reasons are various, but the arrogant American assumption that relations with Washington would continue to be, after independence, all that mattered, stands out as an assumption that Filipinos bought until the present day.

But the Philippine mission was more than a little compromised by the incompetence of the department of foreign affairs even after much time to remedy its lapses had come and gone. The absence of diplomatic sense in Philippine statecraft, with some notable exceptions, stands out by comparison with the strategic sense in, and availability of talent for, business and politics. And the Philippines compares with overwhelming disadvantage to its neighbor Thailand, a nation that used its diplomats and statecraft shrewdly to attain its position as a newly industrializing country.

It was a problem of omission and commission. By omission the absence of a competent ministry meant that there was no guidance for the rest of the government on American developments—that is what foreign affairs was to the Philippines in these years—and thus all the more the predilection for Filipinos (and, in this case, Filipinas) to go their separate directions. Thus the six-month period in 1989, of immense import to relations between the two powers, where there was literally no person at the Department of Foreign Affairs occupying the position of responsibility for North American affairs; and that followed a period of two years when only an "acting" officer was on duty. And when someone was appointed, no one in the American embassy was even minimally inclined to pay her the slightest bit of attention, professionally or personally.[23]

There was commission. Precisely because of a ministry's responsibility to establish boundaries, Foreign Secretary Manglapus deemed it his role to create the psychological reality of Philippine independence. A gifted intellectual, writer, moral leader, senator, and once acting foreign secretary in the old days, Manglapus took his position in the new republic seriously. He saw his role as one of preaching his position on the bases, namely that the psychologically debilitating relationship with the United States had to be cut; the father had to be killed, he was fond of saying. The point is not that his position was right or wrong; it is that it was disconnected from the realities of Philippine discussions of base—and aid—developments.[24] But the secretary's formal position gave him the floor in negotiations. He hurt his own cause by making the Philippine position less coherent, and undercut the Philippine government position perhaps fatally in the process.

Manglapus created another problem, in setting up parallel hierarchies of his own people within the department, out of distrust of bureaucratic channels—and of those left over from the Marcos period. Professor Gabriel Iglesias, a student of public administration, argued that a president, "in trying to push through revolutionary programs, must first destroy the bureaucracy," which he defended Manglapus as doing. "He has practically appointed outsiders to overlap with every career diplomat in the department," something of an overstatement, but one of enough truth to reveal why neither channel got much done.[25] It caused other problems as well. Manglapus did not trust Manila's premier diplomat, Emmanuel Pelaez, its ambassador in Washington. Pelaez, a former vice president of the republic, was an elder statesman par excellence—but Manglapus tried to run relations with Washington through the consul general in New York. Pelaez was in the obvious spot to advise Manila on the base negotiations, but when he returned home in late 1990 he found that nearly every recommendation he had rendered had been ignored, with dire consequences in due course. Nor was Aquino able to remedy the problem from within the palace. "There wasn't anybody there who could advise her on foreign affairs," her one-time press secretary said.[26]

NOTES

1. For an extraordinarily comprehensive treatment done in the Philippines, see Alejandro Fernandez, *The Philippines and the United States: The Forging of New Relations* (Quezon City, Manila: NSDB-UP Integrated Research Program, 1977).
2. C.V. Fonacier, comp., *At the Helm of the Nation—Inauguration Addresses of the Presidents of the Philippine Republic and the Commonwealth* (Manila: National Media Production Center, Republic of the Philippines, 1973), p. 69.
3. Stanley Karnow, the Pulitzer Prize-winning author of a study of Philippine-American relations, commented to the author (on the television show *The McNeil-Lehrer Report*) that the only thing the U.S. Congress was interested in with respect to the Philippines was "the U.S. bases." This author disagreed.
4. Teodoro Benigno, "Here's the Score: This Last Coup: A Postmortem," *Philippine Star* (4 December 1989).
5. Luis D. Beltran, *Straight from the Shoulder:* "The Mouse that Roared," *Manila Standard* (27 January 1990). The question of whether the Americans would leave if they were asked to was much discussed in early 1990, and was another sign of vulnerability. Teodoro Benigno argued that the president "may not be able to boot the Americans out. Then that's when we jump from the frying pan into the fire. That simply means the Americans could link hands with the faction or factions in the military sharpening their knives for another coup. Then we have the Apocalypse." "How does the Republic Cope," *Philippine Star* (26 February 1990).
6. "The Presidency," *Solidarity* Seminar Series on Public Issues, No. 20, *Solidarity* 125 (January-March 1990), p. 160. Hereafter "The Presidency".
7. "Opinion," *Manila Standard* (15 February 1990).
8. And, as an Ilocano, could be assumed to be more instinctively "pro-American"—Ilocanos had, it was thought, more relatives in the United States.
9. "Cory's Lament," *Manila Standard* (15 February 1990).
10. Interview, The Honorable Alejandro Melchor (10 September 1989).
11. Confirmed by interview with President Marcos (21 November 1978).
12. Interview, His Eminence Jaime Cardinal Sin (14 September 1989).
13. *Ibid.*
14. A point suggested to me by Professor Samuel Huntington.
15. See Raymond Bonner, *Waltzing with a Dictator: The Marcoses and the Making of American Policy*, (Quezon City: Ken, 1987), pp. 81-82, for stories—true beyond doubt—of Mrs. Marcos's attempts to use her feminine charms with prominent Americans to obtain advantage for the Philippines and its first family.

16. About which, members of the faculty and student body were less enthused than deans. Some of the former participated in the demonstrations against Mrs. Marcos when she visited the school. Her treatment was sufficiently rough that funding for the chair was never completed, to the obvious relief of many, especially the present writer, whom the acting dean had designated the forthcoming "Ferdinand E. Marcos Professor."

17. Curiously, all the most prominent exiles went through elaborate motions of denying their access to private funds. Marcos had sequestered all of them, Senator Aquino insisted, as did Senator Manglapus. Marcos had done them all dirt; in Aquino's case, his wife's family's interest in the Philippine Long Distance and Telegraph Company was indeed seized—but the ten thousand hectare Hacienda Luisita owned by the Cojuangcos was not. Thus the visible standard of living of the prominent exiles belied their claims. It is pertinent to note that for Senator and Mrs. Aquino it was necessary to accept help from her rival cousin Danding Cojuangco in buying a house, so Ninoy's claims were not entirely contrived.

18. Some also had substantial properties in America. Eugenio Lopez, for example, lived (and died) opulently in San Francisco, while Marcos extorted much of the family fortune from him.

19. Interview, His Eminence Jaime Cardinal Sin (14 September 1989).

20. William Branigan, "American Mercenary's Charge Stirs Political Storm in Manila," *Washington Post*, 18 October 1991, p. A26.

21. Though in terms of raw real power, the American with the greatest influence in the Philippines is the consul general, and was so seen by Filipinos. He issues the visas, for which there are long lines all day, and sometimes all night, in front of the embassy. Even the rich and famous have to husband their influence with the embassy carefully to preserve their own visas—and those of their ahmas, drivers, nurses, and cooks.

22. For a thorough and highly informed study of this subject, see Lewis E. Gleek Jr., *Dissolving the Colonial Bond: American Ambassadors to the Philippines, 1946-1984* (Quezon City, Manila: New Day Publishers, 1988).

23. At a diplomatic reception, a newly arrived and highly knowledgeable senior American diplomat gave the woman in question not even the courtesy of a nod when introduced to her, which anywhere else would have been considered a serious snub.

24. Revealingly, a high-ranking Filipino quoted Chairman of the Joint Chiefs William Crowe as having said, after negotiations with the Philippines, that Manglapus was a "total disconnect." Interview (9 September 1989).

25. "The Presidency," p. 144.

26. Interview, Teodoro Benigno (3 October 1989).

4

Security Through Development?

Development and security have been the purported goals of every third world state since the onset of the era of independence following World War II, as we have already argued. True, there have been other underlying goals, some perhaps more pervasive (for example, the search for power on the part of élites or ethnic factions), others less so, usually classifiable, however, as subsets of our twin study (for example, education). And these two subjects have dominated the literature in their separate incarnations. Recently, the relationship and possible interdependence of these two variables have come under scrutiny, and in this chapter we see how some of this bears on Philippine politics. Most of what has been done is cross-national, and valuable. Here we have a single case study with the detail such affords, a country where the issue of security and development is central to survival in the present period.

The single most impressive achievement of the Aquino era was the government forces' imminent strategic victory over the Communist insurgents, which had almost been achieved—as was proclaimed as the goal from 1989 on—by 1991. Let us clarify what is meant by victory. Richard Kessler, in the first serious post-1986 study of Filipino politics,[1] has argued that so endemic were the problems from which insurgencies had long sprung in the archipelago that a mere defeat of the New People's Army would be no more salient, in the long run, than the defeat of the Hukbalahaps had been a generation earlier. But in the long run we are all—certainly more Filipinos would have been—dead. And it is difficult to see why this achievement of strategy and magnanimity should be minimized.

But now we come to the nub of the argument. It is inequality that drives the "cyclical pattern of rebellion,"[2] Kessler argues. And here is the other part of the story, development. It was the position of the military high command that the insurgency could not and would not be defeated, other than in an even shorter-term sense, without development, without a narrowing of the gap between rich and poor, and without all the other conventional indicators of unrest. But if their words are to be believed as more than rhetoric, then their imminent "victory" would be as hollow as Kessler predicted. The gap between rich and poor was hardly narrowing, after all, and, outside metropolitan areas, it was difficult to find the evidence of real development. So Kessler has a real point. But so does General Ramos: development, "real" or otherwise, could not begin anywhere in the absence of security.

Integrating security and development was at all times difficult. For one thing, the link itself was seen as negative in numerous circumstances—for example, land reform. While land reform was seen as the long-term solution to rural unrest, and while security in the countryside was everywhere admitted to be necessary for the program to work, no one on the development side wished to see security considerations used in choosing (for example) priority areas for the CARL, or Comprehensive Agrarian Reform Law. At the Department of Agrarian Reform (DAR), officials universally insisted that such considerations did not apply.[3] It was their belief that, were such to obtain, the program would be tainted immediately and would fail. They would only make agreements with The Department of National Defense (DND) at the margin—governing, for example, security of projects and people already in the field.

By the same token, given the prevalence of politics and political considerations in the archipelago, most local officials confirmed the suspicion that very seldom could security *and* development be considered in the same breath. Politicians sought the limited funds available for their own sectarian purposes. It was a testament to Ramos's political skills that officials everywhere noted that they were "beginning" to take security considerations into account when apportioning development (or pork-barrel) funds.

In an interview, General Ramos, then Secretary of National Defense, said that it was his goal to make security considerations count about "one fourth" of the decision as to the apportionment of development funds, which he thought had been reached in many provinces. In an ensuing interview, Secretary of Local Government Luis Santos "guessed" that, in the decisions on the allocation of development funds, security considerations had come to count for "about one fourth" of the decision. If nothing else, the two distinguished cabinet members were showing that coordination, at least of some things, was not impossible in the Philippines.

The Americans also tried to achieve the integration of security and development objectives, despite their inability to do so for themselves back home.[4] Supposedly the Americans proposed to President Aquino that they would set up a framework—but the president would have to follow up on it. "And she put it to us that *we* would have to implement it." Nothing happened.

But the Americans worked with Filipinos to integrate the objectives at three levels. There were long discussions, for example, with the economists—at least the conservative ones, such as Finance Minister Jaime "Jimmy" Ongpin, with whom programs were lengthily discussed and then coordinated, until his suicide in 1987. Second, the Americans of course worked with the military to devise theories—preeminently with General Ramos, but also with others, such as General Rafael "Rocky" Ileto, an adviser to President Aquino, who had served as ambassador to Thailand in the 1970s when the Thais had brought their insurgency to an end (with a little help from China). But most interesting was the cooperation in the field, where AID, the Central Intelligence Agency (CIA), and Philippine agencies could work to "clean up" situations, in the usual euphemism. This happened most prominently in Davao, where (as we see later in greater detail) the NPA had come virtually to rule the city. An activist businessman named Chito Ayala, in whom the Americans and Philippine military had great confidence, took matters in his own hands and fashioned a coalition of those forces with the local vigilantes, the Alsa Masa, to rid the city of the NPA threat. It was bloody but successful, and as a result others imitated Ayala's game in other provinces, but never with such substantial results. It did show that development and security could go hand in hand—but the Davao case was not exactly the showcase one wished to make "exhibit A."

Social Contract?

Economic development in the context of economic justice is the highest priority of Filipinos. This is easily shown. The Ateneo survey in 1990 asked what the "programs were that President Aquino should attend to in 1990."[5]

That "economic programs" should have almost twice the salience as the item of next highest priority is significant, especially when one considers that "peace and order" is fourth—with solving the insurgency therein com-

ATENEO PUBLIC OPINION SURVEY[7]					
	Survey area		Socioeconomic Class		
Questionnaire Item	RP	Metro Manila	ABC	D	E
• *Programs that Pres. Aquino should attend to in 1990*					
March 1990					
Economic programs	52	68	55	52	48
Jobs, employment wages	29	49	37	27	28
Agriculture	24	8	22	26	22
Peace and order	22	17	29	24	17
Social services	19	39	26	17	17
Political, social justice, military	13	23	19	13	9
Infrastructure	10	4	11	8	13
Education	8	12	10	7	8
Livelihood	8	6	8	8	8
Health services	3	3	3	3	4

posing only a fraction of the importance of peace and order itself—and military graft and corruption along with associated behaviors, a distant sixth.

And what is meant by economic programs? Eighty-seven percent said "price control;" only a tenth mentioned economic recovery or improving economic conditions. It was a situation of triage.

There are even more surprises. Respondents were asked which of two opinions "comes closer to your opinion about equity and rapid economic growth": Roughly similar majorities are found in favor of government intervention in the economy and against the laissez-faire style that in so many ways had always been practiced.

What Filipinos got in practice was something quite different—albeit with aspects of what they preferred, selected to benefit the élite from Makati, the upper-class redoubt. There were cartels operating under the protection not only of laws but of cabinet ministers appointed to administer the economy. A good example of what was going wrong therein was revealed in congressional hearings in September 1989. It became clear that a flour cartel existed—one that kept imports to just below the country's milling capacity, with an obvious effect on pricing.

How had this happened—and *cui bono*? Allegedly it was the old culprit José "JoeCon" Concepcion, Jr., the Minister of Trade and Industry who had technically divested himself of his enormous interests in the flour industry

---

ATENEO PUBLIC OPINION SURVEY[8]

Questionnaire Item	Survey area		Socioeconomic Class		
	RP	Metro Manila	ABC	D	E

- *The government should give priority to rapid growth of national economy even if at first this will enrich only a few; in the long run, the poor will also benefit.*

	25	27	25	27	23

- *The government should first address the poverty of the majority of the Filipinos even if this slows down our economic growth.*

	74	72	72	72	76

By ratios of slightly under to slightly over three to one, all respondents chose addressing poverty as a key concern; the unanimity by class (as also by region) is striking.[9]

On rapid growth and "self-reliance," there were even more dramatic results.

- *The infusion of foreign capital and foreign debt into our country will result in the rapid growth of our economy.*

	19	11	17	19	20

- *We should not depend on foreigners even if this slows down our economic progress; our economic growth rests on what the government and the Filipinos will do with our country's wealth and resources.*

	78	88	80	79	76

---

but in reality had merely turned over management (and presumably the stock) of the business to his family; José Concepcion III was in fact the president of record in 1989.

Concepcion's benefits went further. He also had substantial interests in appliance manufactures in the country; U.S. embassy analysts argued that reserved items on the B list for trade liberalization often coincided with what it was his interest to protect—refrigerators, for example, which one of his plants assembled. Of course he shared his benefits; reportedly he made the Aquino children partners in his ventures—and made substantial contributions to the church through Cardinal Sin directly. So he did good while doing well.

He finally went too far. In late 1990 he "retired" from government "in the face of strong criticisms that he had assisted in the grant of 'behest loans' to a Taiwan petrochemical firm. His announced divestment of his shares in family-owned businesses had also been doubted by critics who charged him with . . . a conflict of interest."[10]

President Aquino stood by Concepcion, despite the fact that the Senate Blue Ribbon Committee recommended censure. Looking over his long tenure, and that of others whose behavior was similar, there is the more generous view—in this case of another cabinet member—that the problem was just that there had always been two views of Philippine development— the old import substitution school and the export promotion school. By this view, Concepcion was simply doing well while doing good, taking the old import substitution school seriously, one that found selective resonance in the tables of popular preference which we have already seen. But the private view of a delegate to one of the major multinational lending agencies was less generous: Concepcion would torpedo Philippine development and keep the country as poor as necessary, rather than allow a single item to be imported that his own industries manufactured.

Public opinion understood. In March 1990 the "margin of satisfaction" supporting him in the country as a whole and in Metro Manila specifically was the lowest of the cabinet—save only for Vice President Laurel, whose antics had taken him about as low as it is possible for a national politician.[11] Filipinos know; while Transport Secretary Oscar Orbos got a "+41" margin in Manila, where his near-heroic efforts to solve (or at least marginally improve) the disastrous transportation crisis was appreciated. JoeCon's margin of satisfaction was zero. Not surprisingly, Orbos's competence was seen by more than the man in the street; in late 1990 Aquino finally fired her incompetent executive secretary—the ranking cabinet member—and elevated Orbos to that central position, where he immediately became subject to presidential fever. JoeCon was out, but he and his family can be presumed to have become vastly richer during his time in office.

Aid Leverage

As a U.S. Congressional report of the 1985-86 period concluded, the Congress had "used aid effectively during this period as an instrument of pressure and influence in the Philippines. It cut aid in order to penalize the Marcos government but also to demonstrate to the Filipino opposition support for their demands for democracy."[12] And what about the Aquino era: now that democracy was a reality, could aid be a lever for social reform, of the kind that would stabilize the polity while depriving the insurgents of their principal targets?

In quantitative terms, how much support the Philippine revolution achieved abroad is seen in the first year's figures of American aid. In addition to the already granted $125 million, the administration got a supplemental of $100 million in Economic Support Funds (ESF) and in addition $50 million in grant military assistance, on top of the existing $40 million. The Reagan administration went beyond that in 1986 and took another $75 million ESF from proposed allocations to other countries.[13]

PAP-MAI—Implementation of the Social Contract?

In 1989 the notion of a "Marshall Plan" could catch on because there was still romanticism about the 1986 revolution in the United States. As Secretary of State James Baker said at the Philippine Assistance Program/Multilateral Assistance Initiative (PAP-MAI) launching party in Tokyo on the Fourth of July 1989—three and a half years after EDSA: "Few can forget the dramatic days of February 1986 when Filipinos bravely risked their lives for democracy."[14] At the American end it had the obvious additional, but always unstated, advantage of tying renegotiations for U.S. military bases simultaneously. As if the Filipinos needed to be reminded, the Americans stalled talks on the PAP-MAI for a year until Manila stopped stalling on the bases. By the end of the bases negotiations in 1991, both sides were finally calling a spade a spade—and admitting the relationship in the open, indeed for the record.

But from the Philippine end, there was a historic opportunity in the MAI. The country had missed its chance for basic reform under martial law; it missed its chance once more in the heady days, and first two years, after the EDSA revolution. It was hard to see what further chance the country would have to take off economically, in the foreseeable future, if it did not use the opening created by a multilateral $10 billion pledging. This was, after all, its third chance in just over a decade. It was the window of opportunity, an Asian Institute of Management professor said, that could lead to NIC status. As a journalist put it, Philippine development had hitherto been, as it were:

> archipelagic...Filipinos seem to see plans, programs and projects as discrete elements, isolated from each other like islands. Until the PAP came along with

its unified vision of development that covers the whole country and seeks to marshal both internal and external resources in the service of a central vision, Philippine development has been fragmented, divisive and uncoordinated.[15]

But were the Philippine plans possessed of a central vision? True, at Tokyo, donors were impressed by Filipino homework—performed by the impressive banker Villaneuva, brought in to supervise PAP, and his deputy Arthur Aguilar—and that was undoubtedly worth hundreds of millions of additional dollars. There were plans, mainly developed for IMF purposes, for restructuring many aspects of the economy, from the banking to fiscal sectors. And there was little doubt that the United States, which had an interest in such restructuring, could get it through the IMF. After all, as Professor Rudiger Dornbusch rather elegantly put it, "We own the IMF."[16] But on the Philippine side there was no strategy.

Professor Gustav Ranis offered the heuristic comparison with Mexico, which made "rather heroic [internal] policy changes . . . in the expectation that the substantial international financial flow required to make them stick will be forthcoming." But the sequence in Mexico is instructive: the society assessed what strong medicine it had to take; it negotiated "an internal social contract involving a good deal of pain, and then asks the international community for the necessary support to ease that pain."[17]

There was the view, of course, strongly held in Washington, that if the governmental reforms were undertaken seriously, then the major reforms—decentralization, land reform—could come in their turn, logically and inevitably. That was optimistic. There had been no social contract whereby the powerful Filipinos agreed on their respective sacrifices; rather everyone made individual, provincial, or departmental end runs to sweeten both the individual and the subnational pie.

The American problem is wider, for policy was not made solely in Foggy Bottom. The enthusiasm in Washington for all things Philippine in 1986 and into 1987 was such that it was difficult to put constraints on Manila, or to demand meaningful reforms. In hearings before the House Foreign Affairs Committee, David Joel Steinberg, an old Philippine hand, testified that

we should follow the lead of the Philippine government in determining the current and future mix of military to economic assistance. To do anything other would be a form of neocolonialism, an imposition of our external notions of how best this money should be spent. The United States should permit as much of the economic assistance money as possible to serve as budget relief. In a time of acute fiscal constraint, we do not help the Philippine government by restricting the funds to specific projects, especially ones that *we* define as significant.[18]

Fortunately, the Congress in its wisdom did not let all its controls go, but Steinberg's testimony (along with the similar words of others) was influential in establishing a climate—in which there were few incentives for Filipinos to change their ways.

One reason for the failure (as it ultimately had to be called) of the Aquino development program was in fact the issue of rent again. What was needed, after all, Ernest Preeg has written, was "a strong decision-making process to deal with politically difficult issues;" but the

> largess of U.S. economic aid to support Philippine democratization, and the predominant view within the Aquino government that economic aid was base rental unrelated to economic reforms, distracted the Aquino government from its essential task and inhibited the United States from using economic aid in support of a sound development strategy. The manner of U.S. aid disbursement, if anything, increased factional disputes within the Philippine cabinet, to the detriment of reform-minded ministers.[19]

Conditionality

Was there in fact any *quid pro quo* of the PAP? Of course any multinational initiative will come to have a life of its own, apart from any particularistic *quo* for a specific donor. But the military bases issue (or, more appropriately, the MBA, or military bases agreement) was woven far enough into the interests of the other donors of the PAP that, for them, it was not especially helpful to see it as solely an American *quo*, given the desire of most that the United States maintain its bases in the archipelago.

Yet for all the assurances to the contrary, it was never otherwise than a Philippine-American game, revolving around the bases. In an AID memorandum prepared for the mission of a high official to the Philippines, it was noted that the pace "of further developing the MAI was slowed by lack of progress in the conclusion of the [1988] review of the Military Bases Agreement and the emergence of 'compensation' as the single most visible issue in those negotiations. *Following conclusion of the MBA review in October, discussions with the GOJ [Japan], World Bank, and IMF were resumed.*"[20]

What the Filipinos were attempting to do—had long attempted to do— was to prepare a climate intellectually in which U.S. aid must be given without strings, without leverage to the donor on the projects for which the aid was given, and to be understood purely and simply as rent. It was never clear why American senators would dig more deeply into drained American pockets for increased Philippine rents, if the *quo* were not to stay there, and this tended to be true even for those tending to view an overseas defense structure as a high priority.

The irony of this issue is of course that seeing the aid as rent was in many ways demeaning, in that contriving it as such precluded envisaging base use as a truly joint enterprise. True, the European parallel in military aid was inapt; base-recipient countries there were sufficiently tied into mutual security objectives *operationally* that bases were perforce joint operations, as with Turkey's role on the eastern front of NATO. The difference in economic level or in geography alone made such operations highly difficult in East Asia between the Philippines and the United States. Still, from a psychological perspective, rent was the worst possible construction. The situation that resulted is that every Philippine agency tended to consider American conditionality as untoward interference.

Thus when the National Economic Development Administration (NEDA) began to be—from the U.S. aid agency's point of view—obstructive, the Americans felt forced to use Filipino methods to go around it. For example, in 1989, NEDA was still fighting USAID's position—in the words of a Philippine magazine—"that ESF, or the U.S. bases compensation, was not Philippine money but U.S. aid and therefore to be disbursed as the Americans desired. This did not make [ex-NEDA director Solita Monsod] popular with the Americans."[21] It was the issue of rent again. Thus AID gave a grant of $99,000 to the highly professional and skillful Asian Institute of Management[22] to help with the PAP. Why $99,000? Because only grants under $100,000 escaped the purview of NEDA.

Monsod subsequently testified that there were "vested interests" from which she had wished to insulate economic planning, some of them foreign. When asked to expound, she gave the example of a turbo gas turbine contract put out to bid, on which a Japanese-French consortium made the lowest bid. "Over the weekend, however, a high U.S. embassy official called her up at home requesting that the contract be given to a U.S. bidder on the condition that they would match the lowest bid,"[23] which of course was illegal. When Senator Enrile demanded to know which official, Monsod revealed it was the American chargé, Kenneth Quinn. Senior American officials confirmed the indiscretion, noting it was hardly the only one of its sort.

Land Reform

There is no subject in Philippine politics where the ideal has been so much counterpoint to reality as land reform. The import of the subject is in part due to the significant role land reform played in the economic surges of Japan and Taiwan after World War II. What is little realized is the Filipino connection thereto. When General Douglas MacArthur presided over the Japanese program, Don Andres Soriano, a Falangist Spanish-Filipino of enormous wealth, was his aide and close friend. Soriano had in fact been secretary of agriculture in both Quezon's and Osmena's cabinets in exile in Washington during World War II, so he was considered to be a man of expertise. As a result, what was visited on the enemy was not appropriate for the friend, though the consequences were unfortunate and economically significant.

The history of attempts to achieve land reform in the Philippines thereafter has been told so often elsewhere as to make it unnecessary here.[24] It should be noted, however, that land reform was the single major positive goal of martial law to which Ferdinand Marcos gave a pretense of seriousness, for the good reason that cutting big landowners down to size obviously reduced the threat of opposition to him. Its political purpose, David Wurfel writes, "was to create mass support for the New Society and its leader, legitimize him abroad, and undermine support for alternative leaders."[25] Marcos shrewdly, for example, sent one of his land reform advisers, the former Hukbalahap leader Luis Taruc, on tours of the United States and other countries precisely to build his constituency, with considerable success. Arguably, this success was based largely on disinformation, given the disparity between Taruc's socialism and Marcos's New Society. Once the big landowners had lost their land, Marcos lost interest in the program—especially when it began to hit the colonels and generals who had accumulated smaller parcels (but above allowed limits) after martial law.

One report noted that in twelve years "only 11.48 percent of 94,395 hectares was covered." Only 10 percent of the farmer-beneficiaries paid their loans to the Land Bank, 44 percent remained at the poverty level, 35 percent either sold out or got tenants, and only 13 percent of the dispossessed landowners were paid by the government.[26]

The problem was basic. As Gaston Ortigas, Dean of the Asian Institute of Management, put it, "There is a structure of poverty that is very stubbornly resistant to any administration trying to change it. Land reform has been going on since Magsaysay's time. But up to now, the arguments about land reform are the same arguments. It is stubborn. It is not moving."[27]

Land reform was a popular issue with strong public support. In the 1988 Ateneo survey, the views of which should closely follow the received wisdom of the postrevolutionary atmosphere, "agriculture" was the top-priority item of respondents asked to name five—followed by government services, employment, peace and order, and so on. The margin was not wide (49 percent for the first, 42 percent the second), but it is still significant. And broken down, "agriculture" overwhelmingly meant land reform.[28]

It was also a high-agenda item at the beginning of Aquino's presidency— at least in declaratory policy; among much of Mrs. Aquino's immediate entourage—and also among her American advisers—it was thought that the new government was not strong enough, in fact, was worrisomely weak, to push through a large program. "The administration couldn't deliver, we felt," an American adviser said. But it was the well-argued view of the dominant economists in Aquino's broader political entourage that land reform must come and come early. In the so-called Yellow Book of the Philippine Institute of Development Studies, something of a Bible to Aquino's administration in 1986, it was noted that land reform's

> demands for a strong political will are so great that significant moves—for better or worse—have always occurred, historically, at the beginning of new political regimes: the "reform" by which the Spanish encomiendas were created, the American regime's purchase of the friar lands..., the ... takeover of the Japanese plantations in Mindanao after liberation, the resettlement program of Magsaysay, the rental reduction program of Macapagal, Operation Land Transfer of Marcos, and, even now, the takeover of some of the lands of the Marcos cronies.[29]

But Aquino did not use her emergency powers to move land reform forward in the first year; her oft-stated reason was that she was doing away with dictatorship, not perpetuating it. She thus threw land reform to the Constitutional Convention, which while voting for "comprehensive" land reform, left the key issues—coverage, retention limit, and compensation—to the as-yet unelected Congress. The leader of the Kilusang Magbubukid ng Pilipinas (KMP), the "Peasant Movement of the Philippines," Jaime Tadeo, himself a member of the convention, saw the likely outcome—a landlord-dominated Congress that could gut the bill—and so campaigned for rejection.[30]

A turning point for both land reform and reform politics was the "Mendiola" incident, in early 1987, named for the street near the palace at which around 15,000 peasant protesters demanded action on land reform.

Nineteen were killed by police and marine gunfire.[31] As a result, by her second year Aquino's entourage had convinced her that it was in her interest to push through a land reform program, if only to prevent more peasants from being killed in her backyard. NEDA director Winnie Monsod and of course palace radicals such as Joker Arroyo came to the fore.

There was also an important American connection. If the first year was taken up with just getting started, by the second year there was a sense that it was time to get serious, if the government was not to fall apart from the right- and left-wing pressures. Testimony in the U.S. Congress reflected such. A presentation by Harvard's Professor John W. Thomas helped to make the case.

He testified that the "left opposition has moved into the space left by the Government's hesitation on agrarian reform and made it their chief demand. If the Government is to [deal with] the militant left wing threat, and unify the nation around a political center, it must take their principle [sic] issue and drawing card, agrarian reform, away from them."[32] He went on to propose a seemingly feasible and phased program, and gave numbers. At that point the Government of the Philippines (GOP) had asked the aid consultative group for $500 million "to complete agrarian reform program in rice and corn land."[33] But such was highly hypothetical; there was no capability to deliver on a program of that size at that point. Thomas proposed $100 million over two years. Congressman Stephen Solarz picked up on that—$50 million in 1987, for Fiscal '88, and ran with it. As he put it, in response to Thomas's position, such funds would be "intended to be a way of creating an incentive for them [the Philippines] to move in this direction and as a way of providing the resources or, some of the resources, which would be needed to actually implement such a program."[34]

Indeed land reform was the panacea. Solarz said in committee that, by implication, it was established that the NPA used the need for land reform as one of its most important appeals; that a government land reform strategy was essential to a serious counterinsurgency program; that there was enough unutilized land and a need for crop diversification; that there are millions of landless laborers; and that the program would cost more than the Philippines could afford—and that therefore, the Congress should transfer the requisite sums. The Congress could not have been more enthusiastic.[35]

At that point Solarz was on a first-name basis with President Aquino, and called her frequently. Here now was the possibility of $50 million of *extra* funds, but targeted specifically for land reform. "It was the lowest risk means of our associating ourselves with the program," an American administrator said, in that the money was strictly reserved for transfers *already* completed, title and all, which is the kind of program Washington understood.

But the idea of extra funds was the kind of argument Manila understood. And not surprisingly, the Aquino government did in fact get serious about land reform thereafter—though it was to be more than yet another year before the Filipino Congress passed the emasculated bill that did get through its committee compromises.

The Garchitorena scandal of 1989 slowed the process down almost to a halt, for the better part of a year, and well illustrates (as Filipinos said) Murphy's law: if anything can go wrong, it will. On one hand was soaring Senate testimony by agrarian reform officials: "a foundation stone that will usher this country to a regime of justice and dignity, especially for our impoverished millions . . . CARL [land reform] is the consummation of our vision of a fair society, where the tenant is freed from age-old burdens of poverty;"[36] and on the other hand the reality of a Filipino Senate investigation showing how venal the system could be. The Garchitorena parcel was 1,889 hectares, bought by a bank in 1988 for P3.2 million. But shortly thereafter the Department of Agrarian Reform bought it, in December 1988, for P62.7 million. Only thirty-seven hectares, or 2 percent, were arable. The land-bank president admitted, during the Senate investigation of the scandal, that the comparative basis for valuation was a piece of land of one thousand square meters.[37]

True, the scandal was in a sense well motivated; because in that stage of the program the mode was "VOS," or Voluntary Offer to Sell, and the DAR wished to make the program look inviting to landlords. But it went a little far. Of course the press had a field day, and Senator Enrile, an inveterate enemy of land reform, could call the parcel the "most overpriced" agrarian land in Southeast Asia.[38]

The scandal at least had the virtue of showing the most significant weaknesses of the program for what they were. Marcos's program compensated landlords on the basis of productive value of the land (at two and a half times the annual harvest). But the Aquino era concept was "fair market value," paid a fourth in cash and the rest in government bonds. This shot the cost up enormously, and thus slowed down the possible rate at which the program could be funded and accomplished.

President Aquino seemed to become serious about the program after the Garchitorena scandal, by appointing a tough reformer to the head of the Department of Agrarian Reform, Miriam Defensor Santiago. A law professor at the University of the Philippines (where, as a columnist-"adviser" later put it, "Nobody who has ever crossed your path . . . could . . . have failed to smell ambition in your very breath"),[39] she had a breakthrough in her appointment as immigration commissioner, in one of the most traditionally corrupt government agencies. She was famous there for refusing favors and payoffs,[40] and her off-the-cuff crusty comments became favorite newstime discussion; she also became a new favorite in discussions of who would succeed Aquino.

When Aquino appointed her to the DAR, Santiago calculated that by playing hard to get she would accumulate the power to make the program work. She refused calls from senators whose votes were needed to confirm her. She made unprintable comments about other Solons; one she referred to as "fungus face." She set up Senators Enrile and Osmeña, the latter of whom was backing a program of Filipino federalism as a way of killing land reform, in such a favorable position that they were able to appear unselfserving in opposing her. Opponents now painted it, not unfairly, as a picture of hubris. "By acting high and mighty, you unleas[h]ed the mean streak that lurks behind every politician's mind, especially against those, such as yourself, who are out for the big prize."[41]

So she gave her opponents a sword. Enrile discovered a bill requiring the DAR secretary to have five years experience with land reform, which Santiago had not. It was a meretricious argument, but it hardly mattered.

Of course during this period little land reform was accomplished. At the DAR, there was perceptibly little work of any sort being done. Bureaucrats lined up for or against Santiago in parallel to politicians.[42]

Aquino in the meantime was taking heat for the disposition of Hacienda Luisita, her family seat. There was obviously a symbolic importance to her decision that transcended even the importance the hacienda held as the country's largest. Lucy Komisar describes the setting.

Hacienda Luisita remained a microcosm of the country's problems. . . . There was severe unemployment; only a minority of the 30,000 people who lived there had permanent jobs. Others were seasonal workers employed during the milling period. The rest of the time they worked two to three days a week . . . for a few dollars a day. The workers and their families lived in villages of grass-roofed huts or concrete block houses. . . . Some of them had electricity when the mill was running.[43]

David Steinberg told Congress that Aquino was "the social equivalent of a Rockefeller or Du Pont. . . .There is a symbolic importance of about [sic] what she does with her own lands or her family's lands which transcends immediate public relations. In other words, if she is a traitor to her class in some important way she will retain her position as heroine to her nation."[44] But the Cojuangco family turned out to be loyal to their class. When the president was asked about her election promise to convert the hacienda into a model for land reform, her spokesman said, "This is a very democratic president. She will have to talk to her brothers and sisters. There is a ticklish problem of family and interpersonal relations there." Indeed.[45]

After trying to delay the court's decision that the land must be distributed, by appealing to the appellate court, what the family did was to offer tenants a choice: a stock-sharing scheme or, if they chose to own their land, a leaseback option, whereby management would lease their land and manage it centrally. According to DAR officials, there could not have been undue pressure for tenants to choose the former, given the amount of publicity around the event and given the controversy attending this.

This reasoning ignores the nature of power in the Philippines. One report—echoed by numerous other observers— said that management threatened that "medical, education, housing and other benefits being accorded them [tenants] would be forfeited if they chose the leaseback option."[46] The problem with the stock-sharing scheme in the best of circumstances is that the shares were to be distributed within thirty years—and in the meantime would be unfungible.

There was another problem; the CARL's objective was, in the words of one editorial, "the transfer of the ownership and control of land to tenant farmers." The reason, it went on, was only partly economic; "land reform at bottom is a massive effort at social restructuring, inducing changes in power alignments by making tenant farmers a social and economic force."[47] A peasant could not use a nonliquid stock certificate as leverage for sending a child to college or to buy a tractor, much less to finance a political campaign aimed at social reform.

In fact, neither the scandal nor Santiago's delayed confirmation were important issues as such. As a study from the University of the Philippines School of Economics said, more important than either "is the fact that the actual process of transferring land to the tiller is going too slowly with too narrow a scope." Its point was that the government did not have a clear plan for the extension of support services for beneficiaries, was not including sequestered lands, and so forth.[48]

The deeper issue was, as Teodoro Benigno put it, "a serious rupture in the relations between the executive and legislative branches." Aquino, he pointed out, was weak, and the Senate would thus refuse to ratify an appointee she had every right to have confirmed—"at a time when the President and our politicians have to link arms, if only for survival."[49] Miriam

Santiago's appointment of course was withdrawn, after she had been left hanging in the wind far longer than even she deserved; the cause of land reform had lost another year. And a year later still other appointees were hanging with equal futility in the wind as the program withered.

Of course, as is obvious, where it has been successful, real land reform has not just been attempted at the start of a regime; it has been started with an animus against the landlords. "These [successes] have tended to be based on a government's confiscatory powers, justified within a framework [in which] landlords already had been inequitably imposing rents on a politically-acquired natural resource for decades," a *Far Eastern Economic Review* reporter wrote.[50] Indeed, Conrado Estrella argues that land reform "cannot be implemented under a normal democratic situation. Marcos succeeded in his program because he declared martial law."[51] The flavor of a report by the radical KMP, the Philippine Peasant Movement, is more what traditionally precedes land reform: "Phase 1. Confiscation and distribution of lands by the deposed dictator and his crony fascist landlord compradors."[52]

In fact, the Philippine Congress was in sufficient measure dominated by landlords and landlord allies, such as Senators John Osmeña and Juan-Ponce Enrile, and Congresswoman Maria Clara Lobregat, to postpone real land reform almost indefinitely. There was no animus against them, and there was at the very least thus no animus in favor of the program. One congresswoman, Hortense Starke, openly exhorted fellow landlords, at a convention in March 1988, to "bribe" the press to see things their way.

But the blame goes higher. President Aquino failed to use her emergency powers at the start of her term to effect land reform, on the good excuse that she was not to be a dictator, that important programs had to be enacted constitutionally, and that the established interests had to have a chance "to weigh in," as Malacañang officials often put it, to make their points and achieve a satisfactory law. She may have believed her excuse. But it is hard to avoid concluding that the real reason, if held consciously only in part, was her lack of real enthusiasm for a program that might confiscate her birthright, the great hacienda that her family had owned for a generation. Her brother certainly gave out enough confusing signals to raise the question of whether her family was serious about land reform.[53]

There is a legitimate argument as to whether land reform was, has been, and could be the answer to Philippine problems—or even to any Philippine problems. One cabinet member, for example, said, "Land reform misses the point—which is productivity," but this person at least understood that *some* program for the landless peasantry was necessary, if only for psychological reasons involving not only the health of the polity but its image abroad. The real point is surely again that there was no social contract. The Philippines had not decided what it wanted. Landlords knew what they wanted and in the Aquino era had the scope to pursue it. Reformers knew what they wanted. But for them it would be difficult enough to accomplish land reform given the lack of resources with which to pay compensation, especially in comparison with Taiwan and Japan. Given a real commitment, the external resources would almost certainly have been available; it was an issue on which the donor countries simply could not say no. As it was, land reform was simply another failure, and the failure was of domestic political will.

The issue, ultimately, was also one of class. Land reform was anathema to the ruling élite, by and large. They could argue in terms of its inappropriateness to the agrarian needs of the archipelago or whatever; ultimately they were arguing interests. Mrs. Aquino had been humane enough to register shock at the carnage of the Mendiola incident and to invite the agrarian leaders along with her incompetent land reform minister, Sonny Alvarez, for a discussion. But as the KMP asked, "Did it have to take nineteen lives of farmers before this government would pay attention to their problems? Where is justice? Where is reason? We fought against Marcos and supported you, Mrs. Aquino. Now you turn your guns against us." Aquino, for her part, "relegated [the formulation of a definite land reform program] to a cabinet action committee," which is to say, to oblivion.[54]

Local Government

There is a long history of heavy-handed control from Manila of developments great and small in the provinces. In the nature of things, control tightened under martial law. Imelda Marcos, for example, controlled the flow of ESF funds going to the provinces for building construction under the Rural Development Fund (RDF), and thus could reward and punish friend and foe through the placement of buildings. According to Ambassador Ernest Preeg, the program worsened under Aquino. The new minister under whom the RDF program came, Solita Monsod, insisted that the program's funding was base rent and not subject to anyone's advice, especially not the donor's. Because of the fungibility of the money, it was traditional to use ESF funds where foreign exchange was needed while designating them for such low foreign-exchange projects as rural buildings. Monsod would not allow a peso of foreign exchange for the RDF program. Small wonder that "the implementation of the program bogged down, decisions could not be made, and the peso account accumulated large amounts of unused funds."[55] The interests of the locals was hardly likely to be taken into account. A U.S. AID official wrote, at the end of his tour, that "the anguished pleas of governors and mayors for sufficient public funds to offer some semblance of response to local development needs underscore the lack of efficacy in the machinery of the new government."[56]

To be sure, there was an attempt at reorganization of the Department of Local Government (DOLA), in 1987, the avowed purpose of which was to revitalize local governments. But the executive order for accomplishing it makes clear that there were competing principles. In its "declaration of policy," the order observed that "it is necessary to reorganize the Department in order [1] to make it more capable of assisting the President in the exercise of general supervision over local governments, [2] in promoting local autonomy, encouraging community empowerment, and in maintaining public order." But the first and second objective were somewhat contradictory.[57]

In affecting security and development, nothing was more symptomatic than the structure and hierarchy of the Peace and Order Councils (POCs) at every level. General Ramos, in conceiving the strategy and organizing the councils, knew that the military could supply the horsepower as well as the force, but that the real problem was galvanizing government at the local level so that Filipinos would see themselves in control of their own fate. In designing the strategy he decided to make the local government officials (hereafter DOLA) as chair, Defense as vice chairman, and this at every level from national, down through province, to barangay. Thus at the highest level he, as vice-chairman, backed up DOLA secretary Luis Santos, an old-style politician, while station commanders (police chiefs) with an equally theoretical secondary status backed up the mayors at barangay level. Alas, as a well-traveled U.S. embassy officer neatly put it, "The military is carrying the whole burden . . . civilian ministries are not carrying water in the countryside."[58] And he who carries the water acquires (more) power.

A hearing of the Senate Finance Committee in late 1988 reveals some of the problems. DOLA Secretary Santos, in addition to making the usual claims of departmental poverty, tried to convince Senator Neptali Gonzalez, the chairman, and his colleagues that decentralization—and indeed the president's Committee on Decentralization—was succeeding in breaking Manila's hammerlock on seemingly all decisionmaking in the archipelago. Gonzalez, after all, had started by telling Santos that his job was to "make true and effective this Constitutional guarantee of local autonomy."[59] Mayors, Santos responded, were now authorized to negotiate contracts up to P200,000 (c. $10,000), governors maybe to P2 million. Moreover, he said, regarding the payment of local officials, there was a deadlock on "only" two—the treasurer and assessor, no less, which the Department of Finance insisted on maintaining control of. There was the rub; as a canny city bureaucrat in Baguio said of the treasurer there, "he's the most powerful person in the city. He can hold up any check, and often does."[60] At a discussion in Washington, a senior Philippine official defended the continuation of this practice, on the grounds that if the Finance Department could not move its officials around the provinces at will, their professional development would suffer. So not much power was likely to devolve by that route, when the "only" officials under Manila's control are the only ones that matter.

As if granting a dispensation, a DOLA assistant secretary said his department was now allowing provincial development councils to select development projects. The chairman came back with the charge that there was "almost monolithic control" by national government and its "layers of bureaucracy." "The funds are there and they are remaining idle in the vaults of the bank," he said, noting that "we lack the political will to exercise powers which are already within us" for, in this case, the release of funds.[61]

Santos confessed that the system was not working well, "because there is a distance between our Constabulary people and local officers even at the moment." How do the mayors re-exercise their operational control? the senator asked. Santos replied, through the POC. But, the chairman said, that was "in document alone but not in reality." For in fact, if the local station commander "defies the authority of the mayor under this accord, are we not allowing sergeants" to run the municipalities?

"Yes sir," Santos replied.

The chairman noted that, in the agreement with Ramos, "operational control and supervision over the local police" was given DOLA. But Santos was quick to assure any opponents from DND that the "power is used very discreetly."

Or used at all? Senator John Osmeña, whose family has dominated Cebuano politics seemingly since Magellan, and as mayor of Cebu must have had as much power as any mayor ever, said that as officer-in-charge there he "could not even replace the station commander." Santos agreed, noting "some military officials are reluctant to relinquish the power also. But in time, this martial law syndrome is beginning" to wane.

But a significant revelation came when Osmeña asked if the local executive could not, in some circumstances, fire the station commander. Indeed, he said, suppose he "reversed the flag on August 28"—that is to say, joined the 1987 Honasan coup attempt, as Cebu's mayor did—"is that good enough reason to replace him?"

"I can take the hint, your honor," Santos said.

A gifted American AID officer, in an informal paper circulated within the Philippine government, could conclude at the end of his tour:

> Despite a widespread rhetorical consensus on the virtues of decentralization, the Government of the Philippines remains centralized to the point of constipation. Even in the four "model provinces" selected two year[s] ago by President Aquino to demonstrate that her government *can* deliver meaningful development little has changed.[62]

Transition

President Aquino had divested herself of the left prior even to the 1986 election, in rejecting the terms of Bayan, or People's Party; but several shrewd associates of the left stayed in her entourage and captured key positions in her cabinet, particularly Joker Arroyo, a gifted lawyer who had worked as a largely selfless human rights lawyer for victims of military abuses during the late years of martial law. He got the critical job of executive secretary—"little president"—through which he could hold up appointments, determine agendas, and influence policy on every front: for example privatization, on which there was broad agreement, appears to have been at least in part a victim of his prejudices—or to be more cynical, his position on the boards of a number of state-owned enterprises.[63]

By late 1986 at least the far right had cut itself off from the administration. Minister of Defense Johnny Ponce-Enrile, the immensely rich (he had published assets of over P2 billion)—and immensely corrupt—co-organizer of the EDSA revolution, had painted himself into a corner and was forced to resign following an abortive coup with which he was known to be associated. That meant that Aquino was rid of a great annoyance—but more saliently, that ironically she now needed the reformists less. For Enrile was replaced by retired General Rafael Ileto, who was a conservative centrist, like Ramos, and Aquino could now comfortably rely on both of them. No wonder radicals could charge that their "ascendence in the corridors of power marked the beginning of the Aquino government's Rightward drift."[64] What was left, however, was the centrist corp with its establishment business support (most of the cabinet) with the exception of Joker Arroyo—and possibly the most brilliant member of the cabinet, Professor Solita Monsod, the head of the National Economic Development Agency.

"Winnie" Monsod had clear and well-articulated views on government economic policy and is another example of the transition occurring. She believed that the international leverage of the EDSA revolution brought entitlement of debt repudiation in the international financial community, and—after her demission—argued widely that Aquino had simply been transfixed by fright at the repercussions that would flow from selective repudiation.

Her position was certainly arguable. There *was* credit from EDSA to be spent one way or the other. The problem was that all of the cabinet and their support groups beyond her had a different strategy: no repudiation, but use EDSA to garner the largest aggregate aid figures possible. After all, the issue was *net* inflows, which could be a function of debt reduction *or* aid increases. Monsod was stuck on repudiation, and undermined national strategy for a year before she finally "resigned" in early 1989—by which time over $100 million of American aid had also been stuck—in the bank—for more than a year, over her insistence that "rent" aid be left to the Philippines for disposition.

In fact it was not the 1987 coup attempt by which Monsod was thrown out; Colonel "Gringo" Honasan was less concerned with economic development strategy than the commies-vs.-good guys scenario in his coup attempt. But the new policies of 1987 doomed her, despite her popularity in her agency and a genuine following among the intellectual élite. After all, the notion of debt repudiation was seductive, even if at the time that siren song was sung "Jobo" Fernandez, the powerful central bank governor, was working miracles with the international financial community.

The 1987 change is not just best illustrated by what happened in the countryside; it is best explained by that. Aquino had been swept to power by the cause coalition, but these were intellectuals, and upper- and upper-middle-class activists in Manila. True, it was necessary to undertake some degree of mobilization in the provinces to achieve that political revolution. But the long and short of it is that, by the next year with elections coming, the cause coalition was unprepared for and inexperienced in the matter of provincial politics. The old élite moved in to do what it did best (in terms of its own interests) and what it knew how to do. As with wartorn countries rebuilding when peace breaks out, it is easier to "rebuild" than to learn new traits (as in the development experience more generally).

Thus as one astute (if aggrieved) observer wrote, the "vast majority of candidates . . . were . . . former elected officials, relatives of powerful political families and/or members of the business élite. The citizens who had demonstrated to bring down Marcos . . . were left out of the process."[65] Candidates of the left were left out in the cold; "only those with money and muscle could be elected."[66]

True, there were differences between the old and new élites; Lucy Komisar is perceptive in noting that it was the "middle and business class that had put Cory in power."[67] But it is not true that the "old families of the landed and commercial oligarchy and their representatives" were gone. She argues that Marcos's land reform had broken their economic power, that Cory's people were the new rich. And there were no people in her cabinet of "working class or peasant origins." But Aquino herself was from the pinnacle of the landed and commercial oligarchy, and the parliament was to be loaded with her relatives. The vice president was a Laurel, the family that had dominated Batangas for generations, and the Senate had his (much more) distinguished brother to boot. Senator Osmeña's family had dominated Cebuano politics since before his grandfather had dominated national politics. There were many others.

Nations like the familiar path; that is to say, the groups that make up the *nation*, within a territory, find it easy to resurrect old patterns, even after considerable periods of disruption. The provincial élite knew how to fight elections with—in the case of these elections—basketball uniforms,[68] or sardines, as in earlier cases. It should have come as no surprise that families and networks that had, in many cases, suffered immensely in the interregnum would swiftly resurrect old networks and move back into power. They did it. The new parliament was the old parliament. "Paternalistic patrimonialism" was back at work.

And *pari passu*, the new president was the old president—at least it was fair to say that her presidency was soon back in the mold of the pre-Marcos era. Indeed as one observer noted, active and passive presidents had alternated in the history of the republic, and she was predictable at least in that regard. Professor Iglesias did a one-year analysis of Aquino's appointment schedule and found "that most of her time was spent in meeting petty businessmen, innocuous groups, and military men. The key cause-oriented groups and the farmers do not appear in our analysis."[69]

The old patterns of national campaigning had also reemerged by the end of this period, late 1987. It was generally agreed that one needed P2 billion—$100 million—to launch a campaign. So—as former press secretary Francisco Tatad put it succinctly—"the class issues will always be resolved in favor of the rich."[70]

As we have elsewhere noted, however, the infrastructure of the country had deteriorated in the interregnum, making the old patterns even less adaptive than they had been before.

The factiousness of politics at the top, which emerged within months of EDSA, had more consequences than mere instability in the executive branch. As the Davide report put it, it is a "price for democracy which often leads to a dilemma."

> Its essence is openness and accommodation. But without firm institutional moorings and a unifying political vision, this becomes sterile and even destructive, often leading to chaos. The ensuing turmoil in civilian politics is an invitation to military intervention. As Fr. Joaquin Bernas sees it, "Once politics gets into the military, the danger is that the military will get into politics." The ultimate result is a political polarization in society at the expense of national consensus and unity, and the danger of military adventurism.[71]

Indeed nothing could have more tersely foretold the central point of the chapter to which we now turn.

NOTES

1. Richard J. Kessler, *Rebellion and Repression in the Philippines* (New Haven, CT: Yale University Press, 1989).
2. *Ibid.*, p. 21.
3. This author's interviews with DAR officials (November 1989).
4. See this author's essay "Security and Development in the Third World: Some Policy Perspectives," in Saadat Deger and Robert West, *Defence, Security and Development* (New York: St. Martin's Press, 1987).
5. Ateneo de Manila University, *Public Opinion Survey* August 1989 (Quezon City: Ateneo de Manila University, 1989), Table 8, p. 36. Hereafter Ateneo Survey. Explanation pertaining to table quoted above: Roughly, A class is the rich élite, B and C are the middle classes, D is the lower-middle class, and E is the proletariat.
6. *Ibid.*, p. 36.
7. Unlike the figures presented in February 1988 report, here the data pertain to percentage of respondents reporting a particular program area and not just the program ranked first.
8. Roughly, A class is the rich élite, B and C are the middle classes, D is the lower-middle class, and E is the proletariat.
9. Ateneo Survey (1990), Table 14.
10. "Aquino Accepts Trade Secretary's resignation," *Manila Chronicle* (17 December 1990), in Foreign Broadcast Information Service-East Asia-90-242 (17 December 1990), p. 40. Hereafter FBIS-EAS.
11. Ateneo Survey (1990), Table 6, p. 30.
12. Committee on Foreign Affairs, "Congress and Foreign Policy," (Washington: Government Printing Office, 1988), p. 174.
13. *Ibid.*, p. 173.
14. Official Text, USIS, American Embassy Tokyo, "US Statement on the Multilateral Assistance Initiative," by The Honorable James A. Baker III, Secretary of State (Tokyo: 4 July 1989).
15. R.V. Diaz, "Calabar [acronym for provinces surrounding Metro Manila] Will Profit Most from PAP," *Daily Globe* (16 September 1989).
16. Committee on Foreign Affairs, p. 659.
17. Gustav Ranis, "The Philippines, the Brady Plan and the PAP: Prognosis and Alternative" (photocopy, May 1989), p. 9.
18. Committee on Foreign Affairs, p. 591.
19. "Neither Fish nor Fowl: U.S. Economic Assistance for Noneconomic Objectives in the Philippines" (draft, Center for Strategic and International Studies, October 1990).
20. Doc. #51650, "Multilateral Assistance Initiative" (Internal Agency for International Development document, undated), emphasis added.

21. "PAP Goes the Weasel," *Philippine Free Press* (2 September 1989), p. 14.

22. A graduate business school set up with Harvard's help on its business school model, and which had come to have a reputation of the highest quality work.

23. "PAP Goes the Weasel."

24. See for example *IBON Primer Series*, "Land Reform in the Philippines" (Manila: IBON Databank Phils., 1988); *United Nations Development Program*, "Expanded Assistance to Agrarian Reform in the Philippines, Project Findings and Recommendations" (New York: United Nations Development Program, 1986); and David Wurfel, *Filipino Politics: Development and Decay* (Quezon City, Manila: Ateneo de Manila University Press, 1988).

25. See Wurfel, *Filipino Politics: Development and Decay*, p. 166.

26. "Why Landlords Think CARP Won't Work," *Nation* (20 March 1988).

27. "The Presidency," *Solidarity* Seminar Series on Public Issues, No. 20, *Solidarity* 125 (January-March 1990), p. 146. Hereafter "The Presidency".

28. Ateneo Survey (1990), Table 9.

29. "Economic Recovery and Long-run Growth: Agenda for Reforms," *Philippine Institute for Development Studies* (1 May 1986), p. 115.

30. *Dictatorship and Revolution: Roots of Peoples' Power* (Manila: Conspectus Foundation, 1988), p. 240.

31. *Ibid.*, pp. 140-41.

32. Prepared statement by Professor John W. Thomas, March 12, 1987, Committee on Foreign Affairs, *Asian Trade Problems* Y4.F76/1:As4/22, p. 625.

33. Quoted in *Ibid.*

34. *Ibid.*, p. 653.

35. *Ibid.*, pp. 915-16.

36. Senate investigation (5 May 1989), p. 7.

37. *Ibid.*, 9 June 1989, p. 49.

38. *Ibid.*, p. 23.

39. "Unsolicited Advice to Miriam," *Malaya* (21 October 1989).

40. Though one (unbought) automobile reportedly ended up in her husband's hands as a result of her stewardship of the agency.

41. This author's interviews with DAR senior officials (October-November 1989).

42. *Ibid.*

43. Lucy Komisar, *Corazon Aquino: The Story of a Revolution* (New York: George Braziller, 1988), p. 181.

44. Committee on Foreign Affairs, p. 644.

45. Quote in Komisar, *Corazon Aquino: The Story of a Revolution*, p. 181.

46. Romy Roosevelt, "Luisita Farmers Pressured to Opt for Stock Sharing?" *Malaya* (16 September 1989).

47. "The Meaning of Luisita," *Daily Graphic* (21 October 1989).

48. Quoted in Hernan Melencio, "Government Projects Deplored," *Daily Globe* (27 December 1989).

49. Teodoro Benigno, "Miriam, the Commission, the Scorpions," in "Here's the Score," *Philippine Star* (22 November 1989).

50. Rigoberto Tiglao, "Caught in the Act," *Far Eastern Economic Review*, (13 July 1989), p. 44-45.

51. "The Presidency," p. 142.

52. *Dictatorship and Revolution*, p. 787.

53. See editorial, "Land Reform and the Landowner," *The Sunday Times* (20 March 1988). Representative Cojuangco in this instance called for the "consolidation of small landholdings into what he calls economic-sized farms."

54. *Dictatorship and Revolution*, p. 241.

55. Preeg, "Neither Fish nor Fowl: U.S. Economic Assistance for Noneconomic Objectives in the Philippines," p. 20.

56. Blackton, John Stuart, (see Chapter 2, Note 25) p. 4. See also the controversy aroused by this document, when leaked to the Manila press. "Make My Day!" column by Hilarion M. Henares, Jr., "Congrats AFP, Winning with Rule of Law," in *Philippines Daily Inquirer* (30 July 1989), in FBIS-EAS-90-147 (2 August 1989), pp. 42-43.

57. Malacañang Palace, Executive Order No. 262, "Reorganizing the Department of Local Government and for other purposes," mimeograph.

58. U.S. Embassy (7 November 1989).

59. *Republic of the Philippines*, Senate Finance Committee, hearings, Department of Local Government (27 October 1988).

60. This author's interview with mayor and senior officials, City Hall, Baguio (October 1989).

61. Hearings, Philippine Senate Finance Committee (27 October 1988).

62. John Stuart Blackton, "Counterinsurgency: Winning within the Rule of Law" (June 1989), provided the author by Filipino officials.

63. By late 1989, when progress toward privatization was still modest, it was widely assumed that the chief impediment was the enjoyment of board membership by numerous government officials. See also Stephan Haggard's excellent overview of privatization before and after Aquino, "The Philippines: Picking up after Marcos," in Raymond Vernon, ed., *The Promise of Privatization*, (New York: Council on Foreign Relations, 1988), esp. pp. 112-113.

64. *Dictatorship and Revolution*, p. 261.

65. Gary Havens, "Aquino and her Administration: A View from the Countryside," *Pacific Affairs* 62, no. 1 (Spring 1989); 16.

66. *Ibid.*, p. 18.

67. Komisar, *Corazon Aquino: The Story of a Revolution*, p. 128.

68. Given out by local officially and blessed candidates.

69. "The Presidency," p. 161.

70. *Ibid.*

71. Davide Commission, *Republic of the Philippines*, "The Final Report of the Fact-Finding Commission" (pursuant to R.A. No. 6832) (Manila: October 1990), p. 101.

5

Military Culture

How do we classify the Philippines with respect to the military role? Robert Looney considers countries "under military control" if they meet one or more of these criteria: key political leadership by the military; existence of a state of martial law; extrajudicial authority exercised by security forces; lack of central control by national political authorities over large sections of the country where official or unofficial security forces rule; or control by foreign military organizations.[1] In the Marcos era, the first four of these conditions obtain; if one can consider an insurgent force equivalent to a "foreign military organization," then all of them did. Under President Aquino, General Ramos first served as chief of staff of the armed forces, then became secretary of national defense. The president at all times was dependent on him for survival. Martial law was not in force, but the armed forces endured continual accusations of exercising extrajudicial authority in rural areas, and the accusations were at least sometimes correct. Armed citizen's groups (e.g., the Alsa Masa) at times ran cities (such as Davao) and always were objects of fear in the populace (as revealed in polls), particularly when they were on the rampage. And with the NPA having influence in 20 percent of the country's barangays in the late 1980s—a conservative figure—it is clear that Manila's writ did not run everywhere. And yet the Philippines was not under military control under either Marcos or Aquino. It is one of the paradoxes of this study.

In contrast to each of its neighbors, a military subculture never established itself in the Philippines. There were implications for the patterns of civil-military relations during the Aquino era. Unlike Thailand, there was no historic basis for the military in government; unlike Indonesia, there was never a long period of military rule (and entrenchment); unlike Vietnam, no revolutionary victory, and unlike Malaysia, not even a colonially derived gentlemanly context for soldiers. True, Filipinos fought bravely for their independence at the end of the last century—and Muslims continued to fight for theirs from the republic up through the end of the next century; but mainstream Filipino culture had no military sagas on which to draw in modern times. As a Philippine scholar accounted for the "strong nonmilitaristic tradition in Filipino political culture," since the military "did not win independence for the nation from the Americans, its image throughout the country's colonial past has on the whole been negative, from the Spanish *conquistadors* to the Japanese Occupation Army."[2] Thus a journalist could actually complain of the treatment meted out by a Malacañang junior clerk to an AFP general. "The general was made to wait endless minutes, totally ignored by office personnel who were engaged in buying or selling food. . . . Summoned before the unsmiling, totally unsympathetic factotum, the general was treated like a school boy being called to task for not having this report or that. . . . In all my life, I had never seen a general so browbeaten by a mere bureaucrat."[3]

Pertinent also were the circumstances of independence and the subsequent role of the United States. All the other colonies gaining their independence from Western powers were gaining it from declining powers—at least declining at the time. The Philippines alone was gaining it from a rapidly rising power, and was laced with bases of that power as part of the terms (and assumptions) of that independence. The Philippine military could not even buy weaponry from other powers without American permission, under the terms of the treaty. It was not so easy either physically or emotionally to unshackle itself in these circumstances.

There is a second implication. Precisely because of the bases and the *American* military subculture in the archipelago, Philippine security never needed to be taken seriously, or so it was perceived. And as islands, the country was far safer, at least from external threat, than, say, Thailand. The result was an atmosphere in which debate could go on endlessly about Philippine security objectives with respect to the bases, but it was usually an unserious debate. At least the real issues in the debate were never really security issues, as we see later.

Hence when the AFP attempted to increase its share of the budgetary pie—for the arguably good purpose of fighting the insurgency—"solons"(as congressmen and senators are so often referred to in the Philippines) argued relentlessly in both Senate and House that there were better ways to spend the money. The guns-versus-butter issue could not have been better stated, on one side, than by Representative Bonifacio Villego, from the poor—and heavily infiltrated—Sorsogon province, who was a member of the House subcommittee on oversight. The military should realize, he argued, "that the real enemy is not the Filipinos in the hills but the problems of poverty, the destruction of the soil and food supply through environmental degradation, and the problem of social justice."[4]

But in fact there was never any division on the guns-versus-butter issue among the military themselves; they knew they could not win the insurgency without land reform, for example, and said so at a conference in 1987 called to develop a national agenda for the twenty-first century.[5] At the conference Professor Carolina Hernandez summed the issue up well:

> While a military solution to the twin insurgency is bound to fail in the absence of socio-economic change which addresses the causes of insurgency, a solution which has no military component will similarly not work. Like it or not, battles are being fought by both sides and the use of arms will have to be accepted as given. The question is how innocent lives can be best protected as socio-economic solutions are put in place.[6]

If the threat of an NPA takeover was more real than many wished to imagine, it was at least more hypothetical than a military takeover, which after all came close to occurring in August 1987 and probably would have occurred in 1989 but for an American intervention. The first coup by an armed force "is always the most traumatic," as one organizer of several African rounds once admitted to the author.[7] So it was always idle to dismiss the possibility of more attempts.

Nor was it dismissed. At the Solidarity Conference, Commodore José Lansangan, Jr., president of the National Defense College of the Philippines, said in a discussion "that the February revolution [of 1986] can still be considered a precedent by the military and can be likely used again."[8] Teodoro Benigno, a former press secretary to President Aquino, wrote explicitly of the possibility that Defense Secretary Fidel Ramos would—if forced to it—seize power.[9] Professor Filipe Miranda tells of briefing Aquino in May 1987, three months before Colonel Honasan's attempted coup, and notes that there were people "plugging for the military when the military's interests are legitimate. . . . We informed her that not only was there disaffection but possibly, a dramatic action of the military should certain things continue to take place."

Miranda noted his then discomfort—in November 1989—of the same feeling, rather presciently, weeks before the great coup; General Florencio Magsino, President of the National Defense College, put it more bluntly: "If our politicians do not watch out, there is no choice for the military but to take over."[10]

The military, after all, had long had its own reform movement within it, born out of disgust of the Marcos regime, but in the aftermath of the 1986 February revolution there were those who wished to use even an Indonesian precedent, and use the armed forces as the basis for a mass party, which was viewed as a very serious threat to democracy indeed.[11]

Although prior to martial law the military had been kept more or less at arm's length from national politics, it did have experience that prepared it for a larger political role. Its role in the counterinsurgency campaign against the Huks in the 1950s manifestly had a political dimension, especially in its training for socioeconomic activities. And then, for example, President Marcos had yielded to President Johnson's pressure for military support in Vietnam by sending "PHILCAG," a civic action unit, from the armed forces, which did a successful stint at civil engineering in Vietnam—and (ominously) gave its leaders experience in nonmilitary affairs of various sorts.[12]

It is a very real question why a military culture did not develop more than it did under Marcos. With the declaration of martial law came an almost instantaneous increase in military emoluments and privileges; soon colonels and majors were ruling in the provinces—as mayors and governors—and by all accounts taking *tong* and all the other privileges that go with unaccountable power. They also headed up sequestered corporations and executive departments, and several general officers and colonels had cabinet or subcabinet status. A retired general wrote that "Martial-law sanctions and rewards led to unprecedented corruption and abuse in the armed forces. Patronage replaced professionalism. The military establishment became Mr. Marcos's partner in maintaining political power and accumulating ill-gotten wealth."[13]

In fact, the actual substantial increase in military spending began *prior* to martial law, as Marcos readied the stage for personal rule. The sharpest increase was, however, between 1974 and 1975, as the war in Mindanao was being fought. After that military spending declined, as a percent of GNP, almost continuously until Marcos was ousted.

Although Marcos relied on the military, his regime was sui generis in nature. A canny, even brilliant, politician, he was so skillful at playing or buying off factions that it was never necessary to make the military the full partners they remained to Suharto in Indonesia, for example, or to every Thai leader save one since 1932. It is odd that the chief prebends of government would go to the famous cronies, who could do nothing whatever for Marcos save transport cash to hidden accounts, and who were a powerful drag on his (declining) popularity from the late 1970s onward. The literal billions siphoned off by such men as Roberto Benedicto, Danding Cojuangco, and Antonio Floirindo were gifts of presidential generosity. If he needed them for cover, he paid a large multiple of what their services were worth. The point is that Marcos did not cut the military in on those dispensations in any substantial manner. Instead he used a bluntly loyal fellow Ilocano, Fabian Ver, never known for sophistication or erudition, who used fear to keep a critical mass of soldiers in line to protect the president. Ver did get rich, it is said, but he was one of the few in the military to benefit on the scale of the cronies.

One writer, noting the bad state of Aquino-governmental relations with the military, notes that many had not forgiven the AFP for supporting martial law—and then goes on to argue that, if "the military enjoyed pre-eminence in rank and pelf" in that era, "by no means were all benefitted. Discontent rankled. . . . There is a sense then in which the military was a hostage to martial power just like everybody else." And if Marcos's downfall was due to many factors, "it is an open question whether he would have fallen so easily if his rapport with the military had not been ruptured by miscalculations about its proper leadership."[14] In other words, had Marcos acceded to the almost universal demand that he get rid of Ver, he might have bought more time.[15] But Marcos knew what they did not—he could not survive without Ver, who knew precisely how vulnerable his master was and alone had the ferocity to fend off attacks. So Marcos's rule ultimately was one of personalism; the military role was always a distant second.

The other side of the coin was a growing sense of frustration with government inefficiency and corruption, in some sectors, that as everywhere else in the world at one time or the other manifested itself as a desire for military intervention. "This past week, we have heard too many generally sober executives and businessmen saying that the only solution to the mess that is government is for the military to intervene."[16] In stepping down from the leadership of the governing LDP party, House speaker Ramon Mitra said that, merely three years after throwing out "the world's biggest *kleptocracy*, so many of us should once again seem prepared to give up our fledgling democracy to the first strongman who could make our trains run on time."[17] Teodoro Benigno relentlessly deplored the lack of leadership in the country, implored the church to mobilize support for President Aquino, and then painted a pained picture of what a military intervention would amount to. "One doesn't really have much of a choice," he complained, between the flawed democracy and military regimentation.[18]

But it was not as if corruption were confined to the civilian sector. There were too many scandals covered up to mention. Senator Maceda observed that "we have a tremendous number of complaints coming in with regard to overpricing and/or ghost purchasing in connection with AFP construction."[19] And when the intelligence budget was debated there was general mirth, since that area, with its secrecy, lent itself to graft and corruption. General Brawner, Senator Maceda's aide, noted that the Rangers—the cutting edge of coups—operated on Intelligence, but that no one wished to give them any now because "they will keep it for themselves." To which Maceda responded, amid committee laughter, "What do they keep for themselves? The Intelligence or the Intelligence funds?"[20] Revealing of the situation at Intelligence—*inter alia*—is the apparent fact, reported on sound authority, that the palace, in precisely the manner of Marcos's day but in more generous fashion, handed out monthly winnings from government-controlled casinos to General Ramos and all provincial commanders; Ramos's take was a monthly P2 million, or about $75,000, which he passed directly to G-2, or Intelligence, precisely to improve its performance.

In fact, there were serious problems. One very senior American official with direct access to Filipino military structures noted how he attempted to persuade the army's logistics command to accept some American computers for maintaining inventory. It took some time for the real reason for the refusal to sink in. The pilfering at Logistics Command (Logcom) was systematic; reportedly warlords could put orders in for advanced weaponry and pay an agreed-upon price that represented a fair percentage of the real value. One editorial noted that a new command at Logcom relieved sixty officers and three hundred enlisted men, who had overstayed, for obvious reasons.

> Graft starts at procurement. From airplanes to tanks to combat rations, Logcom officials are said to be quite diligent in exacting their 10% from suppliers. The bidding procedure is a joke, and the supply contracts are awarded to whoever offers the biggest commission. Insiders at the Logcom say only the purchases covered by the U.S. Foreign Military Sales Credit can reasonably be expected to be above board . . . but not even these were above suspicion. [21]

Nor was education clearly the answer. With respect to a proffered revision of the military academy's curriculum, Maceda observed that "most of your

Military Expenditure (ME) 1978-88[24]
(in thousand dollars)

Year	ME	ME	GNP	CGE	ME/GNP	ME/CGE	ME/ per cap	GNP/ per cap
	(current $)	(constant $)	(const)					
1978	393	661	32920	4869	2.0	13.6	14	683
1979	522	806	35200	4790	2.3	16.8	16	711
1980	505	715	36950	5275	1.9	13.5	14	727
1981	539	695	38190	6024	1.8	11.5	13	731
1982	531	644	38910	6080	1.7	10.6	12	725
1983	544	635	39390	5519	1.6	11.5	12	714
1984	390	440	36560	4629	1.2	9.5	8	645
1985	408	446	35070	4700	1.3	9.5	8	602
1986	632	673	35720	6386	1.9	10.5	11	596
1987	653	675	37830	6451	1.8	10.5	11	615
1988	680	680	40380	6672	1.7	10.2	11	639

GNP=Gross National Product
CGE=Central Government Expenditure

provincial commanders are PMA (Phillipine Military Academy) graduates, but when they reach the level of provincial commander, they also go into illegal gambling, illegal logging, etc. etc. . . . if he's promoted and offered 500,000 as *jueting* [betting] protection, he can't resist it."[22]

But what was the solution? General Magsino made the pregnant observation that "sometimes the solutions are worse than the problem, sir." Senator Maceda, getting the drift of the statement, responded "especially if the solution . . . is a coup d'état."[23]

The budget is the obvious place at which to examine priorities and trade-offs. The budget debate is also the place where special pleadings and special interests are focused. As we have noted above, there has been, in the past generation, an almost inexorable rise in defense spending throughout the developing world—with the Philippines being a remarkable exception for the most part.

Nevertheless, the pressures were on in the late 1980s, after the three years of economic growth, to increase the defense budget. There had already been one substantial budget increase, in the form of a supplement, after the 1987 coup attempt. But the pressure built up for more. Although the chart shows how The Arms Control Agency in Washington translates pesos into dollars, the reality in Manila was very different. There the pesos debated in the Senate had competing purposes. When, in 1988, a budget was presented that was a third larger than even the revised 1987 one, it was clear that the military could get what it minimally needed.[25] And it was by far the best organized department for making its case.

Subsequently the pressures were the more normal ones—service rivalry and the like—for increases. Senator Aquiliño Pimentel, in 1989, for example, made a powerful case for naval expansion. The country's naval vessels were, on average, forty-four years old—those of Malaysia were only twelve and of Thailand, sixteen. Thailand was budgeting over ten times as much for its navy as was the Philippines. Since EDSA there had been 520 "foreign intrusions" into territorial waters, including fifteen submarine sightings. The government must spend, Pimentel concluded, $1.25 billion to purchase needed vessels, over ten times its then budget for the navy.

Of course there was no money for such an expansion, and the debate in any case degenerated to accusations against the United States, from which the Philippines was obligated to obtain permission prior to buying ships, planes, or matériel, under the Mutual Defense Treaty. As a result, his country "has been turned into a veritable dumping ground for discarded or obsolete U.S. military equipment."[26]

Factionalism

There was good reason for the civilian leadership to be nervous about military loyalty to the Aquino government. The army itself had grown from 18,000 troops in 1970 to 66,000 in 1988, and in the interval had experience running—and abusing—provinces, administering martial law, killing Marcos's opponents.

Factionalism had a full history in the armed forces. The underlying problem was none other than the basic personalistic structure of all Philippine politics. Soldiers aligned themselves with personalities rather than fully accepting the hierarchy, wherever they were assigned. General Renato de Villa, when AFP chief of staff, tried to deal with this, and at a turnover ceremony pressed personnel not to "align themselves" with groups or persons for purposes of promotion. The problem became obvious whenever commands were changed. "It behooves all men and women . . . to rally behind their new commanding general. Indeed, it is a pillar of the chain of command that subordinates must adjust to their superiors and not the other way around," de Villa said, in the process underlining how in fact matters had worked in the past.[27]

Factionalism was compounded by regionalism. Marcos moved very fast after becoming president in 1965 to "Ilocanize" the armed forces, that is, to install fellow Ilocanos in the senior ranks. A report a year and a half *prior to* martial law noted that, "except for the chief of staff, General Manuel T. Yan, who, incidentally rose on account of merit,[28] almost all other officers now holding key positions are Ilocanos." The report suggested that an "explosive" situation was developing as a result in the armed forces. "Should a nation-wide civil strife explode, the President will for sure be faced with a divided armed forces, how sure is the President that non-Ilocano officers and men who have been harboring a grudge will not revolt?"[29] Of course Marcos knew precisely what would happen in those circumstances, since he was obviously already planning his autocracy, to be buttressed by those same Ilocanos.

But Marcos's manipulation of the military went further. As Richard Kessler writes,

> Marcos played to the military's inherent factional weakness under the guise of strengthening it. The periodic claims of reform, reorganization, and personnel reassignments were meant not to improve the military but to lessen American pressure for change and to enhance his control. . . . Marcos feared that a strong, professional military might ultimately overthrow him, and at times he even promoted the idea that the military might take over in order to discourage opponents. Ironically, he was right.[30]

The problem of factionalism was compounded following martial law, when two of Marcos's cousins, Fabian Ver and Fidel Ramos, began competing for influence. Ver had the upper hand almost throughout thanks to his rather basic and crude loyalty to Marcos (he had been his driver) and command of the Presidential Guard Battalion, on whose loyalty Marcos and his family had to depend totally in the latter years of martial law. Ramos however was always able to build a stronger institutional structure of power through his command of the Philippine Constabulary (PC), where his net was national.

Another cause of factionalism might well be what Professor Miranda called the building up of a "military class," the operational indicator of which is the number of relatives a Military Academy cadet has; 8,000 between 1951 and 1991 were studied, yielding an increasing concentration of what was obviously becoming a "military class." Moreover, the cadets were increasingly coming from higher socioeconomic backgrounds, similar to those at the University of the Philippines, resulting in "an erosion in the democratic characteristic of the people entering the military academy," thanks to this new elite's unwillingness automatically to respect civilian authority.[31]

There was also the matter of size. The AFP increased in size eightfold during the Marcos presidency. Emmanuel Soriano, a member of the Cabinet's Crisis Committee in the aftermath of the 1989 coup, noted that it was inevitable that fraternal organizations would develop as the size increased, to "soften the impersonal and stern facade of military life," in a situation where the old informal ties were insufficient.[32]

But, he went on, the problems became serious only with the "perceived turn toward the left by the Government" on Mrs. Aquino's assumption of office. In the first year, the issue was played out in the form of factionalism in the cabinet; the problem started with civilians. Juan-Ponce Enrile, the fabulously rich defense minister, secured his place—still as head of the Ministry of National Defense—in the new order by being the first to defect from Marcos's inner entourage.[33] But he thought he deserved to be president; indeed during the coup, he was one of three people asserting his own right to the palace, and believed at the least he had the right to rule jointly with Mrs. Aquino as the leader of the military faction in a civil-military regime. "The tension started to build up when Aquino and her advisers pushed for civilian 'supremacy' over the military."[34] He was frustrated by Aquino's incompetence in office and even more by her hints of populism.

Radicals, on the other hand, suspected him, not without reason, of championing the corporate interests of the military if only because he was increasingly isolated in the cabinet; they saw the military in turn as feeling threatened by a peace process that, while ending the insurgency, would vastly curtail its role and influence.[35] Until the November 1986 coup collapsed around him—and he was forced to resign—he ran circles around Malacañang, openly criticizing Aquino and her administration at Rotary Club meetings and wherever else he could get a forum. Worse, he used his office to circumscribe the president. Typically, "when Cory wanted a plane to take her to a disaster-relief mission, Johnny refused to give it to her," her then press secretary, Teodoro Benigno, said. "We felt we were under siege."[36]

Closest to Enrile at Camp Aguinaldo was his fellow hero of the revolution, RAM founder Gregorio "Gringo" Honasan.[37] RAM's Hotspur, Honasan was a swashbuckling and courageous lieutenant colonel who helped motivate his boss, Defense Minister Enrile, to start the coup. Ambitious, charismatic, and clever, he had a wide following in the military and used it to organize opposition to Aquino's government. Thus in the first year of Aquino's administration, her opponents had a veritable free rein within the military elite and established many precedents that were to make the Great Coup attempt of 1989 possible.

The first of these precedents proceeded from the first coup attempt, that of a band of Marcos loyalists operating from the Manila Hotel in July 1986. Allegedly, the Honasan network had intelligence of the forthcoming coup and did not pass it on. More important, once the coup had fizzled, the defense minister—*their* patron, Juan-Ponce Enrile—meted out the most modest of punishments, some pushups in the field. Having done their pushups, the men returned to their units, ready of course to try again.

But most important, the Marcos loyalists moved a substantial step toward reconciliation with the very men who had ousted them from power the previous February, owing to their mutual and growing disaffection with the government in power—though it would be only after five more coup attempts that the "loyalists" could reward the Honasan faction for its generosity by joining them in another coup attempt.

By November 1986 Enrile was ready to strike, but he delayed and postponed. What he had, in addition to Honasan, who from his Camp Aguinaldo office did not hesitate to call in officers senior to himself, were elite units recruited for one purpose (for example, antiterrorism) but usable for another (for example, to make coups). With these forces he dominated the concerns of the government for the month. Repeatedly, Chief of Staff Ramos had to call in major commanders to find out if they were loyal. At one point, after movement of troops and all possible signals of a coup, Ramos and the service commanders confronted Enrile, who realized that a coup must fail in circumstances where no service chief supported him.

The next move, on 22 November, was a coup that "became a chess game with each side trying to anticipate and block the moves of the other. In the end, the rebels backed down without firing a shot."[38] And then the queen moved: Aquino, finally after over nine months of his disloyalty, fired Enrile.

But that is as far as the consequences went. Charges were never filed against coup plotters. One Davide Commission informant "explained that Ramos's moves had always been conciliatory, not wanting to deepen the cleavages existing within the AFP."[39] And if an "iron fist" had been used, the leadership was unsure of what would happen. Ramos himself testified that there was little he could do as the plotters were mostly under the jurisdiction of the Ministry of National Defense, as if an organized government meeting to consider a very basic threat to its survival could not have dealt with that obstacle.[40]

For that matter, what was Aquino's problem? She had absolute power as president and commander in chief over both Enrile and his aides. Of course there was *utang* owed for their role in bringing her to power, but *utang* does not last forever. Her own perception is too clever by half—that were she to fire Enrile (as she is quoted by Komisar), he might not "want to vacate his office. Who's going to enforce it?"[41] If such does reflect her view at the time (and it is consistent with her behavior), it says little for her courage and much about how traumatized she and her government still were by the dramatic events that brought them to power. Leaders, in this respect as in all others, are made of the same clay as the rest of us.

Small wonder in the circumstances that Honasan was able to recruit some two thousand officers and men for an attempt to overthrow Aquino on 28 August 1987—and all but succeeded, but for the loyalty of Chief of Staff Ramos.

RAM actually had got going in 1985 and made itself felt throughout official circles, from DND headquarters to the American embassy. At the least it wished to redeem the army's professionalism; at most it saw the possibility of ruling the country. Although it was to be tagged a "right-wing" faction—especially as counterfoil to the NPA—RAM started out, and largely remained, less defined by ideology than by personal ties and ambitions. "It is true that for many coup participants, the rallying call seemed to be anti-communism but the network of RAM-HF [Honasan Faction] recruitment still frequently relied on personal relations," the Davide commission observed.[42]

The sense of betrayal by Aquino's government grew in AFP circles between the revolution and Honasan's unsuccessful coup attempt a year and a half later. It derived from President Aquino's association with her cause-oriented associates who had organized her campaign and who had been at her side from 1983, including, in the cabinet, Joker Arroyo, a shrewd human rights lawyer who had litigated against individual officers for human rights abuses; Arroyo did not trust the military, with reason. But as executive secretary at the palace, he and his associates convinced the president to take the risk of releasing all five hundred plus political prisoners, including NPA leaders known to be—according to the apprehending agents—committed Communists.

Once the Presidential Committee on Human Rights (PCHR) was established shortly after the revolution, soldiers began to be tried for human rights abuses while the enemy in whose pursuit they allegedly committed the abuses went free; it was to them a Catch-22, made preposterous by the facts of power: the revolution may have been a victory for People Power, but it was started out of the barrels of AFP guns. As one is quoted saying, "We toppled one government, and can topple another if reforms are not made. In fact, Cory didn't give us our jobs; we gave her a job; before that, Marcos could have annihilated all of them until we preempted his plans and Ver's forces."[43]

And the fact that only after Gringo's 1987 coup did the soldiers get a long-sought pay raise tended to reinforce in many of their minds the justice of the failed leader's cause. Nor does a pay increase bring loyalty. As a serving officer wrote, "Because these improvements in military life were brought about by coup attempts there is a feeling among coup non-participants that they owe these improvements not to a concerned government but to coup pressure."[44] They had a point. Until the president replaced Arroyo as executive secretary (and speechwriter Teodoro Locsin), the soldiers had a burning grievance. But after the coup human rights investigations of the military were virtually halted for a time.

The serving soldier also felt that the military leadership was corrupt, something any researcher could confirm routinely in discussions in the camps with soldiers. Senator Maceda, in a speech in which he proposed to go on "asking questions" whether or not the DND liked it, said it was "notoriously known that a substantial portion of this intelligence fund was pocketed by the commanding officers concerned,"[45] as we have already seen. But a year later his knife was sharper still, this time picking out General Montaño as his victim, accusing him of pocketing huge percentages of the gambling takes in central Luzon; of course hundreds of Montaño's lieutenants rose up to demand Maceda's resignation, in somewhat amused horror at the accusation, which they all knew to be true; indeed many of them were a part of that action.

Some of the "corruption" was even "legal;" if Ramos got P2 million a month from the palace, the provincial commanders reportedly got P1 million; and if they pocketed it, in all likelihood the smell of money, at least, surrounded the transaction. And what junior officers may know, the enlisted men will soon find out. There are few secrets in the Philippines.

The mood in Congress was thus to try to keep the armed forces on the defense. They had a free ride in 1987 after the revolution, the chairman of the Armed Services committee, Senator Maceda, said; but in 1988 they were asking for a P13.8 billion increase in their budget, to P21.2 billion—the biggest jump in any year since 1975, when it increased 122 percent. "Some questions will have to be asked," he kept repeating,[46] in special reference to reports that the AFP was complaining about those questions.

It was a general view that DND reports on the insurgency were part and parcel of a "budgetary insurgence" (or Budgetary Huks, Victor Corpuz, the one-time NPA officer, was to call them); there were those claiming the AFP, "for purposes of the budget . . . inflate the number of NPA regulars; for purposes of justifying presidential trips abroad, you will claim that there is now a declining number of NPA regulars."[47] Senator Santa Nina Rasul, for example, in the 1988 budget hearings, noted that between 1986 and 1987 there was purportedly a decline in the insurgency; at least such was claimed. "But your budget has not decreased in that period . . . how come?" he asked an army representative.[48] Senator Maceda, a professional who was himself once executive secretary in Malacañang, said he did not trust the statistics "being issued by General Headquarters" on casualties in the war. He proposed to go down to the company level and find out for himself.[49] He did that, making over forty trips to camps in one year alone.

General Ramos did not always escape criticism. He was sometimes pointedly, though usually without evidence, accused of playing his own hand at the palace rather than undertaking controversial reforms in the military. Former chief of staff General Rafael Ileto is one of the few who went public with the charges.[50]

By early 1990, in the months after the Great Coup attempt, strains between civilians and the military were so open that the military was put on full alert when Aquino traveled to Baguio to deliver a commencement address at the Philippine Military Academy, a center of unrest. Cars and drivers were searched and her speech was interrupted eighteen times by "spurious signals."[51] It was the sort of intelligence noise that often precedes coups. Intelligence was, however, one of the areas most suspect institutionally in the AFP. Maceda's insinuations were typical. Congresswoman Hortense Starke charged in what is called a Privilege Speech (one legally inviolate) in the House, that intelligence on the NPA was being hoarded by one service to the exclusion of others, that only P30,000 per month was trickling down to regional units in the PC, out of an overall budget of more than P500 million. The proof of inefficiency, she pointed out, was the failure to anticipate the 1989 coup—though she admitted, and made public, the suspicion that "many senior officers knew that Honasan was just around the corner but they also knew that by keeping him at large, they would have an operational leverage against the civilian government."[52]

Factionalism had become so pervasive, and so seemingly insoluble, that Filipinos looked for outside solutions. Ambassador Melchor, then Manila's envoy in Moscow but a former under secretary of defense and executive secretary under Marcos, wrote a report to the Department of Foreign Affairs, arguing that the "primary source of instability to the Philippines" was the AFP, not the NPA. To remedy the problem, he recommended "deep structural reforms," preceded by an "audit" of the AFP. Basically, he did not feel that Malacañang or any local entity was capable of asking the tough questions that needed to be asked or looked into in order to have a meaningful reform of the AFP. Hence, his recommendation for an external group—read American—of advisers to assist a board of AFP officers earmarked to take over the major command assignments in the AFP.[53]

The report not only was not heeded; the Department of Foreign Affairs, whose head did not get on well with Melchor, leaked it to the press confident that the notion of an external auditor would catch headlines—and land Melchor in trouble, both of which happened. Calls went out from the Senate floor demanding an investigation—until Melchor was able to get the uncensored version, so to speak, in relevant hands. In fact, it was to become clear in time that the DFA had leaked it selectively; and Melchor was in large measure able to vindicate himself by the turn of events. One of his old alumni associations—the Philippine Military Academy's—passed a resolution supporting his recommendation. And the fact that one of the most internationally respected and nationally prominent citizens of the Philippines could campaign for the idea indicates how bad the situation was—and how great the legitimacy of the United States was.

The Creation of the Philippine National Police

The Philippine Constabulary (PC) was always an anomaly in the country's security structure. It was created out of the remnants of the Spanish Guardia Civil and acted as a U.S. security force shortly after the war for independence, by the American victors, and was commanded by an American. It did much of the mopping-up operations. "Repressive police action did not endear the PC to the masses who continued supporting agitators for independence," a Philippine naval officer has written. "On the other hand, the PC enjoyed the support of the elite classes cultivated by both Spanish and American colonizers. The PC was important in quelling labor strikes in factories, farms, and plantations."[54]

In 1936 the PC was merged with the army and then, during the war, absorbed by the U.S. Armed Forces in the Far East. After the war it was a Ping-Pong ball bouncing from one institutional home to another—outside, then inside the national defense structure[55]—but it maintained its character as, essentially, a national police force. Its importance grew dramatically with martial law, because at that time *all* police forces were brought under the Integrated National Police and therefrom subordinated to the PC. "Mayors and governors were stripped of their control over the local police, and control was handed over to the PC provincial commander who concurrently served as provincial police superintendent,"[56] Max Mejia writes. Marcos was, of course, the true beneficiary of the system, getting as he did the additional benefit that, by putting the PC under the military, he could even frustrate the will of the U.S. Congress, which had recently determined not to permit U.S. aid to go to police training anywhere in the world. But in Manila, the PC, under the armed forces, could claim it at will.

The PC always had three problems, the first two being virtually stigmas. As Congressman Bonifacio H. Villego put it, the PC had a "peculiar history as colonial instrument against Filipino nationalists."[57] As we will see, though its early stigma may have eroded, it acquired an equally strong one in public assumptions of the graft and corruption amid which it seemed always to be found, whatever its institutional home.[58] As the president of the National Defense College said,

> the joke has been going around that when one is assigned to the PC, whether you enrich yourself or not, you will be corrupted. You are already destroyed. . . . If you do not play to the music, you are not given any important assignments. In almost all our social affairs, the PC always shoulders the expenses. The Congress also found out in their surveys that among academy graduates, the assets of those in the PC are bigger.[59]

The third problem was even more basic, however. The PC's basic assignment was crime; but insurgency is a crime, and as the field force closest to the ground in the provinces, it was inevitable that the PC become involved in fighting the insurgency. In fact, it was as head of the PC—for twelve years—that the then president's cousin, General Fidel V. Ramos, began to develop his doctrines and strategies for a "total" campaign against the NPA.

That of course would—and did—inevitably lead to competition between the army and the PC over who would lead any given campaign against the NPA. Victor Corpuz, the one-time NPA commando turned AFP author, wrote of this "disunity" that "a constabulary unit, for instance, that receives A-1 information concerning the enemy would rather act alone . . . than pass the information to other army units . . . for concerted and coordinated action."[60] And the army, he says, plays the same game. But precisely because of the differently pointed institutional objectives, as General Brawner put it, the PC was always able to define its own agenda and evade instructions from general headquarters. "If it didn't like the orders on the counter-insurgency front, it could just say it was busy with crime. If it was given instructions it didn't like on the crime front, it could preoccupy itself with the insurgency."[61]

There was a long-standing constitutional predisposition to give the PC a more civilian character. The 1935 constitution provided for a national police force, as did that of 1973 and 1987—"national in scope and civilian in character," as the latter document's widely quoted words put it. Without doubt the PC would have preferred to keep things as they were in 1989, when the palace and both houses of Congress finally proposed legislation to put into place what was constitutionally mandated. Surely Ramos himself, as secretary of national defense, would have so preferred, given his personal links to the men he had commanded for a dozen years and still within his hierarchy of command. But the bias was too great for bucking the constitutional provision. The question became how much the PC would be changed as it joined with the Integrated National Police under civilian authority, outside the DND.

If the main motive for detaching the PC from the AFP was suspicion of the police, a new motive arose as the government battled, especially in 1990, to secure the loyalty of the armed forces. In matters of coups, the police's loyalty had in large part been continuous. Thus the effort to "develop the civil police and the NBI [National Bureau of Investigation] as the counterweight against the military rebels and against coup conspiracies," Amando Doronila argued. After all, it was the police who had to flush out military rebels during the 1989 coup's struggle over Channel 7.[62]

The problem of civil-military relations was exacerbated as never before on this issue, to the point where the possibilities of a coup d'état were openly bruited as leverage against the lawmakers. It started with Senator Maceda's barrage in a Privilege Speech against PC commander General Montaño, for his alleged benefits from—inter alia—jueting (gambling) and assorted other irregularities. Maceda's legislative proposal provided that all PC generals —and all top-ranking sergeants—be automatically retired from the service, while the rest be given the choice of joining the army or the new national police. "Let the generals retire and enjoy their loot," Maceda said. And that hit home enough for Montaño to threaten a class action suit by the top PC brass against the senator, and to accuse him of doing more damage to the PC than the National Democratic Front, "which has been fighting a 20-year insurgency war against the government."[63]

True, it was not as if military corruption was confined to the PC; in 1989 there were 581 officers and enlisted men facing graft and corruption charges before the AFP Anti-Graft Board.[64] Colonel Honasan reportedly took advantage of the fury in the PC to recruit forces from within for a coup, telling them "we told you so, that's what you get for backing up this government" (in the 1986 revolution).[65] Ramos lent his immense prestige to Montaño's cause—but without defending him on the specifics. "The demoralization within the PC created by these discriminatory provisions [in the Maceda bill] should not be overlooked as it could seriously affect our six-year campaign to improve internal security and national stability."[66]

Ramos, of course, knew how true the charges were; he was amused, for example, to find the troops cheering enthusiastically when he required all commanding officers in a province publicly to sign an oath against gambling involvement—and the noise was greatest when the provincial commander signed.[67] It was an open secret that the gambling syndicates paid for their protection in large amounts of money, and the troops resented that the fruits were not spread beyond the commanders' immediate entourage.

Indeed corruption in the PC was a larger issue than jueting. Illegal logging—which had reduced the country's forests from 19 million hectares in 1965 to less than a million today, with incalculable consequences for the environment—was always thought to be a major preserve of the PC. Congressman Padilla, of Nueva Ecija, made a Privilege Speech bringing such charges out in the open ("nefarious activities of PC-INP men ranging from extortion to brazen thievery") and linking the depredation of the forests to all the other problems the republic was suffering from.[68] It was said that there were two kinds of PC commanders—millionaires and stupid ones.

Whether the removal of the PC from the AFP into an integrated police structure that was "national in scope and civilian in character" would remedy any of the inherent problems of the PC was not clear in the early 1990s. Nor was it evident that the challenge of coordinating development and security was being made easier by this move, the origins of which, after all, were reactive rather than creative. Although it was much too early to make a definitive judgment, it looked as if the PC was unlikely to get less corrupt under the new dispensation; rather it seemed likely to become less effective, given the more distant coordination that would thenceforth obtain with its sister organizations in the fight against the insurgencies and crime.

The Young Officers' Union

Possibly the most serious threat to the established order emerged with the realization that RAM was outflanked on the left by younger, more idealistic, less senior, and more committed soldiers, with the rank of major and below, in the form of the Young Officers Union, or YOU. At first it appeared to be a phantom organization, perhaps a faction within RAM; the first real intelligence on it was on 4 October 1989; according to the Air Intelligence and Security Group it was "reportedly poised to stage a coup if the Aquino government did nothing about" recent scandals.[69]

YOU's role in the 1989 coup attempt became publicly known only in mid-1990. It seemed clear that they had been a driving force, possibly the catalyst in the coup, and they were what differentiated it from the 1987 attempt. That is to say there was more momentum and drive in 1989 because there were ideas invested in it beyond the mere question of "who-whom" or who governs. In fact, YOU personnel talked an honest language of radical reform—not the Marxist rhetoric of the small band of Marcos opponents who had picked up international radical slogans, but genuine populist phrases that, however much they may have resembled those of Communist movements elsewhere, were tied to specific Philippine problems—land tenure, an elitist ruling class, social stratification, and so on.

It is ironic that this movement began coming into its own as a serious force just as the AFP as a whole was mastering the threat of the NPA. Indeed, the question arose as to why YOU took so long to make a tactical agreements and common cause with the mountain-grown guerrillas. The answer is that their origins were genuinely separate, born of their own view of their country's problems seen from the metropolis as the old elites reestablished themselves, rather than nurtured in the mountains out of an internationalist ideology at a time when such held much currency, and whose analysis bore considerable resemblance to the problems in the archipelago. So as 1990 wore on it became clear that YOU had a distinct identity and had allied itself with RAM in the 1989 coup for tactical reasons only—because they had "wanted to validate something," a spokesman said.[70] By mid-1990 YOU had openly broken with RAM, which it accused of having a "hidden political agenda"[71]—meaning here what it usually means, namely personal ambition. It had precedent throughout the third world—particularly in Egypt with the radical Free Officers and the Ba'ath in Syria and Iraq, but also in Latin America and Africa, as also in the revolutionary forces in the Philippines itself, during the ill-fated war for independence. Amando Doronila saw it symbolizing three important tendencies in the AFP—the reawakening of nationalism, the inroads of leftism, and the further segmentation of the armed forces.

The first tendency was made evident when YOU came out in opposition to retention of the bases—a major heresy to main-line soldiers, who saw their matériel, weaponry, training, and legitimacy as tied to their American partners. Doronila correctly differentiated YOU's position from RAM's anti-Americanism, which was "plain opportunism. They denounced US intervention because they perceived it turned the tide against the [1989] coup."

The second tendency came with the realization that the AFP was associated with entrenched forces that prevented land reform, economic justice, and everything else associated with Philippine stagnation. There was, therefore, "within the most strategic organs of state power, an embryonic force addressing fundamental questions of distribution of power and wealth and prepared to link itself with likeminded, youthful forces in civil society."[72]

Segmentation came when YOU, Doronila went on, realized that RAM lacked popular support. True, Honasan was personally popular, and there was visible public cheering during the 1989 coup attempt, but it was not sufficiently structural or widespread enough. YOU realized that "it is hard for a coup to succeed without popular backing and if the population is not sufficiently outraged against the regime." It was therefore developing a political program and could organize pressure, within the constitutional system, for change.[73] A spokesman said it was like the Communist movement with a party, a united front organizing the grass-roots level—but was not allied with the Communists.

There was indeed a significant difference with traditional Communist strategy—which, when on the outside, could be summarized "the worse the better." YOU's Captain Danilo Lim, a West Point-trained Scout Ranger in detention, commented that "conventional or traditional coups are now passé." "The compelling necessity which Philippine conditions dictate is a nationalist revolution. Bombings and death threats *do not create the revolutionary situation* but they create an atmosphere of anarchy and violence which only aggravates the present situation."[74]

General Ramos, for example, noted the similarity between the YOU's efforts among young people and the efforts of the Communist Party of the Philippines's "Nationalist Youth" during the 1960s and 1970s.

> The YOU's progress, based on what we see and on our evaluation of seized documents, is that they are trying to picture themselves as the pillar of the youth and the military corps. . . . They are trying to enter campuses and integrate themselves with workers and other sectors to prove that they are dedicated to the new nationalism they have allegedly discovered.

Those tactics had brought their Communist predecessors up from 300 members in 1970 to almost 23,000 by the mid-1980s, he added.[75] And YOU opened every door; two military officers and a young police lieutenant "are being closely watched by the military intelligence for recruiting followers into" YOU. A Camp Aguinaldo source added the ironic touch that the three officers "belong to the intelligence service."[76]

Whether a coherent YOU, well armed, would stay within the system and resist the temptation either to strike through a coup or to ally with the CPP-NPA seemed highly implausible. The CPP-NPA certainly saw the parallel course. In an interview from his Dutch exile, José Ma. Sison, founder of the CPP and purportedly still its leader, noted that compared with RAM's conservative platform, "YOU appears to have a more progressive and nationalist stance." And if it was allied with RAM, he could compare its trajectory to RAM's—which, after all, had been part of the Marcos government, and then joined the Aquino government, and then became dismayed by that. Making the predictable and classic analysis of "objective" elements of alliance, Sison added that "even if some elements espouse anti-communist ideology, as long as they speak of good proposals in the economic and political arenas, [the CPP] would look at the advantages of those proposals."[77]

Indeed by October of 1990, YOU claimed already to be forging tactical alliances with Communists to unseat President Aquino.[78] A front, the "Democratic Front for Filipinism," was announced as a step toward coordinating antigovernment forces "in preparation for a civilian-military uprising." There was to be no small military steps, just "one big bang only;" "muscle flexing" was ruled out, the game was "to prepare the masses" for the important strike.[79] By December the alliance may have still been tactical, but it was operational. For one thing, YOU was quarreling with RAM, at least so claimed General Biazon; YOU after all wanted a protracted struggle, RAM a "short struggle or the speedy grab of power."[80] But the fact is that the alliance was confirmed by a senior alliance leader and renegade, Abraham Purugganan. Step by step YOU was moving toward revolution.

NOTES

1. Robert Looney, manuscript, "A Topology of Third World Countries," 1989.
2. Carolina G. Hernandez, "The Philippine Military in the 21st Century," in Solidarity Conference, *A Filipino Agenda for the 21st Century*, 7-8 February, 1987 (Manila: Solidaridad Publishing House, 1987), p. 245. Hereafter Solidarity Conference.
3. Nelson Navarro, "State of Insecurity," *Malaya* (6 September 1989). Though, given the general efficiency of Malacañang, one might say the general was being treated like everybody. ("At Malacañang, there isn't much to do," one official said in an interview. "You call your friends, you play card games.")
4. Efren L. Danao, "P3-B Cut in Defense Budget Proposed," *Star* (6 Sept. 1989).
5. Solidarity Conference.
6. *Ibid.*, p. 236.
7. "It's like first sex," he explained. "It's easy—and great—the second time." Conversation, General Robert Kotei (Accra: 1975).
8. Solidarity Conference, p. 52.
9. See Teodoro Benigno, "Eddie Ramos, the Man and the Enigma," *Philippine Star* (7 September 1989).
10. "The Presidency," *Solidarity* Seminar Series on Public Issues, No. 20, *Solidarity* 125 (January-March 1990), p. 148.
11. This author's interview, Alejandro Melchor (10 September 1989).
12. See this author's case study of PHILCAG in his 1976 study, *Unequal Partners: Philippine and Thai Relations with the United States, 1965-75* (Lexington, MA: Lexington Books, 1975).
13. BGen. (ret.) José T. Almonte, "The Soldier and the State," *Manila Standard* (13 November 1989).
14. Adrian E. Cristobal, "Marcos and the Military," *Philippine Daily Inquirer* (11 September 1989).
15. Ambassador Alejandro Melchor, who negotiated in Washington at the end of the regime, repeated the extent to which Marcos's survival was deemed—at the highest levels of the Reagan administration—a function of his willingness to get rid of Ver.
16. Luis D. Beltran, "Government Is Immobilized," *Manila Standard* (18 September 1989).
17. Ramon Mitra, "I'm Not Deserting LDP," in *Ibid.*
18. "Here's the Score," *Philippine Star* (8 September 1989).
19. Hearings, Philippine Senate, Committee on Armed Services (4 August 1989). Hereafter, Hearings.
20. *Ibid.* (7 August 1989), p. 45.

21. "Off to a Good Start," *Malaya* (5 March 1991), in Foreign Broadcast Information Service-East Asia-91-043 (5 March 1991). Hereafter FBIS-EAS.

22. Hearings (8 August 1989).

23. *Ibid.* (8 July 1989), p. 64.

24. Arms Control and Disarmament Agency, "World Military Expenditures and Arms Transfers, 1989," p. 61.

25. Though, as General de Villa was quick to point out in testimony, the AFP budget was still only 7.9 percent of the national budget—so other departments were growing too. Budget hearings, Philippine Senate (30 June 1988), p. 88.

26. *Manila Standard* (7 June 1989).

27. Photocopied address, AFP (24 February 1990).

28. And who was sent as ambassador to Thailand soon thereafter, presumably precisely because of his professionalism as a soldier.

29. Leon Meer Manipol, "AFP Ilocanized!" *The Weekly Nation* (1 March 1971).

30. Richard Kessler, *Rebellion and Repression in the Philippines* (New Haven, CT: Yale University Press, 1989), p. 122.

31. "The Presidency," p. 158.

32. Quoted in *Business World* (5 July 1990), cited in FBIS-EAS-90-131 (9 July 1990), p. 43.

33. Though the fact that Enrile's position was slipping was not irrelevant to his decision.

34. Dante Simbulan, "Can Cory Rely on Her Soldiers?" *Philippine Witness* 15 (September-October 1987), p. 2.

35. See *Dictatorship and Revolution: Roots of People's Power* (Manila: Conspectus Foundation, 1988), p. 258.

36. Interview, Manila (September 1989).

37. RAM was coined as an acronym from another group, namely "R.E.F.O.R.M. the AFP Movement," standing for Restore Ethics, Fair-Mindedness, Order, Righteousness, and Morale. Davide Commission, *Republic of the Philippines*, "The Final Report of the Fact-Finding Commission" (pursuant to R.A. No. 6832) (Manila: October 1990), p. 139. Hereafter Davide.

38. *Ibid.*, p. 181.

39. *Ibid.*, p. 183.

40. *Ibid.*, p. 183.

41. Komisar, *Corazon Aquino: The Story of a Revolution* (New York: George Braziller, 1988) p. 230.

42. Davide, p. 246.

43. *Dictatorship and Revolution*, p. 232.

44. Lieutenant Maximo Mejia, Jr., " 'Bantay O Bantay-Salakay'?: The Philippine Military as a Source of Instability" (MA thesis, Fletcher School of Law and Diplomacy, 1990), p. 55.

45. Hearings of the Joint Committee of National Defense and Finance (27 June 1988), p. 34.
46. *Ibid.*, p. 22.
47. *Ibid.*, p. 47.
48. Philippine Senate, Budget hearings on Philippine Army (11 July 1988), p. 54.
49. *Ibid.*, p. 33.
50. See "De Villa—Ramos Clone?" *ASIAWEEK* (12 February 1988), p. 14, cited in Mejia, " 'Bantay O Bantay-Salakay'?: The Philippine Military as a Source of Instability," p. 58.
51. El Macaspac, "Denounce Power Grab, Cory Tells New PMA Graduates," *Manila Standard* (19 February 1990).
52. "The Message in the Mutiny Cited," *Privilege Speech*, reprinted in *Manila Bulletin* (22 January 1990).
53. Ambassador Alejandro Melchor to author, 20 April 1991.
54. Mejia, "Bantay O Bantay-Salakay'?: The Philippine Military as a Source of Instability," p. 28.
55. See Michael Dueñas, "The Proposed Philippine National Police," *Philippine Free Press.*
56. Mejia, "'Bantay O Bantay-Salakay'?: The Philippine Military as a Source of Instability", p. 39.
57. *Ibid.*, p. 13.
58. See the discussion in "The Presidency," p. 155.
59. *Ibid.*, p. 156.
60. Victor N. Corpuz, *Silent War* (Manila: VNC Enterprises, 1989), p. 130.
61. This author's interview, office of Senator Maceda (2 January 1989).
62. "Institutional Conflicts Can Bring Anarchy," *Manila Chronicle* (16 July 1990), in FBIS-EAS-90-137 (17 July 1990), p. 44.
63. *Philippine Daily Inquirer*, 24 October 1989.
64. As announced by General Ramos. The release does not, however, break down the service of those charged; it merely indicates that it *does* include the Integrated National Police. There can be no doubt that all the services were well represented. Roy Sinfuego, "Antigraft Court Charges 9 Generals with Graft," *Manila Bulletin* (22 June 1989), in FBIS-EAS-89-119 (22 June 1989).
65. Dueñas, "The Proposed Philippine National Police," *Philippines Free Press.*
66. *Philippine Daily Inquirer* (24 October 1989).
67. While author was traveling with General Ramos.
68. Congressman Padilla, speech before the House of Representatives (20 January 1990).
69. Davide, p. 299.
70. "Alliance of Military Rebel Groups Breaks Up," *The Manila Chronicle* (17 May 1990), cited in FBIS-EAS-90-096 (17 May 1990), p. 34.

71. *Ibid.*
72. "YOU Reflects New Thinking in Army," *The Manila Chronicle* (18 May 1990), cited in FBIS-EAS-90-097 (18 May 1990), p. 44.
73. *Ibid.*
74. Manny Mogato, "Coup Plot Denied by YOU Officer," *Manila Chronicle* (8 August 1990), in FBIS-EAS-90-154 (9 August 1990), p. 46. Emphasis added.
75. "Ramos Claims RAM Adopting Communist Strategies," Manila Diyaryo Filipino in Tagalog (27 September 1990), in FBIS-EAS-90-188 (27 September 1990), p. 62.
76. Joey Caburnida, "Military 'Agreeable' to Amnesty," *Manila Chronicle* (31 October 1990), in FBIS-EAS-90-211 (31 October 1990), p. 56.
77. "Sison Predicts Aquino's Fall in Four Months," *Malaya* (17 September 1990), in FBIS-EAS-90-181 (18 September 1990), p. 59.
78. "YOU 'Forging' Alliance with Communist Rebels, *The Manila Chronicle* (22 Oct 1990), in FBIS-EAS-90-204 (22 October 1990), p. 59.
79. *Ibid.*
80. Manila Broadcasting Co. (4 December 1990), FBIS-EAS-90-233 (4 December 1990), p. 44.

6

Development Through Security?

The leitmotif of the Philippine armed forces was to accentuate the interdependence of security and development. General Biazon, while commanding Manila's security forces, warned against military budget increases. "If we siphoned off more for the military establishment," he said in a public forum, "then there will be more hunger. The poor will now become easy prey for the communists who will seize the opportunity to stage a revolt and grab power."[1]

The problem was always how to find the appropriate balance between civil and military—and how to coordinate between them, as we have seen. The problem was not just hypothetical or for the long run. In the Bondoc peninsula, the secretary of national defense explained how a German development commitment was held up because the workers had no security; this lack of security accounted for a number of the projects being held up in the multibillion-dollar Philippine aid pipeline. The problem went the other way too; as John Blackton put it, "a situation will [otherwise] arise in which military operations produce no lasting results because they are unsupported by civil follow-up action."[2]

Moreover, the military developed a new approach to their operations that emphasized what Colonel Villanueva, in Senate hearings for the army, called a "human ecology" approach, in which 90 percent of the counterinsurgency (CI) budget was being used for human ecological protection, 10 percent for tactics—or operations.[3] In appearing before a Senate committee, one AFP general, in justifying the new Special Operations Teams—SOTs—being funded, noted that their seventh and final phase was in fact economic development. "Please take note that we . . . include the economic development although it is not the work of the military, but we just like to accentuate the fact that through the military, we can invite local officials, per persuasion, to perform the roles in the delivery of the services."[4] As a U.S. Embassy official put it, however, the problem with the SOTs was that they went to a given area—and then stayed.

The book *Silent War*, published by a one-time senior New People's Army (NPA) leader who went over to the government, is an analysis of guerrilla strategy and a proposal for a successful counterinsurgency strategy. It is unique in the annals of CI in being published and discussed in "real time" (that is, during operations). The book's only appendix is the outline of the SOT concept in its seven phases. Its brilliant analysis notes that the old strategy, looking at body count, left "the enemy political structures in the barangays . . . practically untouched and intact . . . [but] To catch the fish, we must first drain the water from the pond." So in enumerating the seven phases of "draining the water" Corpuz comes to number seven: "Economic Development"—"bringing basic services to the people and uprooting the basic causes of dissidence and discontent."[5] But how? Where were the resources? It was as if the entire explication were a gigantic tautology.

For that was always the problem—the provision of services. There is little doubt the interface was between government and Juan de la Cruz. It was down just below the Municipal POCs—the Peace and Order Councils, made up of local government officials and their military counterparts, with which any Filipino could have contact. But as a vice mayor said, in a municipality in the relatively prosperous province of Laguna, adjoining Metro Manila, "we take our work on the POC very seriously. We meet for several hours twice a month. The problem is, all our recommendations require resources. There are no resources."[6]

An example of the problem of coordination and follow-up arose in a Senate committee hearing. Senator Rasul asserted that the rebel-returnee program was not working: so why appropriate P4 million? At issue was the payment for weapons turned in. General Ramos conceded that some of the firearms turned in had come in previously. And furthermore, that all too often the benefits to a unit were not distributed: the leader kept all. So in mid-1989 Ramos suspended payments for firearms and gave DOLA the lead in the reconciliation and development program.

The bigger part of the program is really what we call the "downstream services" rendered by other departments like Agriculture, Labor and Employment, Trade and Investment, and also, of course, local government. And these are in terms of training, farm assistance, farm animals, fertilizer, tools, seedlings, and where this is feasible, relocation and resettlement.[7]

It was asking a lot.

The strategy is flawless. And much of the implementation has been impressive, accounting for at least some part of the CI turnaround in 1988-89. Alas, where the POCs tended to fall down is where local officials had relatively great flexibility and autonomy. In Baguio, for example, the POC did not meet for over a year, after a new station commander arrived who considered them supernumerary.[8] For that matter, neither did the development council meet. Of course Baguio is unique—not least so for these purposes in that unwritten understandings existed with the NPA not to violate the city's peace. In return, the NPA was able to use Baguio for rest and relaxation—just as the military itself could.

CAFGU

The Citizens Armed Forces Geographical Units (CAFGU), on paper, look familiar. Their objective seems identical to Marcos's CHDF—Citizens' Home Defense Forces—few organizations were more discredited by virtue of their abuses of power—untrained men with arms terrorizing, intimidating, abusing villagers. And it is thus that Ramos found it necessary to scrap the CHDF and start anew. In fact, the opportunity to charter CAFGU came with all the other booty of the failed 1987 coup. In its aftermath Ramos tacitly obtained palace approval for a new CHDF—of course with assurance that this time there would be no abuses.

The emphasis Ramos gave to CAFGU can hardly be accidental. There were certainly good reasons. As he pointed out,[9] CAFGU forces, being recruited from the area of operations and confined thereto, need no budgetary R&R. They need no perks. As they were from the region they were motivated to protect their own people and public infrastructure. The creation of a 160,000-man CAFGU force would, at low cost, more than double the manpower available to fight the insurgency. As they were under military control—indeed as they were *not* a citizen's army but a military auxiliary— they should be susceptible to coordination.

Why, then, was CAFGU the only line item of the AFP budget for 1989 and 1990 singled out for serious cuts—at least cuts of the programmed increases (from 65,000 to 80,000 men)? Senator Maceda spoke openly in committee of CAGFU abuses, relating them to those of its predecessor, the CHDF. Newspaper reports appeared with regularity citing them: "CAFGU: A bungling monster," said one. It told of recruits waiting in ambush for NPA forces, but killing a carabao instead, and of another instance where one soldier killed his comrade. Governor Vicente Y. Emano "condemned the violence involving CAFGU members and traced it to the haphazard screening of applicants and very poor discipline. . . . Unless major changes are made . . . the CAFGU will soon become a 'Frankenstein's monster' among the people it is tasked to protect and safeguard," he said.[10] A prominent editor, in a report on the AFP, accused the military of "forced recruitment to paramilitary forces (CAFGUs)."[11] A columnist noted that CAFGUs were accused at times of renting out themselves—and their powerful guns—for private purposes, of which there was no doubt.[12] A thoughtful American official wrote of the rising concern as more and more weapons were issued to CAFGUs:

> the long term concern over who will ultimately control those weapons remains at issue. The interest of some GOP elements in upgrading the CAFGU arsenals from semi-automatic M-1s to fully automatic M-16s raises the stakes even higher. Just as Vietnamese self defense forces often sold automatic weapons to the enemy to raise cash, rural CAFGU members may find that with an M-16 worth a year's income, the temptations to sell will be irresistible.[13]

In Negros Occidental, CAFGUs could be hired by landlords[14] for the private purpose of guarding their sugar holdings—though this last blending of public and private purpose is historically Filipino in character.

Still, it was not clear that such was the larger pattern. Ramos argued that after one year CAFGU generated fewer complaints of abuses than the regular forces, and there was no reason to doubt his claim, based on his department's excellent data.

The kind of exemplary discipline that would tighten up the armed forces is reflected in a report on the eve of the 1989 coup. Brigadier General Cesar Fortuno, commanding general of the army's 101st Infantry Brigade, "recently dismissed two soldiers and one member of [CAFGU] for alleged grave misconduct." One was dismissed for "indiscriminate firing of firearm while drunk causing panic among people" in a barangay, another for threatening, while drunk, "to shoot several public school teachers"; and a third for "harassing with his firearm several farmers."[15]

It is thus possible to see, as the military tightened up on CAFGU's (and others') abuses, why towns began to rebel against rebels. In the Bicol, deep in what was generally deemed NPA territory, a town "has defied the power of the rebels by not giving to their war funds and yet survived." The mayor said this was because "of the Bantay Bayan volunteers [army-trained civilians] fighting the rebels side by side" with CAFGU members. Where once NPA guerrillas patrolled the barrios with their tax collectors seeking out those with money to give to their war funds, Bantay Bayan volunteers "have taken their place, freeing the residents from the collectors," he said.[16]

Even the conflict between the two paramilitary groups could be assuaged—CAFGUs having been trained by the PC and Bantay Bayan by army Rangers. A "near shoot-out once occurred," but the mayor summoned both groups to a conference, and explained to them the urgency of close cooperation against the rebel movement. "My people can now sleep well at night," the mayor claimed.

In fact, the larger reason for the budgetary attacks on the CAFGUs was the suspicion that their real purpose was to fan Ramos's political purposes, to serve as rural vanguard for his presidential ambition. Yet that accusation, made often by Senator Maceda and his staff, was unworthy of those using it, even apart from Maceda's own unrealistic presidential ambitions.[17] True, the selection process of CAFGUs, through local leaders, certainly gave Ramos patronage access. But Ramos at most was doing well while doing good in building up the CAFGU; the need existed for paramilitary forces whether or not they would benefit their creator. The fact that the NPA was threatening mayors planning to form CAFGUs was evidence enough of the program's success.[18]

Strategic Victory: Security and the Insurgency

The Philippine Communist insurgency has been well studied elsewhere, most notably in its political context by Richard Kessler, who concludes that even if the NPA is put down, there will be another to replace it, given the government's inattention to the underlying causes of poverty and injustice.[19]

Our purpose is therefore to look at the interstices of the competing and sometimes contradictory efforts to reduce the Communist insurgency. But first, we must ask how it was viewed in the Philippines, which then tells us how important a priority it was for the society. Generally, when the essential structures of a society are threatened in a basic way, there is an understandable tendency to deny the evidence. At least *post facto* it is easy to see that societies whose existence was lost or inherently compromised tended to produce multiple reasons why threats were not taken seriously prior to their actualization: witness appeasement in Britain in the 1930s or the contemporary French reliance on the Maginot line. The fact that the Cassandras sometimes turn out to be wrong—as in the case of the United States in the late 1970s with respect to the Soviet military threat[20]—gives the optimists fresh enthusiasm.

In the Philippines, after twenty years of slow but perceptible and steady growth of the New People's Army, the predominant belief was indeed one of denial. There was a full range of reasons why the NPA would never come to power. Filipinos are too religious, some said, to permit a Communist insurgency to win (though why the rural poor among whom the NPA did hold sway did not seem bothered by that was not explained). The very contradictions of Filipino politics would pervade the NPA as soon as the group became more successful: true of all advancing causes, the salient question nonetheless was whether they come to power before or after they are ensnared in their own contradictions. The archipelagic geography made an NPA win unlikely because the party could never establish itself nationally, it was said; though how it could be denied substantial control of the nation once it had established a tight grip on Central Luzon was not made clear. The NPA had no charismatic leader and no rear bases and thus no outside supply lines—arguments that made NPA gains thus far more impressive than would otherwise have been the case, if they did tend to put some parameters on future gains. And the reality of charismatic local leaders might have been more salient in any case.

Societies always awake to the threats to their existence; the question is whether it is soon enough. In late 1989, at a meeting of bankers and their clients,[21] a rich businessman noted that he had discovered that his daughter was being given National Democratic Front (NDF) tracts at her élite school by a professor; another noted that he could no longer go to his island off the coast of Quezon Province: an NPA ambush the week before killed a dozen soldiers; another had witnessed an NPA killing only an hour from Manila. Yet there was no sense of danger.

Although there had been a dramatic decline in engagements in 1986, thanks to the cease-fire, the number of incidents went back to Marcos-era levels soon thereafter. In fact, some Philippine commentators, as well as this author, worried by the excessive optimism following the 1986 revolution, argued publicly at the time that, after a brief drop in encounters, the lines on the graph would revert to their sharp incline, for at least two years. After all, the insurgency had two decades of steam and its leaders were unlikely to put much stock in reform by a government led by a Cojuangco.

Cardinal Sin was impressed thereafter, however, by reports from the bishops of improved AFP behavior in the provinces[22] and thought as a result that the insurgency would be gone within three or four years. Indeed there *was* real improvement in army performance. There had been an improvement in the figures for "number of barangays influenced" by the NPA and more guns had come in than had gone out.

But it was the National Democratic Front, civil arm of the NPA, that was fighting the real battle, and there was no one and no organization countering it in the Philippine government. Informed opinion generally thought it to be a DND concern—when in fact the NDF was a civilian concern, surely of Malacañang Palace or at least a department of information set up to answer the propaganda charges widely circulating. Malacañang's fear was of the columnists: a department of information would get scorched by the press for propaganda, as if the palace had no tools of its own for dealing with columnists.

In fact, the Philippines was lucky. It seems that the NDF lacked the sophistication, even the "street smarts," to provide the NPA with even a small percentage of the sophistication that Vietnamese Communists had used to win their war.

As it turned out, 1988 was the first year since 1968 that on virtually all measures the insurgency did not gain ground. For an insurgency, it is basic that the absence of gain is a substantial defeat. According to a data sheet prepared 31 July 1989 by General Ramos's personal staff, in 1988 the CPP-NPA declined in number from 25,200 to 23,060, or 8.5 percent. There was a 20 percent decline in the number of communist firearms. A decline in the number of barangays "affected" actually started in 1987, and by 1989 the number declined by a tenth for the first half of the year alone. The number of AFP-initiated incidents increased enough to make clear that the army and constabulary were feeling more confidant and could seize the initiative generally. In his report Lieutenant Alexander Arevalo concluded that the insurgency "plateaued" in 1988:

> *By all indications, 1989 will mark the beginning of their continued decline in*
> *the midst of the relentless effort of the government to contain the insurgency*
> *problem by 1992.* Since the CTs have been losing a lot of grounds in the
> countryside, they are expected to shift their activities, military and political, to

the urban centers in order to keep their presence felt and to further their cause. This will include the conduct of terroristic activities of high psychological and media impact. Metro Manila, the seat of power, and other key cities in the country are expected to be a primary site of [this] terrorism.[23]

The 1991 data tend to show that the trend continued, including the predicted terror. If the percentage of improvements continued to seem small, it had to be remembered that this kind of war is won at the margins. Improvements of 5 or 6 percent per annum, compounded, are highly significant, not just for the magnitude of the threat but, more significantly, for the momentum signified.

Ramos's goal as SND was a strategic victory by 1991. "To win does not require that all the knights have been cleared from the chessboard," he said,[24] only that one has achieved strategic dominance of the archipelago. The timing was of course coincidental with the start of the presidential campaign, which would powerfully benefit Ramos, whose achievement this would clearly be. And despite the 1989 coup, it was beginning to look like Ramos would achieve his goal. There were many reasons why the NPA began to fail, perceptibly in 1989, then more substantially in 1990. But first in importance is the perception that military abuses were on the decline—and there seems little doubt that the reality matched it.

The military leadership was winning its battle to end the martial law-learned abuses by the troops. The situation in the past had been unattractive in the extreme. Victor Corpuz notes, for example, the exemplary behavior of NPA commandos in the countryside with their strict code of discipline ("Do not damage crops; Do not take liberties with women," etc.).[25] In contrast, "when government troops enter a barangay . . . people see the exact opposite. They see arrogant, disrespectful, and foul-mouthed soldiers. They see drunkards and gamblers. . . .They see suspects being tortured, mutilated, and 'salvaged' [summarily executed] . . . ."[26] Thus the seriousness with which Ramos and his circle took the clean-up campaign.

In a survey—the one that Cardinal Sin took with great seriousness[27]—forty-four out of seventy-six bishops responded to questions of human rights violations in their dioceses—including arbitrary killings, torture, arbitrary arrests, looting, arbitrary executions, and so on. Twenty-six bishops rated the military as having improved, twenty-three rated it "the same," and four found a deterioration. Seventeen bishops also rated the police as having improved, with twenty-three the same and four also down. The NPA, however, came off much worse. Only three bishops found improvements in its behavior; twenty saw NPA as "worse."

There was no reason for celebration, however; all the groups were still committing violations. Moreover, as a Jesuit sociologist points out, "while at first glance the NPAs seem to be top violator . . . yet if the government groups are totalled, they come out neck-and-neck with the NPAs with scores of 39 each, followed by the police with 37."[28] The NPA got sixteen points, followed by the police and CAFGU (civilian units) each with five; the military and vigilantes got four each. Twenty-eight bishops said the military had done better in 1989 than 1988: sixteen the same, two said worse. As for the NPA, twenty said worse, eighteen the same, three said better.[29] In one particularly violent area, southern Luzon, the regional director of the commission on human rights, Apolinario Florencio, said that the military was facing two hundred human rights complaints, from illegal arrest to salvaging. But the military filed about the same number against the rebels. Florencio admitted part of the problem: it was easier to identify, and thus apprehend and try, soldiers than rebels.[30] Amnesty International found the situation sufficiently serious to warrant a report on disappearances in the Philippines, between mid-1988 and 1989.[31] But on the whole, it not only looked like the AFP was behaving better; the NPA was having to be more daring—or more violent.

The National Defense 1990 report showed that finally, the services were cracking down. From the revolution to just after the Great Coup, 679 military and civilian personnel were investigated on graft and corruption charges. From the AFP, 251 were terminated. In the first half of 1989, out of 1,224 cases investigated, there were 406 court-martial cases in the AFP and police.[32] The word was getting around, if slowly and late.

While it is true that injustice was rampant in the Philippines, it did not necessarily follow that protest correlated with injustice—as if it ever did. The war was being fought where the NPA could take a stand, regardless of the "objective conditions." Thus while Negros was traditionally an NPA stronghold, it was seen to be that as a consequence of the feudal patterns of large sugar haciendas and the plight of the sacadas (sugar-cutters). In fact, by the time of the collapse of the price of sugar in the 1980s the large haciendas—and the extravagant life-styles that went with them—were largely a thing of the past, and the famine furthered the change. As Tom Marks has pointed out, 75 percent of Negros land in sugar cultivation was in farms under 100 hectares, with over half in farms of 50 hectares, the level of viability.[33]

Thus in the summer of 1989 the AFP mounted a major campaign against the NPA in Negros Occidental—but it was not in sugar land, it was in the "CHICKS" area (an acronym of the major towns in the southern part of the island), in which there is little sugar—and not much more government presence of any kind.[34] The reason why the campaign got so much publicity and attention, especially from European human rights activists,[35] is that the armed forces, in an admitted stupidity, evacuated 31,000 civilians from eight rebel-infested towns prior to the campaign but did it with no plan for the interests of the townspeople; Major General Mariano Adalem, the army chief, said it showed a "lack of planning and poor coordination with local officials."[36]

But basically the government's strategy was working—as it did in CHICKS—in reducing the NPA's number of strongholds, while also allowing it to choose the terrain of battle. Small wonder that the NPA began to shift tactics, as many predicted, to an increasing percentage of acts of urban terror, which is vastly more manpower efficient, especially in spreading a sense of hopelessness among the masses.

The active strategy of the AFP also began to bear fruit. Ramos began giving increased emphasis to his SOTs, with the goal of preventing the CPP-NPA "from further enlarging the Communist 'Organs of Political Power' " in the Philippines. The goal of these élite units was to neutralize the political machinery of the party, particularly its "logistics, financial and communications capabilities." It was a political-military concept, for weeding out guerrillas, eliminating safe houses and the like, while rendering economic assistance to affected villagers. Soldiers built schoolhouses, roads and bridges, and opened free clinics.[37]

One clear sign of improvement was the relatively peaceful barangay elections on 28 March 1989, the last electoral step in the program of the 1986 revolution. All things are relative, and the fact that there were twenty deaths directly related to the elections paled before the 157 killed in the preceding election in early 1988, for mayors and governors.

As the AFP made inroads on the insurgency in the countryside, the NPA made the predicted decision to shift the venue of the war to the city, Metro Manila in particular. In 1987 it went on one rampage in the capital, sending "Sparrow" units out to kill swiftly and run quickly. The AFP and police reacted by going after safe houses and arresting an unprecedented number of CPP-NPA leaders. A DND position paper gave four reasons why this round of urban terror failed. First there was religion, still firmly rooted in Philippine society. Second, Sparrow brutality shocked Manilans, and third, after the experience of the Marcos dictatorship, no one wished a "dictatorship of the proletariat." Fourth, democracy was in place, after elections in which Manilans had participated en masse.[38] One might add a fifth reason, namely that the economy was then booming and the effect was, if not enjoyed by all, visible throughout the capital region. But when not all of these conditions obtained, in 1990, the Communist leadership could try again—with greater effect.

There was another factor in the impending strategic victory—one for which the military could take only indirect credit (and tactically tried to take no credit at all). This was the efforts of civilian groups, "vigilantes" from one point of view, "civilian voluntary organizations" from another. The important point is that in a country where guns are easily obtainable, groups threatened by a Communist takeover can be expected to fight back on their own. Many did, and in several critical parts of the archipelago, it made a substantial difference. One of these is Davao; with a population of over a million, it is the largest city in Mindanao. By the time of the cease-fire with the NPA after Aquino took office, the guerrillas had all but seized power in the city.

But in April 1986 three former guerrillas, according to legend, shot a rebel assassin and shouted "Alsa Masa," or "Arise, masses," from which time the organization by that name grew dramatically in strength.[39] Its leader was one of these three guerrillas, Rolando Cagay, but the person who galvanized the disparate forces behind it—from Malacañang Palace to local gangs—was an Aquino adviser, Jesus "Chito" Ayala, a man of enormous energy and conviction. Funds went to Alsa Masa from all over the government—for example, from the Department of Local Government, which committed funds for "livelihood projects" for Alsa Masa.[40]

Alsa Masa used some tough tactics to "clean up" Davao. There were summary executions, and recruitment was not done nicely. But even the New York lawyers' committee looking into their activities, while criticizing the coercion reportedly used, added, "This is not to deny that much of Alsa Masa's support is freely given; the group may well be the most genuinely popular vigilante force in the Philippines."[41] And the armed forces, in reacting to the lawyers' committee report, noted, in what may well be a truthful statement, that:

> The genuine popularity being enjoyed by Alsa Masa in Davao is not cultivated by violent coercion and intimidation. Popularity, if it is truly genuine, is not something to be imposed, rather it is something to be earned. . . . A year after Alsa Masa was founded, it has been credited by some local government officials for the mass surrender of NPA rebels after the 60-day truce.[42]

It was so credited by the U.S. Embassy as well, which added its own gory details as to how the achievement came about. "For a few days no one looked, no one asked questions, and the streets ran red. When it was over, Chito Ayala was covered with even more glory than blood and Davao had no more NPA."[43]

In Negros one sees informal arrangements between the military and civilians, armed by themselves or from the arsenals. These arrangements have had considerable success in reducing the NPA threat to manageable proportions. According to the lawyers' report, "More than 32 armed vigilante groups, including several fanatical religious cults, engage in 'anti-communist' activities in Negros, according to local human rights monitors. There are said to be numerous other clandestine groups."[44]

There was, as it were, private "military" initiative. One band of brothers who ran several medium-size plantations had a primitive but apparently highly effective intelligence and counterinsurgent operation. Information on the NPA was stored in computers. Security was maintained by CAFGUs who were, on the whole, ex-NPA and happy to be out of the mountains. The brothers were heavily armed and had plausible stories to tell of executions that they had carried out.[45] If there was to be peace in Negros, it clearly would come as a result of both official and unofficial undertakings.

Newsweek in 1987 made a celebrated case that landowners were building armies to resist land reform.[46] In a technical sense the report was accurate, at least with respect to the first point. They *were* building armies, they were getting the weapons from government arsenals, and the department of national defense was all but turning a blind eye. What the intent was is not self-evident; but surely the immediate threat of the NPA was far more pertinent than the hypothetical proposals for land reform. In any case, the real issue then was the famine caused by the low price of sugar; the landowners were less well-off than ever.

What was far more significant was the rise of private voluntary organizations (PVOs) or Nongovernmental Organizations (NGOs), acronyms that took hold and which were used as easily as at the United Nations.[47] These sprang up to solve some of the more immediate problems of the island, for example helping international relief organizations distribute food to starving children, as well as to build a better community spirit for the long run. The phenomenon of PVOs is well explained by what had happened at the end of the Marcos era; so many people banded together to rid the Philippines of Marcos that, having succeeded, they needed new goals for old organizations. And many of the new Aquino officials were products of the PVOs, hence sympathetic to their style and goals. Negros Occidental was flooded with PVOs—run with the blessing and enthusiasm of Governor Montelibano and the substantial participation of his wife.[48]

The NGOs in Negros developed a full range of additional projects, which were run efficiently and enthusiastically. Lawyers, business leaders, educators, among others, threw themselves wholeheartedly into their work, and Mrs. Montelibano was there to ensure that government delivered what services it could. Small wonder, then, that the army could begin to be effective in eradicating the insurgency in the summer of 1989, and that defecting NPA cadre could become CAFGUs working for sugar planters: popular sentiment was apparently in the process of reversing. At least the beginnings of a social contract were emerging in Negros Occidental.[49]

What happened in Negros Occidental is revealing as a potential model, albeit a pessimistic one, for the nation as a whole. Negros, the Visayan island that exemplified more than any the sugar culture and the way of life of the old sugar barons, was hit hardest by the international collapse of sugar prices in the mid-1980s. Famine hit new heights. So did the insurgency.

In fact, many of the planters had achieved an "understanding" with the NPA—they paid high taxes to the NPA, low wages to the sacadas, and were left alone.[50]

A new spirit motivated at least some of the owners and managers, however. These began enforcing the payment of minimum wages to the sacadas, by imposing real reprisals against those underpaying them.[51] They armed themselves with at least tacit approval from General Ramos, and set up companies of CAFGUs, citizen allies of the armed forces, often filled with returnees from the hills. It was obvious in late 1989 that the NPA was losing its popular base in Negros.

The coup, however, reversed progress. Because alleged coup leaders were in Negros, and thanks to Danding Cojuangco's close ties with the island[52] and the great attention he received on a visit there, Manila issued a National Emergency Memo Order (NEMO) ordering the disarming of the planters—with the result, according to one reporter, that these owners "lost touch and control over CAFGU units on their farms, some of whom may make their accommodation with the NPA, since their patrons are now living in Bocolod," the safer capital of the province.[53] Whatever else was happening, the AFP and NPA once again were engaged in heavy fighting, which had come almost to a standstill after a successful AFP campaign the year before.[54]

Matters took a further turn for the worse when the Sugar Development Fund program of Negros landlords, which had funded the wages, benefits, and matériel of twenty CAFGU companies, decided to cut the pipeline. It opted instead to "rechannel the fund to economic development projects that would address worsening poverty in the island," according to the usually well-informed *Manila Chronicle*.[55] The military said it would delay its plan to crush the insurgency there in two to three years. The report noted that military spending was down 20 percent thanks to austerity measures and that the CAFGUs were now directly under the military—rather than the PC, which of course was defunct. Moreover, half of the CAFGU companies nationally were subsidized by private interest groups and were thus all vulnerable to the kind of belt-tightening witnessed in Negros. The point of course was that security and development were not just a yin and yang of government policy; they were usually a yin *or* yang, down to the local level, given the constraints on resources. One has to presume that the sugar planters had found that, as the overall threat of the NPA declined, it was more cost efficient to put scarce pesos in human investment and tell the military to come up with the funds itself for the CAFGU units.

Despite such vagaries, the NPA continued its decline, for which there were at least four reasons. At the international level, there was the collapse of communism worldwide. True, the NPA was unique for its size among revolutionary armies in receiving so little support from abroad. But it was not so much a decline in monies or arms; the money at least may have been on the rise until 1989. But there ceased to be any encouragement from traditional centers abroad. A Soviet foreign ministry official in early 1990, for example, publicly stated that Communists in the Philippines, like those in Eastern Europe, had "gone astray and lost the confidence of the people, so their common problem now is now to regain this confidence."[56] A Filipino senator in early 1990 could brag that an NPA delegation which went to Europe on a fund-raising mission came home empty-handed—though the more skeptical Senator Maceda was quick to retort that the armed forces' preoccupation with the coup attempt had "allowed insurgents to mount ambuscades that have telling propaganda effect."[57] It was hard to convince cadre to continue their sacrifices in the hills when their political leaders forbad them the use of their radios—lest they hear that the Berlin Wall had come tumbling down, among other things. And of course they did hear.[58]

Second, there were their own mistakes. Their antiinfiltration program resulted in the mass murder of hundreds of partisans. A mass grave on the Bondoc peninsula, for example, was made by the military into a public shrine in memory of the murdered partisans. Art Borjal, a columnist, wrote further:

> The alienation of the Left from its political base and the so-called Middle Forces, which it tried desperately to win over, is essentially a product of two errors: its monstrous revolutionary taxes and the massive recruitment of *lumpens* into its ranks. The drunkards and the tough guys who joined the ranks of the underground during its massive and indiscreet recruitment a few years ago have been

major liabilities. The tax collections, which were really burdensome to small landowners, lowly-paid professionals, and small countryside entrepreneurs, alienated the Middle Forces.[59]

Third and most important, there was, as we have seen, a strategy for defeating them. Fourth, there was the simple fact that, by 1989, the conventional view of the insurgency was in substantial measure incorrect; the facts of the received wisdom were wrong. For it began to be obvious in 1989 that the NPA, like its Huk forbears, would lose its revolutionary struggle, despite the popular indifference to Ramos's effort to defeat it. This did not mean that the cause would go away, as Kessler has persuasively argued. But it would make a real difference for the ability of Aquino's successor to build a viable polity if Ramos could achieve his "strategic victory" in 1991.

Cease-fire

Though Ramos's strategy was still working in late 1990, the sense of crisis throughout the archipelago, as a result of other factors as well, had built to a level where something had to give. The earthquake on 16 July was very nearly the straw breaking the camel's back. In the preceding month urban terror had increased with a rash of bombings, for which a group called "Cobra" claimed credit, but the NDF on 22 July declared a unilateral cease-fire in quake-ravaged provinces and in Metro Manila. This put increasing pressure on the government to reciprocate; finally, two months later, the military agreed to a "selective" cease-fire—no military engagements to be initiated, though rebels would remain subject to arrest.

In fact, as General Rodolfo Biazon conceded, the government was merely formalizing what it had to do anyway, given the devastation of the quake: "And since there is seeming to be a de facto cessation of hostilities—because the [AFP] had to focus its attention and resources toward rehabilitation."

Momentum, however, built toward more comprehensive peace talks; senators, columnists, everyone got in the act. The NPA made as a precondition for talks a commitment to get the Americans out of the bases. The military, while seeking a respite for its soldiers, wished to avoid its experience of the 1986 cease-fire, when the government had no agenda and the NPA was able to move about freely, consolidating gains. This time General Ramos listed four demands: a laying down of arms, proof that the rebels "respect their unilateral cease-fire calls," a formal request of the president, and an acknowledgment of the Constitution—with a commitment to act within it.[60]

In the meantime, however, the international crisis in the Persian Gulf, with its devastating impact on Filipinos, thanks to the loss of remittances and the increase in petrol prices, added one more element of crisis, straining Aquino's ability to govern to the breaking point. The NPA, not surprisingly, ended its cease-fire. As the *Manila Chronicle* editorialized, that decision had nothing to do with the oil price rise per se but rather with the perception "that the goal of overthrowing the government through revolution is better served by fuelling unrest than by taking part in the peace process" with a weak government. "Put differently, the NPA has sniffed blood."[61] It realized within a month that it had gone too far, however. The CPP reprimanded its urban guerrillas for random violence and ordered them to focus on "imperialist" targets—this after twenty-four buses were torched by guerrillas during a general strike.[62]

On balance, the Philippines must be given considerable credit for beginning to get the insurgency under control, something that is nothing short of remarkable given the diversity of the institutional players competing for roles in that game. That in looking to the insurgency the AFP leaders lost sight of a still bigger threat, within their own house, does them no credit, but given the paucity of resources available, their achievement with the insurgency stands on its own.

NOTES

1. "No Coup Try This Year, Says Biazon," *Philippine Daily Inquirer* (19 January 1990).
2. John Stuart Blackton, "Counterinsurgency: Winning Within the Rule of Law," USAID (Manila: June 1989), p. 8. Provided to this author by the Philippine Government.
3. Army hearings (11 July 1988), p. 54.
4. Joint Committee, National Defense and Finance (27 June 1988).
5. Victor Corpuz, *Silent War* (Manila: VNC Enterprises, 1989), pp. 189-91.
6. This author's interview (16 September 1989).
7. Senate hearing (4 August 1989), p. 24.
8. This author's interview, Station Command, Baguio (November 1989). Pertinent also is the fact that, at that time, the mayor presiding over the city was generally thought to work, in the views of every official interviewed, "across the grain."
9. This author's interview with General Ramos during field trip.
10. Greg G. Borja, "CAFGU: A Bungling Monster," *Philippine Daily Inquirer* (12 November 1989).
11. Teodoro M. Locsin, "The AFP under Fire," *Philippines Free Press* (18 November 1989).
12. This author's interview with Tony Abaya, September 1989.
13. Blackton, "Counterinsurgency: Winning Within the Rule of Law," p. 5.
14. This author's interviews, Negros Occidental (November 1989).
15. "Around the Nation," *Manila Bulletin* (27 November 1989).
16. Salvador D. Flor, "Bicol Town Defies NPA," *Manila Bulletin* (22 November 1989).
17. Maceda was generally regarded as one of the most competent legislators— but lacked the enormous war chest for a serious campaign; and the fact that he was widely understood to be gay, though not as total a bar to the presidency as in the United States, was enough to prevent him from getting serious attention in the presidential sweepstakes.
18. See "NPA Warns Mayors Not to Form CAFGUs," *Malaya* (1 September 1990), in Foreign Broadcast Information Service-East Asia-90-171 (4 September 1990), p. 52. Hereafter FBIS-EAS.
19. Richard J. Kessler, *Rebellion and Repression in the Philippines* (New Haven, CT: Yale University Press, 1989). See also William Chapman, *Inside the Philippine Revolution—The New People's Army and Its Struggle for Power* (New York: W.W. Norton, 1987).
20. Though Cassandras would argue that their very warnings were responsible for altering the threat, as America elected Reagan, rebuilt its military, and confronted the Soviet Union head on.

21. A bank's clients meeting, addressed by the author (September 15, 1989).
22. See endnote 29, infra.
23. "Update on the Communist Insurgency Situation in the Philippines," Summary, by Lt. Alexander Arevalo, Military Assistant to SND. Memo provided by SND to author.
24. This author's interview with General Fidel Ramos (November 1989).
25. Corpuz, *Silent War*, p. 132.
26. *Ibid.*, p. 133.
27. This author's interview with Sin (September 14, 1989).
28. Belinda Olivares-Cunanan, "Political Tidbits," *Philippines Daily Inquirer* (1 August 1989).
29. "NPA Committed More 'Abuses' than Military," *Philippine Star* (11 September 1989).
30. Noli Cabantug, "Human Right Body Accuses Insurgents, Soldiers," *Manila Chronicle* (27 May 1989), in FBIS-EAS-89-103 (31 May 1989).
31. Amnesty International, "A Summary of Disappearances in the Philippines since June 1988." The 1990 report claimed fifty disappearances for which government security forces were responsible, with three executions, six detentions, and twenty-five remaining missing. See *Manila Chronicle* (18 March 1991).
32. Department of National Defense, 1990 Annual Report (Quezon City, the Philippines), pp. 7-8.
33. "Insurgency Redefined," *Far Eastern Economic Review* (25 October 1990), pp. 15-16.
34. This author's interview with General Fidel Ramos (18 September 1989).
35. A group of these activists, after their investigations in Negros, met with Secretary of National Defense Ramos. I was present at the meeting and felt they belligerently and inaccurately characterized the situation in Negros Occidental as desperate and treacherous.
36. *Philippine Daily Inquirer* (29 May 1989).
37. "Winning the War Against the Insurgency: Issues and Answers, April 1989," DND handout.
38. *Ibid.*
39. Lawyers Committee for Human Rights, "Vigilantes in the Philippines: A Threat to Democratic Rule," New York: Lawyers Committee for Human Rights, 1988, p. 24. Hereafter Lawyers.
40. *Ibid.*, p. 25.
41. *Ibid.*, p. 27.
42. Quoted in full in *Ibid.*, p. 167.
43. This author's interview, U.S. Embassy (March 1988).
44. Lawyers, p. 41.
45. This author's interviews and site visits, Negros Occidental (November 1989).

46. See "Resistance on the Right: Landowner Armies in Philippine Sugar Country," *Newsweek* (10 August 1987), p. 44.

47. See the special issue of *Solidarity*, no. 127 (July-September 1990), *Nongovernmental Organizations in the '90s*.

48. This author's interviews with Bocolod (November 1989). The author is grateful to Mrs. Montelibano for arranging interviews with numerous PVO directors in Bocolod City.

49. Interestingly, European human rights groups, visiting the Philippines in November 1989, focused almost entirely on abuses by the military in Negros Occidental. The author was in Negros shortly after their visit and investigated their charges, finding evidence of almost none of the "atrocities" alleged—except to confirm that there was a substantial population relocation during and immediately after a major military campaign in the CHICKS region of the province.

50. This author's interviews, Negros (November 1989). Also see Luis Beltran's report, "Marubeni's New Image," *Manila Standard* (18 February 1990).

51. For example, according to one family of managers who treated its own workers with exemplary regard, pressure on recalcitrant planters started with "a little chat," which, if not bringing compliance, was followed by a visit to the bank to see if credit could be choked off. Additional pressure verged on violence.

52. His wife Gretchen is from a German-Filipino family there of great wealth, and he owns extensive properties on the island.

53. Luis D. Beltran, "Government Is Immobilized," *Manila Standard* (18 September 1989).

54. See "AFP, NPA Resume Fighting," *Manila Standard* (18 February 1990).

55. Manny Mogato, "Negros Landlords Cut Subsidy for Militia Units," *Manila Chronicle* (18 March 1991), in FBIS-EAS-91-054, (20 March 1991), p. 54.

56. Romy V. Mapile, "Local Reds' Problem Noted," *Philippine Star* (22 February 1990). The citation is Mapile's paraphrase.

57. *Manila Times* (21 January 1990).

58. This author's interview with NPA defectors, Negros Occidental (November 1989).

59. Art. A. Borjal, "The Left's Last Hurrah," in "Jaywalker," *Philippine Star* (17 November 1989).

60. "Ceasefire Framework Drawn," *Manila Chronicle* (6 September 1990), in FBIS-EAS-90-174 (7 September 1990), p. 57.

61. "NPA Exploits Government's Vulnerability," *Manila Chronicle* (27 September 1990) in FBIS-EAS-90-188 (27 September 1990), p. 62.

62. Hong Kong AFP in English, quoting *Daily Globe* (7 November 1990), in FBIS-EAS-90-216 (7 November 1990), p. 41.

7

Interface of Security and Development: The Bases

However much grumbling there was nationally about the extent of U.S. assistance to the Philippines, within the armed forces there was always a businesslike attitude and gratitude for American weaponry and training. The military, as columnist Tony Abaya put it, "rightly or wrongly, is perceived to be pro-American."[1] Although the roots of this perception are in the nature of the connection, the practical spirit of this cooperation was always a function of senior AFP and civilian DND leaders. During the 1960s and into the 1970s it was Alejandro Melchor, an Annapolis graduate, who incarnated this. As under secretary of DND and then executive secretary at Malacañang Palace, Melchor made it his business to know all the key American military personnel in the Philippines—as well as their bosses back home. Several CINCPACs (Commanders in Chief, Pacific) were personal friends. He came to know weapons issues intimately.

In the period of our study, General Ramos maintained the spirit of this practical cooperation. When military leaderships elsewhere in the world (and in the Philippines) complained of getting second-line or even secondhand American tanks or jeeps, Ramos was quick to note that he preferred to get "five hundred surplus jeeps for the book price of twenty new ones. And Filipinos are the best maintenance engineers in the world. We have a surplus of manpower to keep our equipment running."[2] When it looked like Washington would renege on part of its 1990-91 aid commitment—in part because of new needs in Eastern Europe and elsewhere—Ramos began talking almost immediately with the Joint United States Military Advisory Group (JUSMAG) about getting equipment transferred from NATO that, precisely as a result of those changes in Eastern Europe, would no longer be needed in Western Europe. He had a world view.

At a time when everyone else was bashing the United States, Ramos was negotiating for hardware to fight the insurgency, to be paid for out of an unexpended balance of $29.4 million in previous loans, which would be converted to grants. "This is aimed at synergizing the Philippine economy as the manufacture of the equipment will be done locally by local labor," he commented, claiming that the United States had already delivered numerous additional helicopters and seventy-seven patrol boats for the navy.[3]

The thorniest, and most emotive, issue between Manila and Washington, especially after the lapse of parity,[4] was always the bases. As the republic's second largest employer, as America's largest installations outside the continental United States, and as continuing reminders of the ex-colonizer's enormous military might, the bases were bound to be a tricky issue to negotiate whenever such was called for. With their first use for domestic purposes (in the coup attempt of December 1989), such was sure to be even more the case than previously.

The bases were established, of course, as part of the terms of independence; few questions were asked. As a Filipino historian noted, in 1947 the Philippine government was "eager to initiate conversations leading toward a definitive agreement on the bases in 1946-47, but it did not have a prepared draft of its own, . . . our representatives were merely redrafting the American proposals."[5]

In 1988-89, comfortably distant from the termination of the agreement, the issue became the "manhood" touchstone for Philippine orators. By late 1989, thirteen of twenty-three senators had publicly opposed an extension of the agreement, which on the face of it doomed any negotiations, as two thirds of the Senate would be needed for confirmation of any treaty. Even the still-important player "Gringo" Honasan, from his not-so-very-secret hiding places, could come out and oppose the continuation of the agreement—as if to prove that he was not, after all, the "American boy."[6] The preface to every discussion seemed to begin with "of course I am for the removal of the bases," followed by differing qualifications.

It was a game both sides could play. As senators spoke, Singapore's strongman made known that facilities on his island, to the extent available, would be open to the Americans if they were denied by Filipinos. All the other regional powers were making known their views, which were generally in contrast to those of the Philippines. "Most of the nations in the region anticipate US withdrawal . . . and are preparing for it," a Filipino paper said.

> They are making adjustments in their foreign policy and budgetary priorities for such a worst case scenario. For example, Thailand . . . has sought joint naval exercises with Japan as the first step for Japan to fill the security vacuum that would be left by an American withdrawal. Thailand's move has rekindled fears . . . of a resurgence of Japanese military threat.[7]

Visiting American congresspersons made known to the Filipinos their annoyance at local attitudes, and in September 1989 the U.S. Senate held up construction funds for Clark Air Force Base, to send the obvious signal that the U.S. government was no longer counting on remaining there, especially since according to the previous year's agreement permanent facilities on the bases were to be considered Filipino property, by definition. Americans in the Bush era were beginning to play down the military dimensions of foreign policy. But embassy officers were still seeing the negotiations almost as a zero-sum game, in which the ultimate player would be the pro-base sentiment of the Filipino people, especially outside Metro Manila.

In fact, it was not a zero-sum game. As the supposedly definitive end of the agreement—1991—got closer, there were more and more Philippine proposals—drafted without assistance from the Americans, for the efficient use of the bases. The nature of the bases, with their large tracts of unused, or underused, territory, provided ample opportunity for the two allies to develop options that provided for the security of both and the development of the Philippines. Ambassador Alex Melchor, Jr., for example, came up with proposals discussed with the Japanese for privatizing the bases, leaving secure areas at both Subic and Clark for the use of both armed forces. Other Filipinos, particularly those in favor at the palace, began to lay the groundwork for the transfer of base lands to private use, including some of the most valuable residential tracts in the republic, in what had the potential of being the greatest scam since the end of parity.

The Americans in Manila were well informed of but not well attuned to the realities of Filipino politics in the period leading up to the base negotiations. Prior to the 1989 coup attempt, the embassy position was that the existing agreement, and the attendant arrangements, was working, so "why try to fix what isn't broke," a senior official at the embassy said. That position did not relate to reality. A less senior, but more sensitive, embassy official thought the problems the U.S. team would need to deal with were, first of all, sovereignty, which could be toyed with; compensation, which was "manageable"; on questions of criminal prosecution, the United States could give way. And on the nuclear issue, the United States could keep its freedom of maneuver, he thought. But the critical variable, he said, was Mrs. Aquino. "If she will say, 'it's in our national interest to keep the bases,' then we'll be okay," he said in an interview.

Aquino was not key. She essentially had no choice on the bases prior to the coup attempt, and afterward was compressed on both sides by her obligations. *Utang* dictated giving the Americans what they needed, which was her overpowering inclination[8]; the facts that created the *utang* dictated otherwise. But her own sentiments were never in question, and in the end she was wholly to miscalculate her own ability to affect the outcome of the negotiations in the direction desired by the embassy. If she could have kept the embassy guessing at all, then the embassy diplomats would hardly have been in a position to play the important role historically assigned to them.

The American ambassador had always been assumed to be the second most important person in Manila. A number of distinguished Americans held the post (no less than Charles Bohlen, for example), and most did play an important role in Manila's politics beyond that assigned to them by Washington. Henry Byroade, for example, buttressed Marcos in important ways during the proclamation and carrying out of martial law.[9] But precisely when American leadership was needed to give a weak Philippine leader some backbone, in the aftermath of the 1989 coup, it was not there—at least certainly not in Manila. The ambassador, a rich New Yorker named Nicholas Platt who enjoyed playing palace politics and confused it with statecraft, had very little sense (or even knowledge, for that matter) of the country's problems or direction. The embassy was caught completely off guard by the attempted coup, but shortly thereafter Platt was singing his usual song that everything was well in that best of all possible worlds. So the vacuum of power in the usual centers from which it radiated—Malacañang, the great white American palace, the ministries or even the Senate—was complete.

In the aftermath of the attempted coup, with what remained of the government's coherence unraveling, the United States decided to default on some of its committed aid for 1991. The American justification was plausible; new needs in Eastern Europe, for example, were depleting available resources, and the Philippines still remained the third largest recipient. But the $96 million shortfall must also be seen as a product of so many mixed signals from West to East, especially Aquino's refusal to receive Defense Secretary Dick Cheney on his Manila visit in early 1990, several months after the Great Coup attempt. That is to say, even had money been available, it is likely that the United States would have made some cuts. Such would explain why, for example, the United States member on the World Bank board abstained from voting on a $390 million Philippine loan application, leading to a letter of protest from Secretary of Finance Jesus Estanislao, even though the Philippines eventually got the loan.[10]

In fact, Aquino's snub of Cheney was an almost inevitable outcome of the stasis of Philippine politics at the time. Alejandro Melchor commented that the fundamental problem was that developing countries could not afford to let their internal politics determine their foreign policies vis-à-vis superpowers, and that those policies had to be determined in terms of minimizing losses. He no doubt is right—but in these particular circumstances, it was asking too much to expect Manila to rise above the psychological needs that the "persuasion flights" had created. The United States had saved the Aquino regime using the very bases that were up for renegotiation and from which a majority of senators were on record as wishing to remove the Americans. The United States then cut its aid by almost $100 million. Not receiving Cheney was the only way Aquino had available of trying to demonstrate autonomy. True, it was widely believed in Manila that Aquino was also reacting to what inevitably looked like what was called the "Laxalt woodshed," in reference to the celebrated visit Senator Paul Laxalt made to Manila to drum reality into President Marcos—especially since Laxalt came in the train of other distinguished message-bearers, as did Cheney (for example, then-deputy National Security Council assistant Robert Gates). The American point was being made with little subtlety; as Teddyboy Locsin put it, it was "Shape up or Ship Out!"[11] The pain with which the whole issue was seen in Manila is illustrated by a comment by the journalist Emil Jurado, who noted that "beggars can't be choosers" and that Mrs. Aquino had only the option of sending Washington a "note of disappointment" about the aid cut:

> We simply have to say "Amen" to whatever crumbs Washington can throw our way. And since Cory herself had bartered away whatever options she had in connection with the US military bases agreement when she asked the US government to intervene in the recent coup attempt, we can't even use the military bases agreement talks this year as leverage. Perhaps, by now, the government should realize that the United States does not really have permanent friends, but only permanent interests—meaning, its own.[12]

But the move could not impress Washington, which had other things on its mind. Small wonder that the U.S. president was quoted as saying that Aquino could "learn a great deal from [Cheney] about the way we view the very important United States presence in the Pacific." And a local wag could make the obvious point that "if the Aquino administration should need 'The Flight of the Phantoms' in the near future, Cheney could recommend sending up observation balloons instead."[13] Indeed, as Ambassador Armitage, the American base negotiator, made his way around the U.S. Congress in 1990 eliciting support for a base agreement, senator after senator and congressman after congressman told him of their outrage that Cheney had been snubbed. Certainly the confusion in signals in both directions was baffling to onlookers. The same keen observer, Luis Beltran, for example, wondered why the United States would save Aquino in December and then was "setting up the Aquino administration for the next one," given the difficulties that the reduction in aid occasioned.[14]

Public opinion on the bases was only a factor in the negotiations in an indirect sense—namely that the official position was very distinct from public preferences, and the American negotiators knew that such was a constraint on their Filipino counterparts. The Americans had their own polls, but the Ateneo survey more than makes the point.[15]

Thus opinion in 1989 was overwhelmingly supportive of the U.S. presence. The sum of all the categories that express conditions on the American role is less than those wishing an indefinite presence. Marginally one sees that it is a middle-class preference—or lower middle class (group D), namely base employees—who support the Americans. And in March 1990 support for them increases—this despite another year of battering by "nationalists" and others trying to drive them out.

The actual talks on the bases did not start until April 1990; the American delegation had been ready since autumn 1989 and had an obvious incentive to get them underway; it could only harm the American position were the negotiations to be compressed too much by the September 1991 deadline, when the existing treaty ran out. The Filipinos, to be sure, had other things on their minds in 1990 following the coup and also had great anxieties about the talks. For one thing, there is a sense in the archipelago, not altogether unfounded, that Filipinos have always come out second best in talks with the Americans. After all, the bases were there, in American hands, because of Washington's linking them, along with parity, to independence. And though there had been numerous negotiations revising the treaty, this time was by far the most important; the very Constitution dictated that the treaty expire in 1991. So if any of the bases were to stay, the Filipinos felt an urgency to garner the greatest possible advantage, since it might be the last.

On the American side, there were two underlying strategies. The first was to convince the Philippine side that they *were* sovereign, that the key issue in proving their sovereignty to themselves was that they were making the

ATENEO PUBLIC OPINION SURVEY[16]					
	Survey area		Socioeconomic Class[17]		
Questionnaire Item	RP	Metro Manila	ABC	D	E

- *Which of the following alternatives do you think should happen?*
  (Base: All respondents)

February 1989

A. Remove the bases immediately without waiting for 1991

	6	10	16	7	4

B. Retain the bases until 1991

	7	15	11	9	6

C. Remove the bases only five years after 1991

	3	7	8	3	2

D. Remove the bases only ten years after 1991

	2	5	6	3	1

E. Retain the bases indefinitely

	40	43	46	49	34

Don't know/No response

	6	5	5	5	6

Not aware of US bases

	35	15	8	23	48

March 1990

A. Remove the bases immediately without waiting for1991

	6	12	8	8	4

B. Retain the bases until 1991

	13	24	21	13	9

C. Remove the bases only five years after 1991

	8	7	12	8	5

D. Remove the bases only ten years after 1991

	2	3	5	2	1

E. Retain the bases indefinitely

	41	45	38	42	42

Don't know/No response

	6	4	7	6	5

Not aware of US bases

	23	6	8	21	34

decision, whatever it was, on the bases; rather than that being sovereign required the United States to be given the boot from the bases. As the American negotiator said in an opening statement, if "you wish us to stay, let it be the deliberate act of a self-confident democracy choosing, through the freely expressed will of its people, to enhance a strategic partnership with the United States."[18]

The other American concern was money, given the sense that Filipino financial demands would be utterly elastic. The strategy was therefore to play down the financial negotiations and try to shame the Philippine negotiators if they put too much emphasis on dollars and cents. At the conclusion of the exploratory talks, Richard Armitage expressed "a sense of disappointment that the issue of compensation so dominated our time during these talks."[19]

Yet to the Filipinos, what else was there to talk about? The American attempt to sidetrack compensation issues was just more of the same old game. Pious rhetoric about old ties, about democratic interests, about mutual strategic interests in the Pacific was just that; those interests were there in any case—the question was, what was the real estate worth to the Americans?

And part of the problem for the Filipino side was that the real estate was declining in value very rapidly, even as the negotiations proceeded. The Bush administration had completed its East Asia strategic study in 1990, which recommended a 10 to 12 percent cutback in forces in the region, with further cuts envisaged by 1995 and the century's turn. Between the exploratory talks and the negotiation's conclusion, the remaining issues from the Indochinese war were all but settled, the Soviet Union had virtually bowed out of the region, and the bases kept only their function of preserving America's international network and ability to project power. Several of the smaller installations had become redundant by virtue of advancing technology—for example, relay stations.

True, the Americans did not wish to lose the bases, and they had a powerful arsenal of arguments. Subic Bay, for example, was just too big for the Philippine Navy to absorb; the international investors lured into Clark Air Force Base to look into developing it gave no encouragement; the Philippines was just in too bad a state to justify the kind of money that would be needed. Crow Valley, which the Americans valued above all the bases, was an excellent facility for training, where U.S. and regional allies could all train, and that gave to the Philippines a regional role of value.

The penultimate bargaining position of each side revealed that positions were in fact hardening and, at least on the Filipino side, bitterness increasing. The Americans wanted a ten-to-twelve-year phase-down of its forces, with arrangements to follow for access to the bases. The Philippines was offering a five year "terminal phase-out," which from the American point of view was uneconomic and prejudicial to the possibility of future arrangements. Moreover, the Philippine side wanted something better regarding rent than a "best efforts" pledge that the U.S. government offered, when in fact there was nothing to which the American negotiators could commit the U.S. Congress. Congress had trimmed the previous year's aid—of $481 million—by $96 million, and undoubtedly would do it again; and both sides knew it.

There was bad blood. The Philippines was in a nervous state, not just from all the internal problems that were climaxing at this time, but at the imminent Persian Gulf war, which was bound to have serious consequences for the archipelago. As the Philippine negotiators pressed the Americans to make good on their offers, Richard Armitage shot back that they should "consider the message you are sending as it is perceived by President Bush and the American Congress: As Americans prepare to fight and die in the Middle East, Filipinos define their own victory in terms of how many and how quickly US forces can be removed from their country."[20] It was the toughest language Washington officialdom had ever used openly with the Aquino administration.

The "final" position the American side took—there were to be more—was an offer of $320 million per annum for ten to twelve years, and only on a "best effort" to get Congress to fund that amount annually. Armitage left Manila saying, in effect, take it or leave it, just before the great Gulf war victory. Oddly, Raul Manglapus followed him to Washington, to plead with senators for a meaningful compromise. It hardly looked right; as one paper called it, it was

> a spectacle reminiscent of an Olangapo woman peddling her daughter near the gate of the naval base.
>
> By frantically following Armitage to Washington, we threw away the valuable leverage of a landlord. . . . The way our mouths watered . . . we advertised . . . our abject helplessness and, therefore, our vulnerability at the negotiating table.
>
> The only way we can now salvage the situation is to ask the United States to please package some "creative" items to pad the payments enough to look reasonable.[21]

In fact, there were creative proposals; House Foreign Affairs Chairman José de Venecia came up with a package that was inventive in the extreme, combining debt for equity swaps, expanded U.S. foreign investment, and bonds (instead of the "best effort" commitment) bought and backed by the banks of the region. de Venecia thought the package would be worth $28 billion, and less taxing on the U.S. Treasury.[22] But it was too late; the Philippine house was not in order. When the negotiators returned to the table, although they were to reduce their differences to a few million dollars a year for seven years, they were so dug in to their respective positions that neither would budge. The Americans left *sine die*.

Filipinos awaiting a better deal than what was envisaged by the summer of 1991 got one answer to the question of the cost of delay. Given the incredible number of natural catastrophes in recent years something disastrous might well have been imagined. But after cyclones, hurricanes, and earthquakes, Filipinos might also be forgiven for not sensing that Mount Pinatubo would erupt after over six centuries. It seemed perhaps a message from heaven; the volcano was nearly equidistant from the two bases—being near enough Clark to cover it all with enough ash to render it inoperable for years to come, and close enough to Subic to shower it with a continual reminder of its presence. It was, in this sense, a statement from God on the negotiations, which could be read both ways—getting the Americans off the hook from a declining situation of diminishing interest, or telling the Filipinos that bases were things of the past. Pinatubo's effect on the world beyond was enough to compensate for and cancel out the "global warming" proceeding in the 1990s, happily; it threw out enough ash to bury an area the size of the District of Columbia with over one hundred feet of it.

And so too its effect on politics in the Philippines. Now, of course, since the Philippines had already asserted ownership of the base property and land, and since Clark had not been truly operational since the fighter squadrons were removed the previous year, ending U.S. Air Force interest therein, the Americans had regretfully to inform their Philippine counterparts that the unratified agreement they had deemed not good enough was too good by almost half; however sympathetic Americans might be with the Philippine plight, whatever United States AID might give as humanitarian relief, whatever assistance military near the volcano would render, the U.S. Congress would not pay rent on a base covered under ash.

Had they already accepted the previous offer, a State Department official said, "we would have honored it as best we could, even though half of it would have been for an unusable base. Still, it would have been difficult to get all the aid through the Congress; they were tired of Filipino games; tired of their inability to decide whether they were our friends or not; tired of their failure to tell us what they really wanted."[23]

Thus in the renewed negotiations, there had to be greater realism. Instead of the $483 billion Manila got for each year under the previous interim agreement, it was to be $203 million a year—for 10 years. True, there were

sweeteners. There was to be an Under Secretary of State-level joint conference each December of the agreement, to examine its implementation, in
which not only could all the gripes come out, but Filipinos could, in advance
of the budget cycle, do whatever they could to improve their position for
more concessions. "We knew we were buying trouble with this, and we knew
the Filipinos knew exactly how many opportunities these sessions would
open to them, even though they pleaded innocence," a State Department
official said.

All that was required was for the two senates to ratify the agreement. On
the American side it was somewhat routine—at least the issue had not come
up in a formal sense. On the Philippine side, although a sufficient number of
senators to block ratification still opposed the treaty, Filipino negotiators
continued to assure Americans that this was posturing, that public opinion
(as we have seen) was so overwhelmingly favorable that the senators would
shift their position. After all, they each had national constituencies; they were
playing to the national galleries.

Even those things going well for the Philippines went badly for Philippine-American relations. The very desperation of the NPA caused it to
escalate its attacks on Americans, precisely when the Americans were keen
on any excuse to cut commitments and get on with what was absorbing their
interests—the big game in Eastern Europe and the Soviet Union. But in June
1990 a respected Peace Corps volunteer in Negros was kidnapped, which
sent the message that all the volunteers were at risk. The American decision
to pull the entire contingent out—at 261 the largest anywhere—perhaps did
not need explanation in the circumstances, but it was not courageous statecraft on Washington's part (nor did the Peace Corps concur in the decision).
General Ramos called the decision "hasty," and it was a general feeling "that
the US authorities overreacted."[24] And, as President Aquino herself pointed
out, there were high- and low-risk areas; there were even no-risk areas, where
volunteers could have gone.[25] It was, in effect, the formal commencement
of the unraveling of the ties.

For all the protests in the streets about the bases, however, Washington
did not waver in its public support of Aquino. The Pentagon's negotiator,
Richard Armitage, said in July 1990 that the "central tenet" of U.S. policy
there was "unqualified support for the leadership of President Corazon
Aquino and the permanence of democracy,"[26] with threats anew to terminate
aid in the event of a coup. Ironically, the déjà vu quality of the support made
it suspect, though not the way Filipinos thought.

For ever since the attempted coup, suspicions in the Philippines inevitably dwelled on whether the United States, now that it had shown it could

reverse a coup, would in fact mount one to maintain its bases.[27] Representative Gregorio Andolana, in voicing such suspicions, for example, proposed that a "citizen's army" be formed to defend the country against America. "It would be better if we fought the Filipino-American war again to settle the conflict once and for all," he said.[28] But such a war would have been one-handed clapping; the Americans had ceased to care. The litanylike support for Aquino tended to confirm that no one in Washington was paying any attention.

In the Filipino mind were numerous scenarios to compensate for the sense of anxiety that the possibility of the loss of the bases entailed. One common argument was that the republic should build up its own strength, by getting from America the "stockpile of mothballed military equipment" in the post-Cold War world, and use it "to transform the country into a credible force to build the new power equilibrium in the Pacific region and at the same time give substance to national sovereignty."[29] Of course it was obvious that the Philippines should build up its own strength—but there was little sense of reality to the point. The country was threatened by an insurgency, by a coup, and was rushing to rid itself of what had been its ballast. It was no doubt a good thing in the long run that it was so doing; it was not clear that the timing was good.

The extent to which the old allies were falling apart is seen in how Manila reacted to Saddam Hussain's invasion of Kuwait in August 1990. The next few weeks were crucial for Washington, in creating the alliance system of the post-Cold War world and in creating the key behavioral barriers in the third world to aggression. One suspected that for years to come the pecking order in Washington would have a lot to do with who showed up with what help when.

Old ally the Philippine Republic said in its first declaration, "It's not our fight."[30] Later Aquino said her country would carry out UN sanctions "in the light of their merits in each given case, depending on the facts and circumstances prevailing and taking into account our own national interest."[31] The Senate president, the third in the Philippine hierarchy, proposed the dispatch of a token force, composed of medical teams (which is what eventually went). But at the NSC meeting at which the matter was on the table—the first such meeting of the whole NSC in several years—the issue did not even come up according to Senator Enrile, who was a guest.[32] True, the Philippines had interests involved; as a paper of the Department of Foreign Affairs says, the Philippines may need Iraq's support on the question of Mindanao, and Filipinos in Kuwait.[33] Indeed, there was some tactical shrewdness in delaying any cooperation with Washington until Filipinos had been evacuated from Kuwait. But Manila went much further than that. It recognized the Quisling government in Kuwait and then did not back off, even if its diplomats on the ground, in rather heroic mold, cooperated with coalition diplomats. But at the United Nations, Philippine diplomats continued, according to some sources, to speak out on behalf of Saddam Hussein.

It was a long way from Carlos P. Romulo's time, when he could title a book *Mother America*, and the Philippines was among the first to follow the American lead in world affairs. The more serious point is not what the Philippines *lost* by visibly omitting to support President Bush's diplomacy. It is rather what it *failed to gain* by not using its own vulnerability as in effect leverage in standing by the United States. Perhaps the actual policy was a simple function of Foreign Secretary Raul Manglapus's sour attitude toward the United States; more basically it was a function of the absence of structures, in Manila, for working out policies that take the country forward. Turkey, for example, with long-term strategies to enter Europe, decided to make a virtue of necessity and was far more visible than was minimally necessary in cooperating with the UN alliance. It got an immediate windfall after the war in Washington's willingness to play the Kurdish question its way. Egypt did even better. "Much of the $40.16 billion of Egyptian debt" to Western governments was expected to be chopped off, in gratitude for its front-line role in the coalition; this on top of the $7 billion of military debt the United States had already forgiven.[34] True, Manila could not have earned that amount of gratitude from its geopolitical position. But it made a trade-off. And one suspects that its basis was *not* concern for Philippine interests in the Gulf per se but rather Manglapus's antagonism toward the United States, something that may ultimately have cost his people billions.

The last chapter on the great bases debate began in September 1991. President Aquino began pleading with senators opposed to the bases agreement (including her own brother-in-law, Agapito Aquino), reminding them of the polls, reminding them of the enormous income that would be lost, from base rent to employment benefits and other such spin-offs. It was common to argue that the fact that the twenty-three senators were all elected nationally made them irresponsible as far as regional interests were concerned. It could also be argued in reverse. Their lack of a regional base freed them to think nationally, of longer-term—and larger—issues, including the psychological dimensions of Filipino-American relations. For once, no one argued that theirs was a motive of greed (there was no obvious source of payoffs), nor were there among these senators patterns of difficult relations with the United States. They seemed truly to be looking for ways to free up the Philippines from the psychological gridlock it was in. In any event, the Senate rejected the treaty on 16 September, with 12 of 23 voting against, four more than required.

Mrs. Aquino, with powerful urgings from interested quarters, made moves to challenge the Senate vote through a national plebescite, but that was always constitutionally problematic. Senator Salonga made the most telling retort—one of the best on popular sovereignty since Burke—when he referred the nation to the first such plebescite:

Pontius Pilate, the governor of a Roman colony, skewed the crowd to decide who should be punished, Barabbas, a bandit, or Jesus, a man of peace. "There is no indication that Jesus Christ got even one vote in that electoral exercise," said Mr. Solonga. "We have buried the treaty and it now lies cold in its grave. Do not disturb the peace of the dead."[35]

Aquino was not pushed by the embassy, nor did the United States offer to pull off the plebescite for her. This was no longer the 1950s, when CIA officials allegedly roughed up presidents of the republic to get them to do what was wished in Washington. In the final analysis, Aquino, seeing no compelling pressure from any direction, and not finding enough impetus to overwhelm the senate's vote, made a virtue of necessity. Gallantly she offered Washington three years to get out—"with no obligation to pay compensation to the Philippines."[36]

It should not be surprising that the changes in policies that seemed to be working their way out were undergirded, perhaps driven, by changes in both popular and elite attitudes in the United States. The Chicago Council on Foreign Relations 1991 survey of foreign policy attitudes is most revealing toward the Philippines. To the question on military aid, "Do you think military aid to the following nations should be increased, decreased, kept about the same, or stopped altogether?"[37] we find the following:

	Public Leaders		Public Leaders	
	Increase		Decrease/stop	
Israel	8%	6%	50%	58%
Philippines	6	4	51	63
Egypt	5	10	47	36
Turkey	4	14	46	38
Korea	2	2	55	64

Although the trend is toward less military aid for everybody, the actual numbers are significant. Turkey is presumably being rewarded, marginally but significantly, for making serious efforts to manage its destiny and to bear the burden of being a front-line ally, for years against the Soviet Union, more recently against Iraq. South Korea is simply recognized as too rich to need aid. But the Philippines—to be at the bottom of the heap is something new. And this perception is even further borne out by public opinion on "Vital Interests." In 1986, at the time of EDSA, 74 percent of the public saw the Philippines as vital, 81 percent of the leaders. By 1990, it was *62 percent* and *51 percent*—or a fall of *30 percent*.[38] Seldom has a country fallen so fast in grace in the eyes of its leading peer. But then seldom have countries frittered away their advantages with those same powers so mindlessly.

NOTES

1. Antonio C. Abaya, "Can a Military Take-over Succeed?" *Manila Chronicle* (18 September 1989).
2. Comment to this author during a trip to a provincial command.
3. *Manila Standard* (24 January 1990).
4. At independence, America demanded, and the Philippines conceded, a twenty-five-year period in which Americans would have equal rights of investment in the Philippines with Filipinos, and would also have the right to own land there. It was a deeply emotional issue on the Philippine side.
5. Bonifacio S. Salamanca, "Quezon, Osmena, and Roxas and the American Military Presence in the Philippines," *Philippine Studies* 37 (1989), p. 314.
6. See Noel C. Cabrera, "Gringo Too Wants US Bases Out," *Sunday Times* (17 September 1989). In response to a submitted question, Honasan wrote that the economic benefits had "no significant impact on the majority of our people. On the other hand, their socio-cultural cost . . . has been tremendously high. . . .We must wean ourselves from the Americans as soon as possible. We will survive."
7. "Working Toward a New Power Balance," *Manila Standard* (19 May 1990), in Foreign Broadcast Information Service-East Asia-90-099 (22 May 1990), p. 56. Hereafter FBIS-EAS.
8. Her position was presumably dictated by more than her economic holdings in the province where the largest American base was; her husband had had a highly realistic position on the bases. "Look," he once told this author, "even if I wanted you to leave, I'd be silly to think I could make you do so. Castro's your enemy and he can't get you out of Guantanamo!"
9. And was sent with other concerns in mind as well. Byroade had an international reputation as a womanizer, on and off-duty. As then Assistant Secretary of State William Bundy said to me in 1969: "The thought of having Hank and Imelda in the same country is irresistible."
10. See Luis Beltran, "Blunt and Subtle Moves," *Manila Standard* (8 February 1990). See also his column "Yesterday's Street Parliamentarians," (9 February 1990).
11. "US Message to Cory . . ." *Philippines Free Press* (17 February 1990), p.3.
12. "Opinion," *Manila Standard* (4 February 1990). It might be added that only in the Philippines would the interpretive comment at the end of Jurado's paragraph ("meaning, its own") have to be added.
13. Luis Beltran, "Not a Time for Making Enemies," *Manila Standard* (15 February 1990).
14. "Reconsidering the Death Penalty," *Manila Standard* (10 February 1990).
15. Ateneo de Manila University, *Public Opinion Survey* August 1989 (Quezon City: Ateneo de Manila University, 1989), table 20, pp. 62-63. Explanation

pertaining to table: roughly, A class is the rich elite, B and C are the middle classes, D is the lower-middle class, and E is the proletariat.
16. *Ibid.*, p. 62.
17. Roughly, A class is the rich elite, B and C are the middle classes, D is the lower middle class, and E is the proletariat.
18. Department of State, FM AMEMBassy Manila to SECSTATE WASHDC (14 May 1990).
19. Department of State, FM AMEMBassy Manila (18 May 1990).
20. William Branigan, "US Warns Manila on Base Stance," *Washington Post* (10 January 1991), p. A14.
21. "Did Manglapus Sell Philippine Bases Short?" *Philippine Daily Inquirer* (11 March 1991), in FBIS-EAS-91-047 (11 March 1991), p. 35.
22. "Compromise Bases Plan Presented to Government" *Manila Bulletin* (11 March 1991), in FBIS-EAS-91-047 (11 March 1991), p. 35.
23. This author's interview, U.S. Department of State, 16 October 1991.
24. "The Philippines," *Economist Intelligence Unit Country Report* 4 (1990), p. 10. Hereafter "The Philippines."
25. Interview, *Manila Chronicle* (8 July 1990), in FBIS-EAS-90-134 (12 July 1990), p. 53.
26. "A Muddle-Through Mode," *Time* (16 July 1990), p. 40.
27. As columnist Emil Jurado put it, "the Americans also know that they can change our government if they must." *Manila Standard* (11 February 1990).
28. "Citizen's Army vs. US Invasion?" *Manila Standard* (10 February 1990).
29. "Working Toward a New Power Balance," *Manila Standard* (19 May 1990).
30. FBIS-EAS-90 (8 August 1990), p. 46.
31. "The Philippines," p. 7.
32. "Opposition, Government Discuss NSC Meeting," *Arts Network* (31 October 1990), in FBIS-EAS-90-212 (1 November 1990), p. 41.
33. Cited in Stephanie Gehlen, "The Effects of the Gulf Crisis on Pakistan and the Philippines," photocopy, Fletcher School of Law and Diplomacy (28 November 1990).
34. Clyde Farnsworth, "Egypt's Reward: Forgiven Debt," *New York Times* (10 April 1991), pp. D1, D10.
35. "Pontius Pilate and the American Base," *The Economist*, 21 September 1991, p. 45.
36. Rita Gerona-Atkins, "Aquino Accepts 3-Year Phase Out of U.S. Bases; Fil-Ams Debate On," *Filipino Times*, Washington D.C., September 1991.
37. John E. Rielly, ed., "American Public Opinion and US Foreign Policy 1991" (Chicago Council on Foreign Relations, 1991), p. 29.
38. *Ibid.*, p. 19.

8

The Triumph of the Trapos[1]

By the middle of 1989 it was clear that the old politics had triumphed. Aquino's popularity had slipped to 35 percent approval, according to a "Social Weather Station" survey, down from 77 percent a year earlier.[2] Put another way, the "margin of satisfaction" with her rule, measured as the percentage "satisfied" minus those "unsatisfied," had gone from +58 percent in February 1988 to +22 percent in August 1989.[3] For the opportunistic vice president, Doy Laurel, the margin had gone in the same period from a mere +16 percent to a -18 percent among ABCs. Where there are losers there must be winners: General Eddie Ramos stayed high—around two thirds—among all groups in the same period.

There was also growing pessimism about the quality of life; in the Ateneo Survey, 18% of the ABC group saw its life improved over six months earlier, 30 percent saw it as worse; in the bottom class, 10 percent saw it as better and 51 percent as worse. In both cases the drop was dramatic compared with the findings of early 1988 and early 1989.[4]

There was, not surprisingly, general cynicism about the political realm. The number of satisfied respondents on the government's antigraft measures declined from 56 percent in February 1988 to 40 percent in August 1989.[5] Taxi drivers told foreigners that the corruption of the Aquino government was just as bad as that under Marcos, which was untrue, or not yet true, but both sets of numbers were beyond their comprehension. Certainly the President's brother, Jose "Peping" Cojuangco, was widely thought to be the most open "corruption manager" the Philippines had ever had. If the sums involved by 1992 were not yet Marcosian, they seemed to be getting close. Moreover, there was ample survey evidence, as Professor Miranda has pointed out, that whereas the A and B classes maintained "liberal and democratic" attitudes, the C, D, and E classes, much the bulk of the population, did not share these views. "In the last 20 years of politics in this country, as evidenced by available survey data, the people do not really have a high disregard or even much disregard for authoritarian government."[6] They were interested in results—and wondered, as Francis Sionil-Jose put it, "why can't garbage in Manila be collected?"[7]

In these circumstances, Malacañang Palace was searching for ways of demonstrating leadership and for the president to regain a suitably high moral stance. In late August, in an attempt to respond to the demand for just such leadership from the center, President Aquino had seized a shipment of Uzi guns coming in to the Benigno Aquino International Airport and ordered them burned; in fact they had been ordered and paid for in legal fashion by the Congress, for at least in part the obvious purpose of self-protection. Aquino had to back off, and the incident cost her a falling out with House Speaker—and her party leader—Ramon Mitra.

But she must have suspected more sinister purposes in the importation. The fact is, guns were becoming as pervasive as in the old society. Shortly after her attempt, a more sinister action did occur. Representative Nicanor de Guzman, Jr., arrived from Los Angeles on 7 September and was immediately accused of trying to bring 314 mostly high-powered firearms into the country in his luggage. He attempted to move to the high ground by taking indefinite leave without pay from the House while the incident was investigated, claiming all the evidence against him was circumstantial. In fact, his explanation did not pass the straight-face test,[8] and the fact that he had traveler's checks worth $180,000 in his luggage (and bills from a Las Vegas casino for $41,000) at least suggested he traveled in the fast lane.

A larger issue, however, was the role of the president's younger brother, the powerful representative from Tarlac. "Peping" had been in California at the same time, which he claimed was due to his wife's medical treatment,[9] but there was abundant circumstantial evidence implicating him. The fact that the president immediately went on the offense, revealingly stating at a press conference that "We [sic] have nothing to hide" and clearing her brother *prior* to the investigation she ordered, tended to prove to Filipinos that she had almost irretrievably slipped onto the old political treadmill. Her brother's subsequent attempts to get de Guzman off the hook in the House of Representatives—where they were close associates—hardly allayed suspicions.[10] In fact, it seemed to prove the case.

As one columnist cynically put it, de Guzman would get off the hook and "we probably won't even notice it. We have short memories . . . for we are a nation which thrives on scandals, real or imagined. Just let one columnist write about another bedtime story starring a bigwig and Junior [de Guzman] will be in the past tense."[11] As it happened, Filipinos got star entertainment from the scandal, including the sight and sound of de Guzman quoting scripture in Congress while hiring a public relations firm to get him off the hook.[12]

Yet the affair would not die down, because it symbolized all the brimming sense of scandal in the reading public. After all, Cardinal Sin himself, on the important 21 August anniversary of Senator Aquino's murder, had preached on the subject of corruption in the very presence of the president, who was herself no longer spared suspicion of public venality. On 12 September the House in fact suspended de Guzman; there were not enough votes to expel him, and the two thirds required to suspend were just met. But as a senior executive of the Congress said just prior to the vote, "We are all watching. It is so very important that they do the right thing [and expel de Guzman]."[13]

It is ironic that reform-minded economists in the Philippines could applaud the fact that cabinet members legally held multiple outside posts along with their high-ranking jobs. "Because at least that is atop the table. I was more nervous when such was *not* allowed; the amount of corruption was then far higher,"[14] one said. Thus the government's executive secretary earned P21,000 per month (c. $1,000) as chairman of the Philippine Oil Company, Philippine Air Lines, and Philippine Center for Economic Development.[15] But if the amounts were not large, the power that came with them was substantial, including immense opportunities for family and friends.

Along with the privileges came the guns. Guns had always been loose in the Philippines, at least after World War II, when shiploads of arms—Browning automatic rifles, .45-caliber pistols, and the like—were smuggled into guerrilla hands by the U.S. Navy and which stayed loose in the society, to be used by Huks and warlords alike. In the aftermath of martial law's declaration in 1972, Marcos had collected virtually all the private guns, save those of Muslims, who were willing to fight a war over them. Thus, approximately 400,000 private guns were added to military arsenals, for now there was to be only one army, one king.

Yet guns began slipping back long before Marcos's demise, especially in the guise of private armies, particularly those of the so-called cronies of the president. And after the 1986 revolution, little practical effort was made to limit the right to carry guns.[16] By the end of the 1980s armed guards were everywhere, as were sophisticated metal detection equipment at the doors of the big banks and signs to check guns before entering premises. One estimate is that 150,000 guns were in private hands—and 8,000 were intercepted at the airport in 1989, simply the tip of the iceberg of those coming through.[17] Indeed, General Montaño, the Philippine Constabulary/Integrated National Police chief, said that gun imports increased by 22 percent in 1988—and by an astonishing 75.6 percent in 1989. His numbers were that there were 178,000 loose guns around.[18] It looked exactly like the old society, for it was the old society.[19]

One of the symbols of the old society, gun-toting congressmen, was also around. General Montaño exempted all 196 congressmen and their body-guards from the "ban" against carrying firearms. Ariel Bocobo reflected a widespread belief in writing:

> The solons and their security goons should be the first to be covered by the ban. These bodyguards are notorious for abusing the law and inflicting harm and violence on poor hapless citizens who happen to cross their congressmen masters. . . . Most of these security aides are unsavory characters from under-world mobs who should never be trusted with deadly weapons in the first place. And they are the major factor behind some solons' success in holding on to their political posts.[20]

Guns were, however, part of a vicious circle—as almost always. The issue of private armies was usually misunderstood. The mayor of Malabon had what was called in his town a "private army." In fact, the NPA had ambushed him at one point; he realized that the PC was stretched too thin in his province to protect him and do everything else that needed doing. The ten men making up his "private army" were just the rotated guards he had to protect himself. In Negros human rights activists say the landlords have private armies. Some may. What this researcher found was plantation and farm owners and managers living at great risk, liable to NPA hits at any time, with several CAFGUs working and guarding, being relieved by, often enough, the owner himself. The larger installations—sugar centrals, for example, have large guard forces, which might well be called private armies. As General Ramos put it, however, "these people have a right to protect themselves and their assets. The army and the PC can't protect everybody all the time."[21]

Deus ex Machina

By the end of 1989 the Philippine polity was gridlocked. Traffic patterns in Manila had become metaphor for national politics. Six-hour electrical brownouts on a daily basis in Manila were halting the virtuous economic growth of the previous three years, and no one saw a way out for the politics: Aquino's position as savior had reality as a musical descant, but the two canceled out at paralysis. The country was waiting for a coup d'état, to the extent that it was awaiting anything.

Throughout late 1989 the talk of coups was universal, the desire for strongman rule expressed frequently. Tony Abaya, an intellectual and columnist, wrote how a popular cabinet member, in a university lecture, called for abolition of the Congress and the establishment of strongman rule. He also described a forum of thirty-five to forty executives, precisely the type who had brought Aquino to power, where an "American political analyst gave his reading of the . . . scene." He was asked about a coup.

> He said that as expectations of the Aquino government become lower and lower and disenchantment spreads, a military take-over becomes a more and more attractive option. . . . He then posed a hypothetical question: Suppose the NPA Sparrows escalate their urban terrorism . . .[and] that there is rioting in the streets because of increases in the cost of living. . . . Suppose in such a situation . . . the civilian government falters and the military decides to take over. How many of you would march in the streets to protest such a takeover? Not a single hand or arm was raised.[22]

Although the American was not identified, General Ramos had no doubt of his identity and invited him to dinner at the Army-Navy Club shortly thereafter. He spent perhaps an hour going over his own role in putting down five coups to that point and making clear that he would put down any others, even if (as the guest suggested) he could have seized power himself in any of these (especially that of August 1987). "I did not risk my life in 1986 to restore democracy to make the Philippines into a banana republic," he said with conviction and passion. True, he led opinion polls for the 1992 elections at the time, and democracy was thus not only a good road for his country but, for him, the most advantageous. There was emotion and belief also in his voice, and it was the determination flowing therefrom that made a coup a more expensive prospect for plotters.

Nonetheless, the sense of inevitability of change built up during this period. The would-be deliverance came in a form different, however, from what was expected, at least in first appearance.

In what was surely one of the most remarkable arrivals in any country's political history, Eduardo "Danding" Cojuangco emerged from the skies on 24 November and called a press conference of the faithful (and of those for hire) the next day, literally turning the country's political patterns upside down and setting the stage—wittingly or not[23]—for the frightening coup attempt precisely one week later.

Cojuangco had left Manila with his patron Ferdinand Marcos and settled in California.[24] He never ceased to keep in touch with his network of officers, businessmen, politicians, and mediamen. He had no passport and was on a prohibited list of immigrants. Because he would come in on his own wings, presumably either to his own airfield or through Manila's Benigno Aquino International Airport in some manner of disguise, he did not need a passport in his own name. To make a point, he sought and got one, not from the consulate in Los Angeles, where a medium-size bribe, at most, would have been necessary, but from the main office and the acting director of the Passport Division, of the Department of Foreign Affairs in Manila![25]

How he in fact reached Manila is still a mystery, though less of one since the Davide Commission's inquiries. Though Danding refused to discuss the issue, enough others supplied data that, when put together, makes irresistible the conclusion that he came from Kota Kinabalu in Brunei, on a flight chartered for $6,000 and piloted by associates of his. From there he seems to have gone to one of his farms, in Malita, Davao del Sur, and then managed to hide his presence coming into Manila.[26]

In a press conference he showed astonishing control—mastery of self and mastery of those questioning him; he "appeared on TV like a modern-day Count of Monte Cristo out to redeem his honor. Then his drum-beaters in media [sent] up multi-colored balloons of praise for a great man, misunderstood and maligned in his time," the very courageous columnist Teodoro Benigno wrote.

It was not just the media that were cowed; no politicians dared speak out. Benigno went on:

> Now Marcos's top crony is in town and not one single legislator has the intestinal fortitude to call a spade a spade. If they talk at all, it's excited gabble about how the 1992 elections will shape up as a result of Danding Cojuangco's formidable presence. It proves what many have been thinking all along—that our legislators have no conscience, no principles, no balls.[27]

When Aquino's government talked of charges pending against Danding, he showed up once again at a press conference with his personal lawyer,

Attorney Estanislao Mendoza, President Marcos's minister of justice and thought to be the country's smartest and best defense attorney. No one was going to put manacles on Danding.

In fact, the government's case—more specifically the case of the Presidential Commission on Good Government (set up in 1986 to recover, through prosecution or otherwise, Marcos-related assets)—was thin to the point of incredulity. Of the numerous charges bandied around about Danding, the best the government's apparat could set forth was the charge that the Philippine Coconut Authority (PCA), of which Danding had been chairman, had contributed P10 million to the Cultural Center of the Philippines, the then first lady's favorite charity, and P6 million to the Philippine Coconut Producers Federation, a private entity.[28] The notion that it was actionable for a large organization like the PCA to give several hundred thousand dollars to the largest cultural organization in the country, the pet project—and largest ever—of the powerful wife of the republic's president, could not be taken seriously.[29]

No matter. By February after his arrival politicians and planters were paying homage to Danding at his home, and when he left Manila, as Luis Beltran put it, his presence was drawing politicians "like bumblebees to a flower."[30] As another columnist said, "The only thing between him and Malacañang Palace now is a bullet. The only person who can put it there is Eddie Ramos."[31]

By late 1991 Danding had so shrewdly managed his reentry into the Philippines that all his voting stock in the republic's largest corporation, San Miguel, was back under his control, even though there was still a judicial challenge.[32] San Miguel too could now become part of the campaign kitty.

The Great Coup

In June 1989 military intelligence received information of a plan by Honasan and his new ally, Marcos's man General Zumel, to "destabilize government," and later in the summer had information on Honasan's recruitment meetings with top military officers. He also received *one million* primers used for the manufacture of ammunition for .45-caliber guns, which were confiscated.[33] Although he was able to dart around Manila quite openly, the military was unable to arrest him—because most members of the military were unwilling, thereby making a point, and also because arrest procedures were cumbersome.[34]

On Thursday, 30 November 1989, the *Philippines Free Press* was on the stands, dated 2 December. Gringo Honasan was on the cover, the picture of his charismatic chiseled face worth a thousand recruits, saying "We have learned our lessons and we have learned them well . . . [This time] We will Kill," in contrast to the 28 August 1987 attempt, pictured in an inset, and in which a mere fifty-three people lost their lives. "Looking back to August 28, we were all willing to die, but we were not willing to kill," he went on. And he went on with his now-famous statement that "A coup is basically a function of clear signal from a people to its military."[35]

Astonishingly, another article featured an interview with General Rodolfo Biazon, then chief of the National Capital Regional Defense Command: he made clear just how different were the conditions then from 1986 when "People Power" ousted Marcos—that indeed it was not the question of how many soldiers were on either side, but of the two million Filipinos on EDSA highway, which Honasan would not have. As the magazine summarized Biazon's position, "[The rebels] did not succeed in 1987 when they had the facilities and actual command of units, when they were free to move around to recruit and politicize. Now that they no longer have these, how can they succeed?" It was a salient question. But—not to put too fine a point on it—there was overconfidence. Honasan, the interviewer said, claimed that eighty to ninety percent of the military would sit on the fence in the event of a coup. And asked about the alleged support of a "Young Officer's Union," which Gringo claimed to have the support of, Biazon simply said, "There's no such group."[36] It was his position that a coup was no longer feasible; Gringo Honasan was no longer within military ranks, free to recruit; all was under control.

Although Biazon was to prove one of the government's real heroes during the coup, his indifference to what was plainly building up was somewhat epochal. To the question of whether eighty to ninety percent of the military would be fence-sitters during a coup, he replied with tactical sagacity and public relations foolishness, "Assuming that is true, what of it? Surely, he's [Honasan] not implying that the remaining 10 percent will side with him and that he will prevail," the general said, then denied that any such percentage would fence-sit.

The only thing he was proved right about was that 10 percent could hold the fort. It was lucky that it could, since it was all he had.

In fact, Honasan already had his clear signal. The government's decision to raise oil prices had the usual public effect, but coming on top of the brownouts, the garbage crisis, and continued evidence of corruption, it is easy to see why he was confident.

The Great Coup got off to an inauspicious start—"when a Scout Ranger team *prematurely* destroyed the AFP communications station in Tagaytay," outside Manila, on 28 November. It was meant to take place on the thirtieth, signaling "D-Day for the 1 December coup."[37] On Thursday night, 30 November, Honasan and his allies struck. Manilans were awakened Friday morning by the bombing of the palace itself by the air force's little Tora trainers. If 90 percent of the armed forces did not sit on the fence, nonetheless a high proportion did; the rebels were able to move freely to seize the airport, important television stations, and key military camps. It was easy for a bystander, such as this writer, to conclude that it was only a matter of time before Mrs. Aquino would depart Malacañang Palace in an American helicopter. Indeed General Ramos, from his command headquarters, was in continual contact with her and the American embassy, which was caught even more off guard than the Filipino high command. By late morning, when it looked all but over, the question had been put to the president of the United States, en route to Malta for talks with the Soviet president, as to whether America would "support democracy." The answer was never in doubt. Aquino still had that card—that one card—in her deck.

The impact of the four Phantom jets flying from the north—the location of Clark Air Force Base—cannot be overemphasized, for the light it sheds on Filipino political behavior. The aural and visual sensation of expertly flown and mammoth planes coming so suddenly in the early afternoon, clearing the skies and stunning the populace, was extraordinary. And the effect on the battle was instantaneous. The Americans had voted, and to the average Filipino—including soldiers—that was the vote that, for the moment, counted. It seemed obvious that it was all over but the mopping up.

In fact, there was so much momentum in the Great Coup that it took a week to mop it up. There were surprises on all fronts. At a time when one would have expected all national leaders to pull together, even those at odds with the leadership, the vice president, Salvador Laurel, gave an interview to the BBC in Hong Kong on 3 December in which he excoriated the Aquino government and omitted to criticize the coup-makers. He did not wish to "pre-judge them," he said. "I cannot condemn the cause because they have been quoted as fighting for good government. How can you be against good government?"[38]

Militarily, the coup kept going. The AFP and the palace repeatedly claimed victory, but their claims were drowned out by bombs and artillery. In fact, it was a question at several points as to whether victory was the government's to lose anew. Unique in the history of coups, the continuing coup, with wave after wave of tactical moves, showed the rebels' determination and resilience.

Thus on 2 December, when the chief of staff had already proclaimed victory—not inappropriately by reference to the history of coups—five hundred Scout Rangers began moving into the commercial and tourist center of Makati, and held it until 7 December, a week after the coup began. Although the Davide Report avers not to see the logic of this occupation, it is obvious. Makati is where the money is. In a major way the Rangers were disrupting the financial life of the republic. The army could not easily storm the area without unacceptable risks to the tourists trapped in the international hotels. When the Rangers occupied Makati, second-phase actions were underway elsewhere; for example, the second attempt on Camp Aguinaldo, headquarters not only of the armed forces but of the department of national defense. Makati was a trump card, which gave the rebels leverage of an important sort—at the most, for an assumption of power if troops elsewhere got control of Camp Aguinaldo and other bases and it was necessary to convince the resistance to capitulate since even the commercial center was in rebel hands; at the least, if all else failed, for the kind of treatment that would enable them to put their lives back together and possibly regroup for another day.

Eventually the latter obtained, since the army was finally able to defeat all the other moves that the seemingly relentless rebels were able to mount. General Enrile, commander of the Military Academy, courageously went into Makati without instructions and negotiated the surrender—mainly with a Major Abraham Purugganan, a YOU founder about whom more was sure to be heard. But for the moment, to ensure precisely that, the latter slipped away during the last talks. His men were permitted to return to their barracks; all over the world newswatchers saw the rebels marching back to Fort Bonifacio cheering and giving defiant gestures of victory.

The question of the centrality of the "persuasion flights" will be debated for years to come. At the time the decision was made to request American aid, at eleven in the morning on 1 December, any onlooker was bound to doubt that the Aquino government could get things back together. The evidence pouring out from the radio, the visible evidence as one journeyed around the city and interviewed troops on the ramparts, was of a crumbling defense. Looked at from the roof of a building in the capital city, the sudden southern swoop of the Phantoms, coming so obviously from the seat of the Thirteenth U.S. Air Force at Clark Air Force Base, under the circumstances, had to be one of the most memorable demonstrations of naked power that man could devise. And so, by and large, were they seen.

It is no wonder, however, that Filipinos have later tried to minimize their import. Thus the Davide Report:

> General de Villa contends that, since the tide of battle had started to turn before noon of 1 December with the arrival of more than sufficient reinforcements at Camp Aguinaldo and since the rebel air assets had already been destroyed, the flight of the Phantoms served no real military value for or against the government forces. This view appears to be supported by evidence that several units which intended to support the rebels were not deterred from still moving, even after wide publicity was given to the flight of the Phantoms. . . .
>
> Ramos' view qualified de Villa's. He said that hindsight tells us that the persuasion flights did occur after the government had gained the upper hand. However, at the time of the flight, the AFP command was not fully certain about the capability of the rebels to launch air strikes from Mactan Air Base or to bring reinforcements from Mindanao and Palawan to Manila. It was not until afterwards that the government knew about the refusal of all the pilots to go along with [rebel] Comendador.
>
> The political value of the flights . . . is questionable. The immediate effect to the public was probably one of relief . . . that the US was firmly on the government side. . . . On the other hand, the flights served to give the opposition, at least initially, a platform to put the government on the defensive, some young officers an occasion to express support for the rebels, and the US and its press a propaganda leverage for the bases negotiations. On hindsight, the government would have been better off not calling on [the Phantoms]. But 20-20 vision was not available when the flights were first agreed upon.[39]

Hindsight indeed was not available at that critical hour. One general officer observed that the Philippine Constabulary—the national police—was on the verge of going over, lock, stock, and barrel, to the rebels, when the flights came. If so, had the flights been much delayed, the rebels would obviously have triumphed. The Philippines cannot be ruled without the PC.

Public opinion is equivocal on the persuasion flights. Asked in the Ateneo Survey "whether or not [one] approved of Pres. Aquino's decision to seek or accept the help of the U.S. during the period of the attempted coup," 42 percent nationally approved, while 28 percent disapproved—though in Metro Manila the disapproval rate was almost double, at 50 percent. Approval also varied inversely with class.[40] And those who approved put their reasons most pragmatically: first to "avoid greater trouble," second "to save country from military rebels" and "to stop coup troubles." The notion that

the United States was "our ally" got 3% nationally.
The table for those disapproving is worth examining.

ATENEO PUBLIC OPINION SURVEY[41]					
	Survey area		Socioeconomic Class		
Questionnaire Item	RP	Metro Manila	ABC	D	E
• *Reasons why disapproved of Pres. Aquino's decision to seek or accept help from U.S.* *(Base: All who disapproved)*					
Internal problems to be solved by us	37	50	49	39	25
Cory had no controlover the situation	9	9	13	8	7
Showed Cory's powerlessness against the rebels	8	12	9	8	9
Showed lack of confidence in our soldiers	6	6	7	7	4
We are capable of solving our problems	5	9	6	5	5
Many civilians were hurt	2	1	2	4	1
Others	5	8	4	8	2

Ultimately, the key reason the coup failed, other than the flight of the Phantoms, is that there was insufficient *popular* support at that time for a rebellion's success: enough for a rebellion, but not to succeed, given the rebels' lack of a genuine and broad popular base (Gringo's personal popularity not to be confused therewith). Just before the coup General Biazon was insightful in noting in economic terms that the conditions of popular support for a rebellion, as in 1986, did not exist; the economic conditions and political conditions nowhere equaled that earlier grave period,[42] a point the Davide commission would make in spades:

Year	Real GNP (million Pesos)	Growth Rate (%)	Inflation Rate (%)
84	91,644	-5.50	50.30
85	87,867	-4.12	23.10
86	89,504	1.86	.80
87	94,705	5.81	3.80
88	101,093	6.75	8.80
89	106,830	5.67	10.60

The Real GNP and Inflation Rates 1984-1989[43]

Of course, what the table tells us is something other than that relative deprivation did not exist—as Davide contends. For if in fact a segment of the armed forces would fight as ingeniously, as long, and as hard as it did, something else must have been at issue, as we shall argue.

In fact, public opinion was not unsupportive of the coup, as the Ateneo Survey shows. Asked "which of the following opinions comes closest to your opinion about the failed coup," 36 percent nationally said it was "completely wrong"—while *46 percent* said it was "wrong *but needed to jolt the government.*"[44] The percentage was higher in Manila—53 percent. The survey goes even further, breaking down the reasons in both categories. For those wishing to "jolt" the government, the first and much the most significant reason was "to let Cory and government review weakness," second "to force government to reform," and then tiny percentages for varieties thereof. So Gringo had passive support, at the least, of a plurality of the population, but lacked the diehard support there, from a systematic program, which might have brought victory.

The basic question we must pose about the coup is not why it failed, but how did it come so close? For twenty-four hours the leaders of the republic had the clearest possible signals of the coup's imminence. Gringo said he was going to do it, the oil price rise had occurred, and rebels had seized the Tagaytay station. Intelligence "noise" of a coup was thunderous on 30 November; by early dawn, the Davide Report tells us, "intelligence officers were receiving mounting information which pointed to an impending coup."[45] Honasan was sighted in Fort Bonifacio. Junior battle staff officers called a conference at eight in the morning to disseminate what had been put together. The leaders of the armed forces had met all Thursday evening, and presumably they discussed serious business. Yet they were unable to come up with reinforcements to secure the headquarters of the air force—a logical place to start; they were unable to prevent rebels from seizing Fort Bonifacio on the edge of the republic's capital and from securing the biggest ammunition dump in the country; and they were only barely, by a fluke, able to secure the person of the commanding general of the Philippine Army, General Cacañando himself; they were unable to prevent a bombing of the symbolic center of the republic, Malacañang Palace; they could not maintain control of the skies nor the international airport. It was plainly and simply an open bridge hand where everyone knew the location of every card ever played. The rebels failed only to realize that there was an American joker in the pack, and that it could be played.

Another reason the coup leaders came so close is that they were better armed than the regulars. "Although the rank and file used government-issued firearms and other supplies, the coup leaders had Uzis, Galils, and Ultimax guns, radio and telephone systems superior to those used by government troops," the Davide Report tells us.[46] Four carloads of M-16s and other weapons were thought to have been returned to Honasan in 1987, and associates of his in Customs might well have helped him smuggle other arms into the country. The rebels had Land Cruisers, while the army "had to commandeer private trucks including fish and fruit vendor trucks, in order to ferry . . . troops to Manila."[47]

And yet, and yet: Even in a loosely governed state like the Philippines, the legal and legitimate armed forces have simply enormous advantage in the procurement, storage, and use of weaponry. To have begged, borrowed, or stolen enough guns to arm several thousand rebels *in a timely manner* is a feat that staggers the imagination. The rebels apparently did not even have large stashes of cash. True, the fact that the banking system did not reveal any unusual deposits or withdrawal just prior to or during the coup does not prove much; a big bank roller would not have created such a paper trail. However, the evidence the Davide Report shows is that a lot of small sums were accumulated through the normal sort of illegal activities in which Filipino soldiers engage themselves—logging, jueting, and the like. If Senator Enrile or Governor Cojuangco turned over the kind of sum that a favorable outcome would have made compelling in light of their interests— let us say some tens of millions of pesos for starters—then they certainly hid the disbursal very well. The Davide Commission found no evidence that such had occurred, and this makes the coup all the more remarkable. True, the way in which Danding came in, in a private plane, made it easy for him to have brought as much currency as he wished; and someone with a $20 million stud farm in Australia presumably could have obtained the money needed. All the same, money is not what made this coup so nearly succeed.

As *Davide* points out with understatement, the first four years of Aquino's rule have shown that the Philippines "has firmly been introduced to the phenomenon of military intervention in politics."[48] Although we can eliminate from consideration the first coup attempt, by Marcos loyalists, as a fatuous attempt to regain power, and the second, as Enrile's spite at not sharing the presidential power he thought he had achieved in the February 1986 coup that brought Mrs. Aquino to power, we must consider the 1987 and 1989 attempts as vital and serious, and relevant to our attempt to understand what went wrong in the Aquino era.

How did military reformers of RAM, who had risked their lives to rid their country of a right-wing dictator, come to link up with the so-called loyalists—friends and protegées of Ferdinand Marcos? It happened because both groups had the same objective—getting rid of President Aquino, and the need was more urgent than in the past. But how to come together? "Considering . . . that they were opposing forces during the EDSA Revolt, someone had to act as a middleman. That role was tailor-made for Brigadier General Edgardo Abenina, a known supporter of the rightist movement who was implicated and charged for involvement in the 28 August 1987 attempt."[49] He was a classmate (PMA '58) of General Zumel, moreover, another loyalist.

Far too much commentary has been devoted to the concessions the soldiers achieved, without attention to the reasons such happened. True, the concessions are significant. As the Davide report points out,

> The general reactions of the government to the past coup attempts have included a revamp of the Cabinet, including the ouster of some of its liberal members due to the rebels' demands; the announcement of reform measures; and the conduct of an investigation on the coup attempt. . . . An immediate response has been the increase in budget for the military. . . . There were also measures taken to promote the soldiers' welfare by expediting action aimed at increasing their material benefits.[50]

The reasons are twofold. This process was in effect a perpetuation of the Marcos system—not as such through his own men, such as General Zumel, acting on Marcos's behalf (in Honolulu), but the whole system, the militarization of the Philippines after 1972, in which the military never tasted supreme power but was always a necessary prop of the regime. It could not unlearn those habits overnight.

And certainly it could not unlearn them in an atmosphere of weak government. You do not give way to the demands of men whom you can fire unless you remain intimidated by them even after the collapse of their coups. Enrile had to come virtually out into the open as a traitor to the government he had created before Aquino would fire him, in 1986; this after he had destabilized, indeed terrorized, her government for months. After Gringo's 1987 coup, he was, to be sure, jailed, but when he charmed his jailers and escaped, Aquino could not convince the military to capture him, though locating him and interviewing him was simple—as this writer found. So Gringo could continue recruiting until the Great Coup nearly toppled her, and after that attempt he seemed even more impervious to capture.

So for the Davide commission to say that the coup failed "because the people were not disposed to it, as they were to the EDSA revolt" is to beg many questions. Indeed its own conclusions contradict this in a far more analytical and important appraisal:

> Its failure was a combination of genuine heroism on the part of some government forces, tactical mistakes by the coup plotters and the hesitancy of key rebel figures . . . , timely intervention of military-civilian forces particularly at gateway roads to Metro Manila, and failure of the rebels to elicit a bandwagon effect from major military units in the country.[51]

Yet it is precisely the bandwagon effect that made the coup so nearly succeed. And notable in the list of the Davide report's factors for the coup's collapse is the absence of one that ordinary Filipinos believe to be the most important of all—the Joker in the pack.

What happened is that the incompetence of the Aquino government had not only sufficiently permeated the country so that soldiers believed a coup was feasible—and necessary; the incompetence characterizes the response itself—and that is what explains the remarkable character of this coup *despite* the *relative* absence of "relative deprivation."

The ability of the republic to defend itself became comical in the coup's aftermath. After the coup had failed, the government could not manage to capture the principal coup leaders. The public perception, says the Davide Commission, is that they "cannot be captured because they are protected by elements within the military itself, [which] tends to demoralize those who abide by the law and undermines the system of reward and punishment in the larger society itself."[52]

Senator Enrile, almost assuredly, played a large part in the coup's planning and financing; the government produced long depositions from four hotel employees, sent to cater a party at his sprawling mansion in Das Mariñas Village on Friday evening, Day 1 of the coup, attended by numerous soldiers wearing the white patches of coup participants and (among others) Gringo himself. "Senator Enrile and the people with him were all occupied listening to the radio. Around 8 P.M., when General Biazon was heard to say, 'Everything is under control,' a very angry Katrina, Senator Enrile's daughter, said: 'This braggart!' Then they all looked glum."[53] Enrile denied all the allegations, claiming the government was "fabricating testimony,"[54] though there seemed little doubt that the testimony was true. Honasan darted around Manila and was always recognized by the cooks and drivers.[55]

General Alfredo Lim, the new director of the National Bureau of Investigation (NBI), made the assertion that "an actual clash of arms with the forces of the Government is not absolutely necessary" to establish rebellion. Knowingly associating with organizations dedicated to overthrowing the government was enough.[56] In any case, though rebellion is listed as a "serious" crime, it is a bailable offense with a maximum jail sentence of a year—a very small down-side risk for a coup plotter. But the government briefly managed to jail Enrile, much to the regret of his colleagues. Speaker Mitra contrasted the arrest with those made under martial law, including of himself; in those days one was arrested, detained, and eventually released without charges being filed.[57]

The speed with which Enrile got out raised the question of whether the Aquino government—and, ultimately, the republic that elected it to govern—had the will to defend itself, indeed to survive. Survival, after all, is the only value by which entities ultimately can be judged. The problem was that the only way Aquino could legally hold Enrile, Cojuangco, and other alleged conspirators was through martial law—and that could be overturned by a majority of the Congress. And that body, Teodoro Benigno wrote, the constitutional drafters "imagined . . . would be an assembly of reverends, of right and honorable men moving to the tinkle of harps in heaven."[58] Of course Aquino could attempt to maintain a majority in Congress—but apparently she lacked the will or interest.

Nor was it possible to link Cojunagco with Enrile and others who openly supported the 1989 coup. While the Davide Commission

> did not uncover any direct evidence that Danding was a plotter or participant, the staging of the coup a few days after his mystery-shrouded arrival, in the light of some facts which surfaced during the hearings or which were unearthed through *subpoenas duces tecum*, raises reasonable ground to believe that he had prior knowledge of the staging of the coup.[59]

Indeed: For years newsmen, military officers, and politicians had allegedly been on his payroll. There were several thousand people with knowledge of one part of the coup or the other, and it strains the imagination to believe that not one—not one of the dissident soldiers in need of money, for example—informed Danding. He just happened to arrive at the right time, after three and a half years of exile, to take up where he left off. If it is not true that "there are no accidents in politics," it is close to the truth in the remarkable life of Danding Cojuangco thus far. The intelligence that the Philippine government had just after the coup, that many coup participants trained at a Cojuangco farm,[60] only adds to the belief that he was a principal organizer, and would have been a principal beneficiary, had the coup gone according to plan.

General Ramos joined the soldiers who had made the first coup attempt against the new republic in doing the pushups that were the punishment handed out. Sentences thereafter were stiffer, especially after Filipinos read the sarcastic international references to the affair. The top punishment for the 27 January 1987 coup was twenty years' imprisonment. Nine of the nineteen arrested rebel officers of the August 1987 coup were sentenced to eight years in jail. By late 1990, twenty-eight top rebel leaders of the Great Coup were undergoing trial. Still being investigated were 1,806 and 753 were "restored to duty status." Seven percent were still at large, including the leader, Gringo Honasan.[61]

There was, in effect, little disincentive to strike. Filipino society is gentle, unpunishing. True, Ferdinand Marcos would not have done pushups with rebellious soldiers, which makes the principal point, that it was the character of the regime against which soldiers were striking. Its very permissiveness brought with it a laxity toward societal problems that failed to inspire military confidence. Still, eight years in jail for bringing government to a halt and almost toppling it is hardly a disincentive to rebellious soldiers. Sentences became stiffer only when the regime finally realized how close was the connection between its permissiveness and its fragile hold.

NOTES

1. "Trapos" is an abbreviation of "traditional politician" used in the Manila press; but it is also a Spanish word meaning "rags you wipe up filth with," as a letter writer to *The Economist* pointed out, in reference to the Philippines (21 July 1990, p. 4).

2. Teodoro M. Locsin, "What's He Laughing About?" *Philippine Free Press* (16 September 1989), p. 2.

3. Ateneo de Manila University, *Public Opinion Survey*, August 1989 (Quezon City: Ateneo de Manila University, 1989), Table 6. Hereafter Ateneo Survey.

4. *Ibid.*, Table 2, p. 16. Roughly, A class is the rich elite, B and C are the middle classes, D is the lower-middle class, and E is the proletariat.

5. *Ibid.*, Table 8, p. 36.

6. "The Presidency," *Solidarity* Seminar Series on Public Issues, No. 20, *Solidarity* 125 (January-March 1990), p. 166.

7. *Ibid.*, p. 153.

8. He claimed another passenger requested that he carry the boxes for him. See *Philippine Daily Inquirer* (7, 8 September 1989).

9. And clearly was in part; she was suffering from cancer.

10. See "Junior's Airtight Alibi," Larry Sipin, *The Star* (9 September 1989).

11. *Ibid.*

12. See Federico D. Pascual Jr., "Solon Quotes Scriptures," in "Postscript," *Philippine Daily Inquirer* (11 September 1989).

13. This author's interview, Philippine Senate (November 1991).

14. This author's interview, Asian Institute of Management (1 September 1989).

15. Ernesto M. Macatuno, "Guingona's Wars," *Philippine Free Press* (16 September 1989), p. 5.

16. See Eric Giron, "A Fascination for Guns," *Philippine Daily Enquirer* (21 January 1990). Technical requirements for carrying guns involved a professional requiring a gun for protection and good moral character. As the article went on, "permits to carry firearms are sold [by the police] to Chinese businessmen for as much as P20,000." In practice anyone wishing to carry a gun could do so.

17. *Ibid.*

18. *Manila Times* (19 September 1989).

19. Max Soliven, the gifted columnist, attributed the phenomenon in part to Filipino macho complexes. He quoted a Filipina as saying that Filipino males "are a bunch of little boys . . . toting walkie talkies, car radios, micro-Uzis, their prize fighting cocks . . ." Max V. Soliven, "Are Big Guns Toys for Our 'Little Boys'?" in "By the Way," *The Star* (8 September 1989).

20. Ariel Bocobo, "The Wrong People to Be Exempted," *Manila Standard* (4 February 1990).
21. This author's interview, General Fidel V. Ramos, (18 September 1989).
22. This author's interview with Antonio C. Abaya, columnist and journalist (27 November 1989), and quotation from Abaya's column, *Manila Chronicle*, 18 September 1989.
23. According to Robert Weigend, public relations adviser in Washington to Governor Cojuangco, his client knew nothing of the coup and acted surprised by it at the time.
24. His PR officer in Washington claims Cojuangco left with Marcos in order to facilitate his departure, only to find out afterward that his own return was proscribed. Events moved so fast on that occasion that such may be true: Cojuangco may certainly have believed such in any case. He held no public office. But his strategy in 1990 was to separate himself from Marcos as much as possible in the U.S. mind (though not in Ilocano country).
25. This author's interview, Department of Foreign Affairs (2 December 1989). See also Davide Commission, *Republic of the Philippines*, "The Final Report of the Fact-Finding Commission" (pursuant to R.A. No. 6832) (Manila: October 1990), p. 515. Hereafter Davide.
26. Davide, pp. 291-97.
27. Teodoro Benigno, "More on Mr. Crony, Mr. Tiptoe and Mr. Clone," in 'Here's the Score,' *Philippine Star* (1 December 1989).
28. Both cases are reprinted in *Philippine Free Press* (10 February 1990).
29. In November 1978, two years after the PCA contribution, this author, on behalf of his home academic institution, attempted to negotiate a "Ferdinand Marcos Chair" and was entertained for ten hours by President and Mrs. Marcos. During this period I witnessed a four-hour extravaganza—the birthday party of banana king Antonio Floirindo—in which the First Lady used her considerable charm and clout to obtain contributions to a variety of causes from those attending. It is not plausible that a crony-favorite like Cojuangco could have been excused from contributing to the First Lady's first charity.
30. "Not a Time for Making Enemies," *Manila Standard* (16 February 1990).
31. This author's interview with a confidential source, Manila (29 November 1989).
32. See "Court Rules on San Miguel," *International Herald Tribune* (17 April 1991).
33. Davide, p. 366.
34. Chief of Staff General de Villa, in an interview, pointed out that, thanks to post-EDSA reforms, a warrant from a judge was needed to arrest a suspect, after which he was out in three days in any case; and noted that President Aquino had a "penchant for obeying the law," which was "seen as a weakness."
35. Michael Dueñas, "Another Coup?" *Philippine Free Press*, 2 December 1989, p. 2.

36. Ruben Lampa, "They Don't Stand a Chance!" *Philippine Free Press* (2 December 1989). He was to be rewarded, nonetheless, for his stalwart defense of the capital during the coup by promotion to the highest position in the armed forces—chief of staff—when General de Villa retired.

37. Davide, p. 259.

38. *Ibid.*, p. 572.

39. *Ibid.*, pp. 564-65.

40. Ateneo Survey, (1990) Table 17, p. 57. Roughly, A class is the rich elite, B and C are the middle classes, D is the lower-middle class, and E is the proletariat.

41. *Ibid.*, p. 58.

42. Lampa, "They Don't Stand a Chance."

43. Davide, p. 88.

44. Ateneo Survey, Table 17, p. 55 (emphasis added).

45. Davide, p. 307.

46. *Ibid.*, p. 568.

47. *Ibid.*, p. 568.

48. *Ibid.*, p. 240.

49. *Ibid.*, p. 508.

50. *Ibid.*, p. 246.

51. *Ibid.*, p. 538.

52. *Ibid.*, p. 587.

53. Statement of Romeo Cejero, headwaiter, cited in *Philippines Free Press* (20 January 1990), p. 7.

54. *Ibid.*

55. For example, he came regularly to the Tropicana, where this author lived, to see a relative; hotel servants were abuzz during his visits.

56. Lysander Garcia, "The Rebellion Charges vs. Enrile and Co.," *Philippine Free Press* (20 January 1990), p. 6.

57. "Enrile in NBI Custody," *Philippine Star* (28 February 1990).

58. *Philippine Star* (26 February 1990).

59. Davide, p. 515.

60. Intelligence report provided to the author, Philippines Embassy, Washington, DC. (20 December 1989).

61. "Ramos Reports on Measures Against Coupists," *Manila Chronicle* (3 September 1990), in Foreign Broadcast Information Service-East Asia-90-172 (5 September 1990), p. 58.

9

Presidency under Siege[1]

It is easy for observers, watching a nation in crisis, to conclude that matters cannot worsen, that when economic, political, and security structures are stretched to a "certain" point, "something" must happen. True, coups d'état are a feature of the unstable third world, and generally happen at low points of regimes' popularity and standing, as is true of the Philippines. But regimes have an ability to decline in standing far greater than was believed possible when scholars began analyzing political stability in the developing world. In Africa in the 1980s, for example, numerous unpopular regimes held on to power year after year, even decade after decade, despite the absence of any apparent popular support or *raison d'être*.

In the Philippines, the fact that President Aquino remained "legitimate," that the leadership of the armed forces remained loyal to her, and that nongovernmental forces such as the church and part of the business community saw her as the least bad alternative made a coup still a difficult proposition.

The sensitivity and vulnerability of the Aquino government as it unraveled in 1990 is apparent in the way it dealt not only with real issues and problems, such as the bases, but imaginary ones, such as purported interventions in the republic's affairs by individuals or organizations with symbolic influence, who could be used as scapegoats for the coup and all that went with it.

Thus Foreign Secretary Manglapus struck out at the United States for going in both directions, supporting Aquino with the Phantoms and undermining her at the same time. This was accomplished by another "tendency"; "right-wing thinking people" —represented by the Heritage Foundation, and similarly by an American scholar then writing about the coup, who at the time of it was a Fulbright professor in the Philippines—were allegedly trying to bring the government down, at least in the sense that they supposedly supported the coup. "Even before the coup, some people were already saying there was no more hope for Cory. Who were those people—they were the Heritage Foundation, people of the Right-wing. You have to expect them to say that of any democracy. But that is their ideological position. It has nothing to do with reality." Manglapus, who had known the scholar for two decades, made the allegations without regard to the facts, in a wide-ranging and important interview.[2]

That particular writer, on the day of the coup, had written an analysis of the causes of the coup for the *Los Angeles Times* that, through the wonders of fax and the time-zone change, was published on the same day. Because the article was entitled—by the editors—"Anybody but Cory," it was widely discussed in Manila and seen as possibly inspired by official Washington. Aquino's press secretary, Thomas Gomez III, in an official inquiry on the attempted coup, said two Caucasians had been "behaving suspiciously" just prior to the coup; in the case of the professor, by writing the article in question, "several days before [*sic*] the December putsch."[3]

The same scholar, in early January 1990, published a *New York Times* Op-Ed article suggesting it was time to "state the obvious about the Empress's wardrobe. Mrs. Aquino lacks the skills to govern this sprawling country even in the best of times."[4] And now his mere article could be labeled an "American intervention,"[5] especially given his proposal that Mrs. Aquino use her emergency powers to appoint an "emergency powers administrator," "who could rule the country while she continued to reign, at least until the threat is over."

> The burden of US diplomacy in Manila should be to make clear to Mrs. Aquino that, having performed her historic duty of removing Mr. Marcos, she now must allow more experienced hands to govern this despairing land. General Ramos, who is given the highest marks by professionals in Manila, has a real chance to save Philippine democracy.[6]

The article, according to columnist Nestor Mata, was considered—as he quoted others—a " 'barefaced intervention in our affairs,' " presumably on the assumption that it was inspired by the official Washington with which the scholar allegedly had connections. It was not.[7] But a year and a half later the issue was still a sensitive one.[8]

In fact, the substantive proposal was something advanced in various circles during 1990, the year of continual crisis. Senator Osmeña, for example, proposed that the president remain in office but that the cabinet resign, with the country being run by Senate President Salonga, the National Security Adviser (General Ileto), and wealthy businessman Washington Sycip—who, President Aquino pointed out, in a rare exercise of sardony, is an American citizen.[9] Even YOU advanced a variant—that Ramos and de Villa would take advantage of the unrest to seize power themselves, " 'in the name of the restoration of democracy and the return of order.' "[10]

Like the year before, by the end of the year a substantial percentage of Manila's political talk was of coup or resignation. Advocacy of a coup became open; for example, the radical economist and columnist Alejandro Lichauco called for a coup to solve the country's problems;[11] while no less than Senator Maceda said that the president had lost the support of the ruling coalition party members and the people, and should resign—he used the otherwise inapt comparison of Mrs. Thatcher, who had just done exactly that.[12] But Mrs. Aquino retorted that she would provide "strong leadership" and would not leave her post.[13]

By the end of 1990 there were formal and active organizations being put together to drive Cory from office. One—CARMA, or "Corazon Aquino Resign Movement at Once"—claimed to have two million signatures for a resignation petition, made up mostly of irate housewives, and made itself very apparent in the streets of Metro Manila; it was chaired by the former senator Eva Kalaw, a relative of the president.[14]

The Rolling Coup

If the state of affairs deteriorated in late 1989, it was to get worse; the last half of 1990 and first half of 1991 challenged observers to explain how the government could maintain itself. The natural disaster of the 16 July 1990 earthquake, with its immense human and material toll, is a convenient boundary of this phase. It stretched the capacity of the republic to respond to a natural catastrophe beyond any event since independence, coming at the time it did. And it was followed by the invasion of Kuwait two weeks later, with its devastating effects on the balance of payments, given the immediate effect it had on remittances of Filipino workers in the Gulf region. Things were so bad that Secretary of National Defense Ramos could be forgiven for expressing the view that, given the immensity of the problems confronting the government, coup plotters would surely be deterred. "The sole aspiration of the people at present is to have peace, unity, and stability," Ramos said hopefully. Indeed, "no person in his right mind would give any kind of support to any coup attempt by the rebel soldiers."[15] But rebel soldiers for their part might not be in the "right mind," and peace, unity, and stability—under Aquino and Ramos—were not what the rebels wanted; obviously the earthquake and Persian Gulf crisis were for them manna from heaven. Yet Ramos as usual understood the basic question; the issue was not a war against an invader "but collective-national consensus to bring about social and economic reforms."[16]

In a revealing and candid interview, Ramos and Chief of Staff Renato de Villa analyzed what their television host felicitously called "the best of times" for the coup plotters—"but for the nation and our people . . . the worst of times." Congress, sensing the danger and responding to it with its customary courage, abruptly adjourned and scampered to the provinces, while the Presidential Security Group elevated the situation to "Death Call Two," near the top. "Destabilization moves," as Ramos called them, in the form of urban bombings, began anew in this period. Along with these were "extortions" and what Ramos correctly called "noise," from the vocabulary of Intelligence.[17]

In the middle of this occurred a gun battle between agents of the NBI and army officers during an antidrug operation, in which the officers were wounded by the NBI. The NBI—and its director General Alfredo Lim—had been on the upswing since the 1989 coup, thanks to palace favor; it had been pursuing supporters of that coup with greater enthusiasm than was thought appropriate at Camp Aguinaldo, Armed Forces Headquarters, the PC in fact filed charges. All was quieted down at a palace conference—though the issues still simmered. Soon after, a reported half of all constabulary officers issued a statement denouncing the resolution of the presidential fact-finding committee ordering a stop to all investigations dealing with the gun battle. Aquino waffled at a press conference and denied that the issue was between the NBI and AFP, though it was.

Well into 1991 the issue still simmered, and poisoned the start of the new Philippine National Police, the amalgam of the PC and the civil police forces. In his testimony a Manila police captain, Reynaldo Jaylo, facing multiple murder charges from the July shootings, linked senior military officers to the drug racket—military officers incorporated into the police. And the drug was reportedly heroin.[18] The republic's security forces were having trouble cooperating.

Although the CPP-NPA at their most recent plenum had inaugurated a new strategy that included a higher emphasis on urban warfare, it was clear, de Villa said, that the August crisis was being run by dissident soldiers—changing their name, for the sake of confusion, from RAM to SFP (Soldiers of the Filipino people), and to Tagalog acronyms; and that the Young Officer's Union (YOU) was in fact a subgroup of younger officers within the larger RAM—a hopeful assessment on his part and, as it turned out, untrue.

But there was, in fact, a new CPP-NPA emphasis on urban warfare. As the *Manila Chronicle* put it, captured documents made clear at the least that such "is not a momentary flirtation and is likely to be sustained by the rebel movement in spite of its costs and even after the recent capture of an important segment of the 'sparrow' [Manila hit teams] network in Metro Manila."[19]

There was, in all, something new going on, as Ramos pointed out. "In our very mobile and electronically equipped society," new tactics were possible, he said. One person manning a telephone with thirty numbers could destablilize Manila, with the right message, "within 50 minutes," he said. What really was new—telephones had been around for a long time—was the emphasis on psychological steps in coordination with the urban bombings. It was, on the one hand, a confession of military weakness that such emphasis was necessary; military intelligence had improved and tactical readiness as well.

Yet there was also a much heightened popular consciousness of the kudeta as a phenomenon. "The importance of mass media, especially radio, in informing people of what was happening during the coups cannot be overemphasized. However, it has also been in this environment that the release of misinformation and disinformation about the coups has occurred," Davide reports.[20]

But at a higher level it was not clear that the response was adequate, or at least measured to the threat. Ramos talked of "People Power" and its role in blocking units during the 1989 coup, but it was a thin reed. The Congress was debating a new law on rebellion, making it a capital offense (instead of one permitting bail at P20,000, or less than a thousand dollars). But as usual it was in no hurry, unlike its haste to adjourn once the threat to the capital city's security was manifest. Asked whether the cabinet, or cabinet cluster 'E' (security and foreign affairs) had discussed martial law, Ramos said that, in many hours of meetings, such had never come up. In seven and a half hours of cabinet meetings with President Aquino, Ramos said:

there was no mention of the word martial law . . . But the word law was very much emphasized, which is respect for the law because we are talking about the oil crisis, the safety and the welfare of our Filipino workers overseas, how to get out those that need to be evacuated . . .

How to get everybody in the political, social, economic, and military and police sectors to work together so that these objectives could be maintained. That is principally, protection of our democracy, maintaining our stability, and getting everybody to adhere to the law.[21]

It is true that Aquino made some attempts to respond to the sense of national emergency. She appeared before some garbage mounds and suggested that something be done about them. But it was, Amando Doronila suggested, at this point merely a "cosmetic gesture."[22] She was attempting to put back together the cause coalition that had brought her to power, but it was a little late.

This expenditure of kinetic energy has not reassured the people . . . that the presidency is now providing leadership. Since the . . . earthquake, floods and Gulf conflict, the terror bombing campaign, and the intensification of coup rumors . . . groups of citizens . . . have been meeting and expressing concern about the vacuum in political leadership and about the volatility of politics.

The leadership was not preparing the populace for the inevitable rise in oil prices, which could touch off a "chain of events the government may not be able to control," Doronila went on. And the president's own brother-in-law, Senator Agapito Aquino, said that in the palace, " 'no adrenalin is flowing.' "

By the end of 1990, the NPA alliance with RAM and the YOU front "Soldiers of the Filipino People" was carrying out operations in the field. True, they were, according to the reported plan, "pocket rebellions in remote areas in the country." Nevertheless, in one at the end of November, the rebels took control of a military communications relay station, a sugar mill, a logging firm, and ambushed the responding AFP soldiers.[23]

The real point is that the "objective" condition of the country was worsening; a leaked analysis from military intelligence argued that the Communist movement was gaining ground among the middle and lower classes thanks to the worsening political and economic situation, brought to a head by the oil price increases. "The document cautioned government against imposing drastic measures which would push further the people towards the Communist line. It concluded that 'the national bearing at the moment appears fragile yet explosive in the face of political and deep economic crisis induced by unexpected confluence of events' "[24]

The only thing countering the sense of inevitability of a coup was that the armed forces began to get serious about sentencing coup-makers of the past. Throughout 1990 the sentences that emerged from the slow-moving judicial system increased in severity. At the end of the year, eighty-one officers and enlisted men were sentenced to terms ranging from twelve to thirty-two years for their role in the 1987 attempt. These were the stiffest sentences ever.[25] An informal survey taken at the same time claimed that "Army soldiers are no longer sympathetic to military rebels compared to ... previous years,"[26] the kind of coincidence that usually accompanies such strong signals of intent. Army leaders said that it meant that reform was really occurring and that the majority [sic] would now fight rebel soldiers, and "most of them support civilian authority over the military."[27] Although it was unlikely that the falling-off would be rapid enough to compensate for the increased rebel recruitment thanks to the oil-price increase, at least it went in the right direction and perhaps offered help for the longer run.

The Return of the Cronies

The trial of Imelda Marcos in New York on charges of mail fraud, obstruction of justice, and racketeering again showed the preoccupation—indeed the obsession—of the Aquino government with the past. To be sure, anyone acquainted with the pattern of corruption in the Marcos era and with Imelda Marcos's style of operation could not doubt that she was guilty of the charges made. The judge even, in charging the jury, reminded them that Mrs. Marcos did not have to have physically stolen funds herself, only that she was aware of the process by which money came the way of the first family.

But Manila overinvested in its desired outcome from the start. It hired, at a cost of $10,000 a month, a public relations firm merely to publicize the findings of the New York court.[28] In so doing, however, it helped to create precisely the atmosphere that Marcos's defense was trying to prove existed—a government in the Philippines eager to hound a grieving widow—so as to get Imelda off the hook. In any event, the prosecution had to prove to the jury that she had violated U.S. law on the specific transactions relating to the properties at issue—not merely that she in general knew that great abuse took place to bring her so vast a fortune.[29]

As it happened, the evidence was circumstantial, and the jury acquitted her. Marcos's victory, in July 1990, had immediate and long-term repercussions on

Filipino (or Filipina) politics. Of course it added more venom to relations between the two countries. It emboldened Danding Cojuangco, it amused Aquino's critics, and it took some of the determination out of Bush administration support for her regime. After all, there were those in Washington who had never taken too seriously (or cared about) the reality of large-scale Marcos family corruption. The court decision even raised the possibility of a "war of the widows," as Time termed it,30 with the two women slugging it out in the 1992 election, which would have been one of the more amusing historical exercises of angels versus witchcraft.

Once Imelda had won, however, the cronies began coming out of the woodwork, making deals with the Presidential Commission on Good Government (PCGG), which President Aquino set up to get the money back. The problem was that after four and a half years of research, litigation, and pressure, the PCGG had little to show, and the government was no better off; it had to start making the deals that it could.[31] But that meant that the cronies could come back and reestablish their positions with more money than a strong government would have allowed—needing less of it to assault the fortresses of power.

The first major deal was with Marcos's close friend Roberto Benedicto, who settled for P1.2 billion—or at the declining peso's value, less than $50 million, surely a small fraction of what the sugar king was worth. The PCGG claimed it had got all the "ill-gotten" assets of banana king Antonio Floirindo and of José Campos, by separating what they had to start with and what they acquired under Mr. Marcos.

Danding Cojuangco, however, chose a different path back to respectability—the judicial system—and he went from success to success. Using his excellent legal advisers, he simply battered away in the Sandiganbayan, the antigraft court, until he got his assets back, including his shares in the United Coconut Planters Bank. No less than the Supreme Court, for example, reversed the PCGG in ordering that he be permitted to vote his shares in the largest Philippine corporation, San Miguel, in which he had a virtual controlling interest—and which made that company the presumed de facto paymaster of at least one campaign in the presidential sweepstakes.

The big deal was with Mrs. Marcos—and both sides claimed it was for $6 billion. Since reportedly that included 60 percent of her Hong Kong accounts worth $867 million, we might then presume she was keeping at least 40 percent of her other assets. For one thing, such validated the worst fears of Marcos opponents, when one realizes that $10 billion was the size of the entire Philippine economy when the Marcos couple took office. In fact, it was to prove much harder to get money out of Imelda than was at first thought, and in the end no deal was forthcoming. Nor could the PCGG get the assets in Switzerland that at one point looked forthcoming, in the first such openness of those banks, because Swiss law provided that the defendant be tried and found guilty in the country of origin of the alleged fraud. But Aquino would not take the risk of allowing Imelda to come back until late 1991, when she reversed herself. But there was no danger.

Amando Doronila—an alumnus of martial law prisons—saw the point:

> Whatever the outcome of all the cases filed by the PCGG aimed at the recovery of the Marcos and crony wealth, the overthrow of the Marcos regime had destroyed neither the cronies' economic base from which they can mount political action, possibly antagonistic to the interests of the present government, nor their capacity to play key political roles.

> Either because of the eagerness of the PCGG to enter into compromise deals which are now seen as disadvantageous to the government or because of the less than competent efforts by the government to flush out the hidden assets, the fact remains that the cronies' economic power base has not been broken.[32]

There was to be a simple test of "crony power," namely the 1992 election. A year and a half prior to it, about the time serious presidential contenders get going in the Philippines, a popular preference poll showed Miriam Defensor-Santiago, whom we last encountered slaying dragons at the Department of Agrarian Reform, at the top of the heap, with 48.7 percent, presumably precisely because of her no-holds-barred blunt willingness to take on dragons (but what turned out to be windmills). Second, with 31.7 percent was Senator Estrada, a popular movie star, who more than any of his colleagues was riding an anti-American horse.[33] Senator Enrile came in third, followed by Ramos, Mrs. Aquino, Senator Salonga, Vice President Laurel, House Speaker Mitra, Mrs. Marcos (with 6.4 percent): and last—and certainly not least—Eduardo "Danding" Cojuangco, with 5.7 percent.[34]

The question was, how much would that list correspond to the certified list of candidates when the real race began, after the power and money brokers had looked to their interests? Barring something of a populist miracle, what was more likely was that the list would be turned almost upside down. For one thing, Ramos had far more institutional strength than the poll suggested. Indeed, another survey in mid-1991 showed him topping the list.[35] And he might well end up with a presidential blessing. But the way Philippine politics has always worked is that where the money is, the people fall into line—assuming the candidate is presentable. Danding, "Mr. Basketball," and presumably the man with the access to the largest sums of money, had networks upon networks. He had the surviving Marcos organization and the support of the Marcos children, not to mention his areas of support in Negros, Davao, and Palawan, where he owned great farms. Those were the kind of assets to be turned into votes in the election. And, indeed, by late 1991, six months before the election, Danding's forces could report that he topped a survey, with Santiago and Imelda Marcos sharing second place.[36] Where money not only buys votes but buys surveys, there were bound to be many more of tests—but it seemed that the tide was moving in Danding's favor.

Once again what looked like a revolutionary phase in the Philippines had concluded without a revolution. In an otherwise brilliant analysis of politics in the Philippine countryside, Gary Hawes, a Western analyst, concluded that, because the "peaceful avenues to change" were being closed off by the military and rural elite, "more and more people are turning to the only other avenue for change that seems both available to the poor and weak, and likely to succeed—the National Democratic Front."[37] This expressed the triumph of hope over experience rather than empirical observation. But Hawes's instincts were right. It was just that the still-feudal structures that he himself analyzed so well made revolution unlikely.

It was a measure of how bad things were that anyone traveling to Manila to advise Aquino had to account for her subsequent behavior despite the presumably good advice being rendered. It was reported that she was relying more and more on her prayer sessions with friends, and she was also thinking positively. She told a *Time* reporter that she read only the front pages of eight of Manila's papers, because she wished "to start out the day feeling very positive and confident."[38]

A "revolutionary" new concept and organization was in fact created in 1991 in an attempt to fill the void between government and citizen, "KABISIG," or partnership, about which much was to be written and said. Aquino in her last year seemed to be investing enormously in KABISIG to have something to leave behind,[39] and her ministers devoted much time and energy to finding ways to energize the citizenry in accordance with the precepts of KABISIG.

In a candid discussion of NGOs and KABISIG, one important NGO leader, Dr. Antonio Ledesma, suggested a positive approach to the concept, on the theory that Aquino was desperate for support for her poverty-alleviation program, which the trapos were unwilling to support, "so in desperation she throws out this idea of a KABISIG, hoping that her nongovernmental organization support groups will come to the rescue, for the sake of a common good that was momentarily seen in EDSA in 1986." But Francis Sionil-José, a writer and reformer, immediately poured "cold water" on that notion. "If Cory was really interested, she could have, during the very first months of her rule, issued a very far-reaching decree on agrarian reform which she was capable of doing because she had declared a revolutionary government."[40] And as another said, her impression of KABISIG, from a primer being distributed, was "vague." "From what I got from this primer, it seems like a way of life or an attitude."[41]

Father Ledesma hypothesized that KABISIG represented Aquino's attempt to "break away from the traditional politicians,"[42] to give power back to the people. Such was a very hopeful concept, and it required that one first be hopeful about KABISIG, which looked from afar like just one more attempt to fill the body politic with fluff.

NOTES

1. The phrase is Amando Doronila's, in "Longest Reigning Lame-Duck Leader," *Manila Chronicle* (26 September 1990).
2. "There are other ways of expressing appreciation," interview by Cristina Pastor and Paulynn Sicam, *Manila Chronicle* (17 December 1989). The scholar (and also this author) had no connection with the Heritage Foundation (which, in any event, could hardly be seen to be trying to destabilize the Filipino government), but was closely identified, while in the Reagan administration, with the Democracy Project, which led (*inter alia*) to the creation of the National Endowment for Democracy.
3. Quoting paraphrase in Noel T. Pangilinan, "Gomez Admits Corruption in Cory Gov't," *Daily Globe* (19 May 1990).
4. W. Scott Thompson, *New York Times*, Op-Ed page (5 January 1990), p. A31.
5. See Nestor Mata, "American intervention!" *Manila Standard* (18 January 1990).
6. See endnote 4, this chapter.
7. Though that scholar was a White House-appointed member of the Board of Directors of the United States Institute of Peace and, as known to many journalists in Manila, had served in the first Reagan administration five years earlier.
8. See Yen Makabenta, "Ramos under the Microscope," *Daily Globe* (4 April 1991): "Of all presidential contenders, Ramos clearly is the best known today to the international community. And the name recognition has been alloyed by immodest suggestions from some foreigners in recent times of trouble that he take over from Mrs. Aquino."
9. "Senator Proposes Resignation of Cabinet Members," Manila Radio News (3 September 1990), in Foreign Broadcast Information Service-East Asia-90-173 (6 September 1990), p. 48. Hereafter FBIS-EAS.
10. Manny Mogato, "Military Intelligence Fears Communist Gains," *Manila Chronicle* (10 December 1990), in FBIS-EAS-90-238 (11 December 1990), p. 50.
11. Quezon City Radio (11 December 1990), in FBIS-EAS-90-238 (11 December 1990), p. 44.
12. Manila DWIZ Radio News (24 November 1990), in FBIS-EAS-90-229, p. 55.
13. Manila Broadcasting Company (7 December 1990), in FBIS-EAS-90-238, p. 45.
14. Tokyo KYODO in English (18 December 1990), in FBIS-EAS-90-20 (18 December 1990), p. 42.
15. Manila *Diyaryo Filipino* in Tagalog (8 August 1990), in FBIS-EAS-90-154 (9 August 1990), p. 45.

16. *Manila Bulletin* (27 August 1990).

17. "Ramos, de Villa Interviewed," Quezon City Radio-Television Arts Network in English (23 August 1990), FBIS-EAS-90-167 (28 August 1990), p. 35.

18. "Dark Beginnings for National Police," *Manila Chronicle* (6 March 1991), in FBIS-EAS-91-044 (6 March 1991), p. 43.

19. Alex Magno, "NPA's New 'Pol-Mil' Concept Summarized," *Manila Chronicle* (5 August 1990), in FBIS-EAS-90-152 (7 August 1990), p. 45.

20. Davide Commission, *Republic of the Philippines*, "The Final Report of the Fact-Finding Commission" (pursuant to R.A. No. 6832) (Manila: October 1990), p. 246.

21. "Ramos Comments on Threats," Defense Dept. Radio in Tagalog, (23 August 1990), in FBIS-EAS-90-165 (24 August 1990), p. 27.

22. "Columnist Assesses Aquino's 'Complacency'," *The Manila Chronicle* (14 September 1990), in FBIS-EAS-90-183 (20 September 1990), 52.

23. Manila Broadcasting Company (26 November 1990), in FBIS-EAS-90-228 (27 November 1990), p. 32.

24. Mogato, "Military Intelligence Fears Communist Gains," p. 50.

25. *Philippine Daily Inquirer* (20 December 1990), in FBIS-EAS-90-246 (21 December 1990), p. 56.

26. Manny Mogato, "Army no longer Sympathetic to Military Rebels," *Manila Chronicle* (20 December 1990), in FBIS-EAS-90-246 (21 December 1990), p. 58.

27. *Ibid.*

28. I am grateful to Chwat/Weigend Associates for bringing the papers of registration to my attention.

29. Cited in Karl Jackson, "The Philippines: The Search for a Suitable Democratic Solution, 1946-1986," p. 8.

30. "A Muddle-Through Mode," *Time* (16 July 1990), p. 40. See also Ariel Bocobo's column six months earlier, whose first line is "The War of Widows: A Fanciful Scenario," *Manila Standard* (1990).

31. There were even rumors spreading, some by people whose information was usually accurate, that the PCGG members themselves were getting the first access to the "confiscated" fortunes.

32. "Cronies Potential for Power," Part Two, *Manila Chronicle* (22 November 1990), in FBIS-EAS-90-226 (23 November 1990), p. 41.

33. Amando Doronila observed that Estrada reached his popularity by "blaming the ills of the country exclusively on the prolonged American presence." *Manila Chronicle* (27 November 1990), in FBIS-EAS-90-229 (28 November 1990), p. 55.

34. *Manila Chronicle* (26 November 1990).

35. Conducted by the NIC 2000 Foundation. See Tony S. Bergonia, "Ramos to Meet Aquino on 'Presidential Plans'," *Philippine Daily Inquirer* (20 March 1991), in FBIS-EAS-91-054 (20 March 1991), p. 52.

36. "Danding Tops Radio Survey," News Release, 27 October 1991, Chwat/Weigend Associates, Washington.

37. Gary Hawes, "Aquino and Her Administration: A View from the Country-side," *Pacific Affairs* 62, 1 (Spring 1989), p. 28.
38. Sandra Burton, "A Muddle-Through Mode," *Time* (16 July 1990), p. 36.
39. And, possibly, to go forward to as well. Aquino revealed in March 1991 that she planned, after leaving Malacañang Palace in 1992, to devote her time to NGOs, which might explain her enthusiasm for KABISIG. See Fred Lobo, *Manila Bulletin* (4 March 1991), in FBIS-EAS-91-042 (4 March 1991), p. 31.
40. "People Empowerment for National Development: Nongovernment Organizations in the '90s," Solidarity Seminar Series on Public Issues, No. 23, *Solidarity* (July-September 1990), No. 127, p. 27.
41. *Ibid.*
42. *Ibid.*, p. 31.

10

Conclusion

In the early 1970s—as perhaps a decade before that—it was possible to argue, as many (including this writer) did, that the Philippines would prosper more than Thailand in the ensuing years. Thailand had endured an indolent dictatorship for over a decade, it was nearer the Vietnamese fires, and it had at least the beginnings of a serious insurgency.

The Philippines, in contrast, blessed by geography, had more insulation from the regional wars and a history of protection by its former colonizers in any case. Economic growth was higher, and once martial law was proclaimed, despite the presidential excesses already apparent, it seemed that many of the historic developmental bottlenecks were to be cleared away by palace fiat.

By the end of the 1980s, Thailand was booming and had already been proclaimed the new NIC; optimistic Filipinos could hope that within a decade their country could advance to the state from which it could take off to NIC status, but heroic assumptions were necessary.[1]

To say that the Philippines in the interval endured Marcos while Thailand moved to a more adaptive, more competitive political mode is to say—and explain—much, but not all. For not all the trends reversed with Marcos's removal; in some cases the damage stopped being added to, but did not seem repairable. In the case of the insurgency, things got worse for a time, and the reason is that none of the root conditions had changed or were changing. The example of birth control is also revealing. At a time when United Nations

Population Fund could report that 51 percent of couples in the developing world—up from 10 percent a generation ago—were using birth control methods, the subject was still officially almost taboo in the Philippines, and the population continued to soar, with all the implications for the country a generation from now. But in Thailand, fertility "has fallen steeply."[2]

Some economic data shed light on the comparison of the two countries. Thailand gives few appearances of an egalitarian society—or one even minimally concerned with equity if one's perspective is Bangkok. But whereas in the kingdom average income of the top fifth of households in the mid-1980s was three times the bottom fifth, in the Philippines the top fifth was *ten* times the bottom fifth.[3] The difference, of course, was in the rural sector, and that is where development must start.

The tax effort of the two countries is also revealing. At a time when Philippine per capita income still exceeded Thailand's, the republic was making only a 10 to 12 percent of GNP tax effort, compared to the kingdom's 15 percent in 1986.[4] IMF data show that few professionals and self-employed pay income tax; of those who do, they pay an average of 1 percent of gross income.

An excellent opportunity to see clearly what was going wrong in the Philippines is seen in reports undertaken by the International Monetary Fund between 1989 and 1991, on Manila's request for extended arrangements and possible access to contingency financing and then later on Manila's request for standby arrangements and purchase under the compensatory and contingency financing facility. In 1989 the fund was all optimism; there had been, after all, three years of virtuous growth after the economy's grind nearly to a halt in the late Marcos years. It recommended generous support to the Philippines. By early 1991, however, the picture was far less rosy. While its analysts fully took into account the bad luck the country had had—the earthquake and typhoon, the war in the Gulf—and conceded that these had been sufficient to derail the program, they plainly were not a sufficient part of the explanation of what went wrong. As an IMF official put it, "much of the blame for the collapse of the program lies in the government's failure to sustain a firm consensus among the parties to the policy-making process, along with weak policy implementation. A comprehensive strategy fell apart owing to a lack of determination in the face of all the obstacles, internal and external."[5] Of course, it was pretty much what we have seen along the way in the political arena.

That a serious and solid core of democratic sentiment and commitment existed in the Philippines was never in doubt. Democracy, as we have argued, is, in a young state, a tender and fragile plant to be nurtured. There is no point at which its survival can be taken for granted. And in crisis, democracy is most sensitive. After the Gulf War started, the *Manila Chronicle* editorialized

> it remains unclear whether the government can respond quickly to the incendiary oil crisis. It is required to demonstrate that a democratic system can be resilient enough to cope with crisis and can summon the people's loyalty to constitutional democracy. Unfortunately, it has failed to demonstrate the competence that it can make democracy function. Not many people are willing to swear by an incompetent government even if it piously professes faith in democracy.[6]

If it continued to profess faith in democracy, it had almost ceased to in equity, and did little to hide its indifference. The Senate president and House speaker "announced that Congress is not planning on enforcing new tax measures to reduce the budget deficit," by imposing higher taxes on the rich.[7] And Aquino refused to see the Labor Advisory Consultative Council, since their agenda was the raising of the minimum wage, and technically they should see regional wage boards first. True, there was no money for a raise;

	Survey area		Socioeconomic Class		
ATENEO PUBLIC OPINION SURVEY[8]					
Questionnaire Item	RP	Metro Manila	ABC	D	E
• *Possibility of the Filipino people completely losing faith in peaceful means of promoting democracy*					
February 1988					
Possible	50	58	55	49	50
Undecided	21	19	21	22	19
Not possible	23	21	22	23	23
March 1990					
Possible	40	49	41	43	35
Undecided	23	12	21	26	21
Not possible	30	37	34	26	34
• *Possibility of the Filipino people choosing a military government over a civilian government*					
March 1990					
Possible	31	33	28	32	30
Undecided	21	9	20	25	16
Not possible	42	57	47	37	46

but the president of the republic in those circumstances at the least can give hope—rather than a slammed door in the face.

All democracy had come down to in the Philippines, during the Aquino era, was an attempted guarantee, for the moment, against another dictator. The multiple institutions, the locally elected officials, and the power and prestige of Senate and congressional leaders tended to ensure that another Marcos would not gain power. Or would he? For there were the other possibilities that had to be considered, flowing directly from what has been discussed at length herein. One of these was of course a coup d'état. There were several possible venues for coups. One was that a coup by radical rebels of YOU would be imminent, leading General Ramos to seize power from within, preemptively. It was a scenario long rumored, as we have seen.

If YOU took power, what would it do? It was undoubtedly the most realistic chance for radical reform the republic had ever had. It would not be getting prescriptions from other capitals and in the end would no doubt be Filipino in its spirit and style—and thus kinder and gentler than its counterparts elsewhere in the third world. But it was difficult to envisage how the oligarchy could survive their program. If YOU came to power despite the opposition of the powers that be, then presumably there would be scores to settle.

The other possibility was that the election would indeed take place in 1992, and that Danding Cojuangco, or a cohort of his, would win it. Weak and strong presidents have alternated in Philippine history—but seldom was there such weakness as in the Aquino administration, and seldom had there been such awesomely strong potential as in Danding. And with the backing of the Marcos organization (and of his children), and strong bases in Davao, Negros, and of course central Luzon where his business interests were great, he had a solid foundation for the campaign. The likelihood that he would, once taking residence in Malacañang, behave like a Franco or at least a de Gaulle was strong. He would have the model of his master, but the lessons thereof as well. So no doubt he would keep the institutions of democracy, or a facade. It was hard to see much more surviving.

So there was the very real possibility that the Philippines, always one of the most conspicuous and one of the first of the league of new democratic states, would be the first to leave the club. It would be a sad development, but the sadness could be mixed with the realization that democracy in the form practiced during this period was apparently not the best thing for the largest number of people; it had not worked, or it had not worked well enough.

One of the problems was of course that, although the economy took off after the Marcoses' departure, it could not provide enough new jobs or goods in a few short years to satisfy the pent-up demands, nor enough to forestall the desire on the part of many for drastic change. Although the economy grew, as we have seen, by a respectable 6 percent, give or take a little, for the first few years, it began declining in 1989, with the brownouts, the coup attempt, and then the earthquake, Persian Gulf crisis, and eruption of Mt. Pinatubo. The result was that the Philippines had its first deficit in five Aquino years, of $183 million, contrasting with a surplus of more than twice that the year before. The head of the National Economic and Development Authority, Cayetano Paderanga, Jr., was reasonably optimistic, nonetheless, with the Gulf War over (from which many construction and other contracts should follow), that a successful new ($3.3 billion) pledging session of the Philippine Assistance Program (PAP) donors and a decreasing threat from rightist elements, would lead to faster growth.[9] The *Manila Chronicle*, however, editorialized that Mr. Paderanga was head of a "planning body, not an implementing agency."

> He is also not the source of political will, and the administration, which is, shows no evidence that it is using the euphoria to forge a consensus; it also needs political will to get Congress to form a consensus. We agree with Mr. Padaranga's analysis, but we are looking for the thing called "will." It has never been in evidence during the past six years.[10]

The problem of "getting it together" was well underlined by Senator Paterno, who officially reported that PAP donors observed that the Philippines "could do a better job of 'urging a consensus' on how to put its economic house in order." The PAP would continue, he said, only if we "get our act together," according to the major donors, and another meeting in twelve months would assess whether they had. There was goodwill among the donors, he said, "but also a skepticism about [the Philippines'] ability to deliver, and show-me attitude prevails among them."[11] It was the old question posed, in more analytic terms, by Professor Ranis: Could Filipinos, among themselves, sort out their obligations for their greater good, make some sacrifices for the greater good, and get on with it?[12]

Then what was the problem in the Philippines during the Aquino era? We have periodically mentioned the lack of leadership as the most obvious problem. Yet other comparable countries have advanced without strong leadership.

Consider Thailand anew. Under a series of weak leaders—there being a brief exception—the kingdom became a NIC. But the uniting dimension of leadership was fulfilled by a monarch who had recouped the glory of the Chakri throne in this same period. And the purposive role of leadership was played by a bureaucracy with historic coherence, of a territory centripetally looking to the capital. There was, as well, an evolving but essentially settled societal compact on the role of the military: they were major players. True, the overall evolution seemed to be in the direction of a diminution of their role, even in spite of the 1989 coup. In any event, no one would count them out, and they were there to maintain their view of minimal stability in the kingdom.

The Philippines had no traditional leaders, not even the partial role that the Tungkus or kings of Malaysia play as rotating heads of state. The president therefore uniquely is responsible for bringing together, symbolically and in practice, all the disparate peoples and interests of the archipelago. As Teodoro Benigno put it, "the very person of the president" brings with it "a certain mystique" in the culture and minds of Filipinos.[13] So too do most heads of state—but in most countries with elected leaders, there are intermediate strata of bureaucracy and power that compensate for periods of weak leadership at the top. In the Philippines these were too weak to mitigate Corazon Aquino's defects.

Nor was there adequate leadership below President Aquino. Her most talented official, Fidel V. Ramos, had the same inclination she had to avoid the excesses of dictatorship. With him, as with her, it was also a matter of preferred personal style. There is no doubt that his staff brilliance, hard work, and deep knowledge of counterinsurgency doctrine allowed the orchestration of his program to bring about a strategic victory over the New People's Army. It stopped short of the critical last step—the coordination of security and development; more than 25 percent of security and development in each other's ministerial or political calculations was needed if the republic were to synergize its efforts in ending the insurgency once and for all.

The question is begged; Eddie Ramos would therefore have perforce had to be a dictator, of sorts, to solve the basic development and security conundrum that was at the heart of the regime's and the élite's long-term survival. Probably. He would have had to assume the power for local government, rather than defer to DOLA for leadership at every level of the ladder of cooperation between barangay and nation. He gave them the lead to give them the incentive to produce, but it did not work that way and was unlikely to. He would have had to be the tough guy in style that he surely was by his record—though anything but in appearance.

He nevertheless stands out as the real winner of the period, the person who performed a historical service, gave his country his best, and in the end could point to the defeat of one more iteration of the nation's insurgency. And all this with compassion and dignity.

And if at the time of writing it did not look as if his attempt to "empower" his country through a popular movement with marvelous goals—and little machinery—would work, he quickly made his peace with the ruling Laban ng Demokratikong Pilipino party and moved into a position where he might well again become the candidate to beat, on the road to Malacañang.

The country's geography also works against its leaders; if power gravitated toward the center under Marcos, the archipelagic nature of the republic always mitigated the center's harshness. With Marcos gone, there was nothing but sentiment and the attraction of development funds located in Manila to draw the country together.

What makes a leader effective? The psychohistorical function is one thing: the leader must symbolize, through his or her own emotional development, the aspirations of a critical mass of a people. But then the leader must be able to identify the problems that are soluble and take concrete steps, by their priority, to resolve them: by galvanizing ministries, encouraging local constituencies, giving incentives to democratic politicians, to use their capital to see the program through.

Aquino did represent the republic's psychohistorical development in her first year in office. Her dream of revenge and parallel rise to power synchronized well with the nation's dream of getting rid of the dictator and repairing the damage. But having been the deliverer in the first year and a half, she became the delivered in August 1987—saved from a coup attempt by the military that remained loyal. Her own sense of entitlement meant she never faltered in conveying her right to her office: it is in fact astonishing that the connection between her weakness and the propensity to coups remained unstated until the month before the Great Coup; but that was the function externally of the misunderstanding of her mandate and internally of the respect accorded to the palace in all circumstances.

In fact, any group with a medium and a message seemed capable of seizing power from the Aquino government, so lightly did it hold onto power. Gringo Honasan, working wholly outside the system, was able to organize a coup against a system that had every reason to expect a coup, and that was because he had a *system*—albeit one revolving around his magnetic persona.

Aquino had no system. Her government was always a grab bag of reformers and trapos, and the only litany they had in common was negative, against Marcos, who was history. Businessmen such as José Concepcion were there to line their pockets, trapos such as Luis Santos were there to keep the old Manila-based system functioning, but for the most part there is little to record of ministerial achievement, apart from Ramos's imminent defeat of the NPA.

Even the goal of democracy was kept with more attention to form than substance; elections were held but nothing was done to prevent the large and substantial abuse of the system by an élite whose wealth had made possible the subversion of real democracy over the generations. Small wonder, then, that late in 1990 a usually reliable Social Weather Station survey found that 45 percent of the public thought that democracy was no longer viable—with only 15 percent thinking that it *was*.[14] Malaysian Prime Minister Mahathir might not be the best person to lecture on democracy, but he made an important point in early 1991, one directed at the Philippines in all its disarray:

> In espousing democracy and free enterprise, nations are finding that it is easier to declare the intention, or to overthrow authoritarian regimes even, than to obtain tangible benefits from democratic freedom and the market economy.
>
> People power is fine. It can remove dictators and corrupt governments. But power corrupts and people power can be no less corrupting. Once it is realized that political power can be achieved through getting people on to the streets, the potentially corrupt can also resort to this weapon for their own ends. Indeed, the overthrow of the corrupt often results in the installation of another leader who is or becomes equally corrupt. It is easier to overthrow [an] allegedly corrupt Government than to materialize a Government that can rehabilitate the nation.[15]

And Aquino had done just that; a corrupt government got tossed, but whatever else happened, the new government failed to rehabilitate the nation. For beyond reinstituting the forms of democracy—which it did straight-away—its only real goal was the negative one of getting rid of the Marcos heritage; the rest were just words, words to deceive or at least to distract; or words to appease. Consider the gentle and elegant but still damning metaphor with which the Davide Commission wraps up its monumental work, calling for a "firmer and more direct hand at the helm" for a democracy in a "crisis of transition . . . People understand that a ship is never always on course. But the ship that arrives safely at its destination is the one which constantly checks its bearings, corrects itself on time, and accelerates its speed when it is firmly on course."[16]

Other than the breakup of the cronies' system, the only important reforms that in fact were implemented were largely dictated or driven from outside—

the orchestrated insistence of the IMF, World Bank, and U.S. Government that reforms of the economic system be initiated, and even these were done halfheartedly, especially privatization.

The Aquino era—as opposed to Corazon Aquino's term—came to an end not because of a lack of virtue or good intentions but because of a lack of minimal competence and because of the innate arrogance of aristocracy. Nestor Mata summed it up well when, after the routine praise for her "singular and historic achievement of leading the peaceful struggle to restore democracy," he doubly faulted her, as crisis piled on crisis in early 1990, first for her "inadequacy" in running the government; and second for failing "to remember the wise counsel of her own husband, that 'without criticism no government can survive, and without dissent no government can effectively govern' "—all to have been avoided "with just a little modesty and honesty on her part."[17]

Her presidency was indeed, as Amando Doronila put it, "pushed to the wall" by events in her last two years. But her response was made up of "rhetorical ploys declaring that she is tough." Her presidency was passive, "an ornament in the seat of power, unable to use the levers of power. In effect, she transformed herself into the longest-serving lame-duck president in the history of the Republic."[18] When General Ramos gave an unqualified endorsement to Aquino when she still had twenty months to go, committing himself and the whole armed forces to defending her to the last day of June 1992, he was presumably once again underlining his own constitutionalism—as well as his availability for that office.[19]

The twin goals of development and security, which we defined as the central goals of any country, were not well met in this period. The real opportunity to achieve a breakthrough in economic development, with the enormous flows of aid directed to Manila, was prevented by the absence of any societal compact or contract; everyone just rushed in for what he could get for himself. Security, on the other hand, had improved in the rural sector, since the rapid growth of the NPA during Marcos's last years was arrested, and the insurgency seemed to be in its final phase.

But security of the regime declined, and it is on that that so much of the confidence building in other areas depends. Seven coup attempts, two huge ones, infected the Philippines with the disease of a proneness to coups in the future. The leading cadre of the 1989 attempt could all be captured, but the example they had set was too substantial not to inspire one or another junior alumnus to try again. And the YOU was figuring out something very basic—basic in most other countries, new to the Philippines: radical reform as a slogan could harness People Power again, if it continued to appear that the reality of reform was blocked by an élite that had long had a stranglehold on power in the republic.

President Aquino had chance after chance to make development and security synergistic. But she would have had to be tougher—for example, on the soldiers of the early coup attempts who learned that their efforts to seize power brought sharp increases to the military budget at best, and at first pushups as punishment at worst. She would have had to oversee herself the release of resources through POCs to insurgent-ridden areas in ways that would have led to virtuous development. And she would have had to get rid of corrupt ministers earlier on, especially those in areas where examples of virtuous economic growth were needed. The pace at which corruption seemed to increase in her official family during her term was not unprecedented in the Philippines. The problem is that it was precisely so very normal and predictable—against all her commitments. When the odor of greed on a large scale began to be present, as when the bases were on the verge of turnover to Filipinos, it became possible that Aquino's administration might be known even more for its hypocrisy than its good intentions.

The whole ordeal of the final base negotiations is instructive. It was dreadful and self-destructive statecraft. It is very easy to see the logic, even the glory, of the senate's decision to reject the treaty. But the Philippines is a poor country and needed the money, for which there was no evident replacement. And all Asia wished the bases to remain: the Japanese prime minister allegedly gave that as his top message on his visit *in media res* to Manila; indeed, the highly informed *Far Eastern Economic Review* reported, in the context of the prime minister's visit, that for the Japanese, without a bases treaty, "the billion-dollar Philippine Aid Program (PAP) would be at risk."[20]

The point is that there were so very many other ways that the emotional growth the nationalists sought could have been obtained. On the negative side, an American diplomat said,

> Our delegation arrived to be told that the old agreement had been terminated— several months before that could possibly be construed in the agreement, and in reality well over a year. Then for a year and a half they jerked us around. Perhaps it sounds patronizing, but we had hoped to help educate them to the new realities, of what our congress would support, of the declining importance for the bases strategically world-wide. We intended to guide them through our ratification process so that the money they wanted from us and on which we agreed in principle would in fact be forthcoming. Instead, we got gripes and moans, petulance, arrogance, attitude, and insults, especially about how we were treating

them as lessers than the Germans and Japanese, for example; we showed them the respective agreements—the really relevant difference being that in the German and Japanese agreements, they pay us, instead of our paying them.[21]

In other words, the Filipinos scored points for self-gratification. And in the process failed to notice how rapidly the world was changing. By the time the negotiations were over, no one in Washington was really interested.

The end came as a Greek tragedy — minus, alas the catharsis. After the Senate's September 1991 vote rejecting the bases treaty, Aquino proffered a three-year phaseout (as seen earlier) subject to negotiability. But like a marriage of high-strung partners that has already begun to unravel, the relationship from this point could only go down.

On the American side, there was an almost audible indifference to the negotiations and even to having Subic, in part, of course, because strategy was changing so fast, but also out of pique for being "at the wrong end of the yo-yo," as one American diplomat said of the year and a half of talks.

On the Filipino side, the situation was more complicated. It was simply not believed that Uncle Sam really would leave. One American involved in the negotiation said:

> The day we were to turn Clark Air Force Base over to them, the Army and Police were firing at each other to get in first and rip out all the stoves, air conditioners, and any other valuables. We asked them to wait until the actual hour of change of command. They refused. The streets of Angeles City were littered with American merchandise stolen from the base. They still wouldn't believe we would leave.[22]

Then, there were new personae. In addition to a new American ambassador trying to salvage the talks, there was a new Executive Secretary at the palace dominating the Filipino delegation: Franklin Drilon, a lawyer and law professor, who brought ancient baggage of Philippine grievances on status of forces agreements (SOFA), which had not been an issue in the previous year and a half. It was essentially an issue of the 1960s.

But as the American interest in the outcome of the talks declined — since there was a diminishing gain available — there was a corresponding lack of interest in conceding anything — on SOFA, on nuclear issues, on whatever. So from the Philippine point of view, Washington stonewalled, while Manila self-destructed.

When the talks collapsed at the very end of 1991, with an advisory for the U.S. Navy to be out in a year, Washington said it would comply — and that was that, to everyone's astonishment. Now Manila would have to deal with roughly six thousand new jobless and their families, and much less aid.

Many investors — multilateral and bilateral, commercial and governmental — would put plans on the shelf. Raul Manglapus registered his surprise and irritation, especially that his ASEAN allies were rushing to pick up the profitable American military pieces, even the Indonesians who had privately counseled steadfastness against the Americans, he was telling people.

The Filipinos had killed the father, as so many had urged. They had not yet found something to put in his place. "It was their Bar Mitzvah," an American diplomat commented, "their coming of age. But they blew it — with the international financial community, the Japanese, most of all themselves. They couldn't get their act together."[23] It was perhaps revealing that the campaign of the gentlest and kindest presidential candidate, General Ramos, was foundering, just as Imelda Marcos declared her candidacy. The situation cried out for a strongman, and there were many volunteers, with Governor Danding Cojuangco benefitting the most from the international and domestic political vacuum. Democracy was unlikely to be a beneficiary of the base closures, given the economic and psychological costs at this particular time. There had never been any disagreement that the bases should go, but at this point more than ever there was a need to phase them out in an orderly way, minimally disrupting the economy. The Philippines was to have the worst of all worlds.

Such conclusions in the political arena might well parallel that to which economists at the IMF came in their own field. The Philippines got its act together politically even less than economically; at least economically there are a finite number of decision-making centers. Marks are worst in the leadership class. But then real countries are not like students taking Merit Scholarship exams; there is no choice but to give them chances over and over. And with the combination of the high scores in the counterinsurgency department, along with the almost depleted—but still historically germane—credit from EDSA the country would continue to be taken seriously. It would not occur with the envy reserved for Thailand, but with adequate reserved judgment for the day that could still come when Filipinos got their act together, using the threads of EDSA, radical revolt, and all else that would make the island republic a nation of equity and pride.

What we have seen, perhaps, is evidence that history is not dead everywhere, not, anyway, in the Philippines, a nation in crisis. True, in the article that made this argument famous allowance was made for developments in the "fringes" of the developed world, which is to say about two thirds of the world's people. But the vibrancy of the struggle between contending parties makes it seem unlikely that history would come to an end for a long time yet—at least in the Philippines.

NOTES

1. Ironically, there were social-medical developments in Thailand that, in fifteen years, might reverse this land to the benefit of the Philippines. For reasons having to do with Thailand's success as a tourist Mecca, but more saliently with Thai attitudes towards sex, Thailand had one of the most rapidly rising H.I.V. infection rates in the world. United States AID data shown to this writer suggested that, in fifteen years Thailand would be losing much of its fertile (and productive) generation at serious economic cost. Sexual practices in the Philippines, so vastly different from those in Thailand, especially in the gay community, insulated the country, in large measure, from the disease. It is on such accidents that societies have risen and fallen throughout history.
2. William Booth, "UN Sees Global Fertility Drop, Birth Control Gains," *Washington Post* (14 May 1991), pp. A1, A10.
3. "Economic Survey on the Philippines," *Asian Development Bank* (November 1988), p. 54.
4. *Ibid.*, p. 28.
5. Interview, Washington, DC (April 1991).
6. "NPA Exploits Government's Vulnerability" (26 September 1990), in Foreign Broadcast Information Service-East Asia-90-188 (27 September 1990), p. 62. Hereafter FBIS-EAS.
7. Manila Far East Broadcasting Company, in FBIS-EAS-90-214 (5 November 1990), p. 55.
8. Ateneo de Manila University, *Public Opinion Survey* August 1989 (Quezon City: Ateneo de Manila University, 1989), Table 19, p. 61. Explanation pertaining to table quoted above: Roughly, A class is the rich elite, B and C are the middle classes, D is the lower-middle class, and E is the proletariat.
9. *Manila Chronicle* (5 March 1991), in FBIS-EAS-91-043 (5 March 1991), p. 51.
10. "Surge of Confidence after Gulf Victory," *The Manila Chronicle* (7 March 1991), in FBIS-EAS-91-045 (7 March 1991), p. 51.
11. "Senator Gives Report on Aid, Policies," *The Manila Chronicle* (7 March 1991), in FBIS-EAS-91-045 (7 March 1991), p. 53.
12. Gustav Ranis, "The Philippines, the Brady Plan and the PAP: Prognosis and Alternative" (photocopy, May 1989), p. 9.
13. "The Presidency," *Solidarity* Seminar Series on Public Issues, No. 20, *Solidarity* 125 (January-March 1990), p. 147.
14. Cited in Teodoro Benigno, Interview with President Aquino, Quezon City Radyo ng Bayan (7 April 1991), in FBIS-EAS-91-069 (10 April 1991), p. 39.
15. Prime Minister's Office, Kuala Lumpur, Address by His Excellency Dato Seri Dr. Mahathir bin Mohamad, at the International Conference on "The

ASEAN Countries and the World Economy: Challenge of Change" (4 March 1991).

16. *Davide*, p. 595
17. "Cory's Lament" (15 February 1990).
18. Amando Doronila, "Longest Reigning Lame-Duck Leader," *The Manila Chronicle* (26 September 1990), in FBIS-EAS-90-187 (26 September 1990), p. 56.
19. Amando Doronila, "Ramos Sending Signals for '92 Polls," *Manila Chronicle* (31 October 1990), in FBIS-EAS-90-211 (31 October 1990), p. 56.
20. "The Centre No Longer," *Far Eastern Economic Review*, 13 June 1991, p. 52.
21. This author's interview, State Department (October 1991).
22. This author's interview, State Department (January 1992).
23. This author's interview, State Department (January 1992).

INDEX

W. Scott Thompson was Fulbright Professor in the Philippines in 1989. He is currently on the faculty of the Fletcher School of Law and Diplomacy, Tufts University, where he has taught since 1967. Dr. Thompson is the author of six other books, including *Unequal Partners: Philippine and Thai Relations with the U.S.*, and has served in three U.S. government administrations.